Immigrant Rights in
the Nuevo South

Meghan Conley

Immigrant Rights in the Nuevo South

*Enforcement and Resistance at
the Borderlands of Illegality*

TEMPLE UNIVERSITY PRESS
Philadelphia • *Rome* • *Tokyo*

TEMPLE UNIVERSITY PRESS
Philadelphia, Pennsylvania 19122
tupress.temple.edu

Library of Congress Cataloging-in-Publication Data

Names: Conley, Meghan E., author.
Title: Immigrant rights in the Nuevo South : enforcement and resistance at
the borderlands of illegality / Meghan Conley.
Description: Philadelphia : Temple University Press, 2020. | Includes
bibliographical references and index. | Summary: "Unauthorized
immigrants in the southeastern United States encounter communities
unused to their new Latino neighbors and quick to call law enforcement.
The precariousness of this way of life leads immigrant communities and
allies to organize and demonstrate to secure legal rights, but these
actions risk backlash depending on local context"— Provided by
publisher.
Identifiers: LCCN 2019010530 (print) | LCCN 2019980512 (ebook) | ISBN
9781439916445 (cloth) | ISBN 9781439916452 (paperback) | ISBN
9781439916469 (ebook)
Subjects: LCSH: Latin Americans—Southern States—Social conditions. |
Immigrants—Southern States—Social conditions. | Illegal
aliens—Southern States. | Southern States—Ethnic relations. | Southern
States—Emigration and immigration.
Classification: LCC F220.S75 C66 2020 (print) | LCC F220.S75 (ebook) |
DDC 305.800975—dc23
LC record available at https://lccn.loc.gov/2019010530
LC ebook record available at https://lccn.loc.gov/2019980512

Contents

Author's Note

WORDS MATTER: they can humanize or dehumanize, clarify or obscure power, elevate or subordinate language, voice, and experience.

Our society dehumanizes unauthorized immigrants through labels such as *illegal* and *alien*. These terms are so commonplace that they are perceived to be neutral. They are not. When I quote dehumanizing language in this book, I use [*sic*] to name it for what it is.

I use *unauthorized* to refer to populations of noncitizens who are out of status, including those who enter the country "without inspection," overstay visa expiration dates, or otherwise violate the terms of their visas. This term illuminates the active role of the U.S. government—its power—to authorize who has the right to be in the country, who does not, and under what circumstances. I also acknowledge that people who are directly affected by the politics of illegality often prefer the term *undocumented*. To honor the words that people claim for themselves, I use *undocumented* when referring to specific individuals.

Grassroots immigrant rights activism is often powered by Spanish-speaking Latinx immigrants, and thus my research was largely conducted in Spanish. To remind readers of this linguistic reality, I incorporate Spanish words and phrases throughout the book. Some conversations were reconstructed from field notes; others were transcribed from audio recordings. To distinguish between these versions of voice and experience, I italicize reconstructed conversations. All direct quotes appear in quotation marks.

Preface

I MET JESÚS on July 2, 2011. He was standing in a parking lot in downtown Atlanta, clothed in a white undershirt and faded denim jeans, and he was not happy.

ON APRIL 14, 2011, the Georgia legislature approved H.B. 87, the Illegal Immigration Reform and Enforcement Act. Signed into law the following month by Governor Nathan Deal, Georgia H.B. 87 became the third in a series of copycat bills, following Utah and Indiana, designed to mimic provisions of Arizona's controversial S.B. 1070, which was known at the time as the nation's most expansive restrictionist law. Notably, H.B. 87 was only the first of many comprehensive restrictionist bills to pass that year in the Southeast.

Georgia's new law empowered state and local law enforcement officers to verify a person's immigration and citizenship status in the course of routine traffic stops, mandated that private and public employers use the federal E-Verify database to confirm the status of employees, and established criminal penalties for those who knowingly "harbored" or transported unauthorized immigrants in Georgia. "It's a great day for Georgia," said state representative Matt Ramsey, one of the bill's sponsors. "We think we have done our job . . . to address the costs and the social consequences that have been visited upon our state by the federal government's failure to secure our nation's borders" (quoted in Redmon 2011).

Not all Georgians agreed.

In June, a coalition of civil and immigrant rights groups, represented by the American Civil Liberties Union (ACLU) of Georgia, the Asian Law Caucus, the National Immigrant Law Center (NILC), and the Southern Poverty Law Center, filed a lawsuit against H.B. 87.

July 1, the day that H.B. 87 went into effect, was declared *un día de incumplimiento*: a day of noncompliance. The Georgia Latino Alliance for Human Rights (GLAHR), a grassroots immigrant rights organization, encouraged immigrants and allies to stay home from work, to close their businesses, to buy nothing. Adelina Nicholls, executive director of GLAHR, urged: "No buying, no doing, no caring for their children, no cooking in their restaurants. This is the commitment we make. The first of July will be a day of noncompliance precisely so that they know that the Latino community *está presente!*" In a statement released to the press, Southerners on New Ground (SONG)—a Queer Liberation organization—elaborated, "We will show our economic power by not working or shopping on July 1st and [we] will demonstrate our people power by marching on July 2nd. Those who thought this law would break apart our communities have awakened a movement."

And so, on July 2, we marched.

———

MONTHS EARLIER, before we knew for certain that H.B. 87 would pass the Georgia legislature, I committed to organizing an affinity group from my city—Knoxville, Tennessee—and driving to Atlanta to stand with Georgians against the law. Upon the law's implementation, our small group quickly doubled and then tripled in size. We rented a fifteen-passenger van, and I was volunteered to captain our trip to the demonstration. Although only two passengers were undocumented, our group felt like moving targets as we drove the white, unmarked van down Interstate 75 into downtown Atlanta.

The forecast for the day predicted temperatures in the nineties. Still, the combination of a midday rally and thousands of marchers packed onto the concrete of Atlanta's shadeless downtown streets made it seem much hotter. We sweated through the pre-march gathering, as group after group of demonstrators trickled in and claimed space in front of the capitol building. People amassed everywhere—standing in the road, sitting on sidewalks, leaning against sides of buildings. Lightweight metal fencing had been installed to keep us from treading on the capitol lawn, but a daring few had jumped the fences to spread out on the cool grass beneath shade trees as they awaited the start of the march. All around, people were putting the finishing touches on homemade signs: "*Legalización ahora*," "No racial profiling," "Immigration reform now!" Some used templates to spray-paint "No H.B. 87" in bold print on poster board, the *o* in *No* designed like a Georgia peach. Others carried vinyl banners, their messages echoing similar themes in English and Spanish: "*Marcha por la Justicia*," "Justice for All."

Demonstrators protest H.B. 87 in Atlanta, GA. (Author's collection)

We sweated as demonstrators piled onto the narrow downtown streets, swarming tightly around a circle of people singing resistance songs and playing drums. A group of DREAMers[1] stood in the center, waving flags and chanting, in call-and-response fashion, "UNDOCUMENTED . . . UNAFRAID!" Around them stood people of all ages: toddlers holding their mothers' hands, old women playing trumpets, young fathers pushing strollers. Families. The music and chanting continued, and we sweated as we listened, and sang, and waited, over what seemed like hours, to take our first steps.

Crammed in so tightly, it was impossible to tell that the march had begun until those immediately in front of us moved forward. And then we were off, singing and chanting for miles as the sun bore down. Those marching around me, mostly Latinx people, roared exuberantly, "*Se ve, se siente, el pueblo está presente!*" (You hear it, you feel it, the people are here!). Ahead, we heard bursts of cheers and applause rumble up from the crowd in regular intervals. It was not until we turned a corner and found ourselves standing at the top of a long sloping hill that we realized why: in front of us, as far as the eye could see, was a sea of white T-shirts. Behind us, the same. Announcements for the march urged demonstrators to wear white, and we did. Looking back at photos from that day, what stands out most is how the mass of people occupying the streets of downtown Atlanta on July 2, 2011, of varied immigration histories and racial and ethnic backgrounds, had been remade into a single undulating white line. We, too, cheered.

AT THE END OF THE MARCH, the crowd assembled to listen to speakers testify about their fears of the law, its impact on their communities, and their vows to resist. The testimonies were punctuated by spontaneous, prolonged outbursts of "*¡Sí se puede! ¡Sí se puede! ¡Sí se puede!*" (Yes, we can!).

It was, reportedly, one of the largest marches Atlanta had seen in decades. The sight of so many people was both amazing and overwhelming, and the sheer number of people packed into those city streets, chanting and clapping and singing, seemed to suck all of the oxygen from the air. Gasping for breath and exhausted by the unrelenting heat, I stepped away from the crowd and trudged back to our van, in search of a moment of peace and a bottle of cold water.

It was in the parking lot that I met Jesús. He was standing next to what I supposed was his car, waving his arms frantically in the air and cursing in Spanish. Although he didn't carry a sign, and I hadn't seen him during the march, I recognized him as one of us by his white shirt.

He was shouting at another man, planted just beyond him: *¿Qué pasó? ¿Qué pasó?*

As I approached, the man turned. Seeing me, he asked, in careful English, *Did you see what happened here?*

No, I didn't see anything, I responded, matching his English. Then again, for good measure: *No vi nada.*

He gestured to his car, a worn but well-maintained sporty sedan, nothing fancy. Painted candy apple red, it stood out next to our van, which was parked just beside it. *Someone broke my window*, he said. *Look.* He pointed at the passenger side of his car: *Mire.* He must have noticed my reluctance to get involved. But I had to walk past his car to reach mine, so I obligingly peered around him as he gestured. Sure enough, glass lay scattered inside and outside the car, the window shattered into hundreds of shiny crystals that danced in the sunlight.

Lo siento, I said spreading my hands wide. *I'm sorry. I didn't see anything.*

I shrugged, and he nodded. It was hot—much too hot to care. And, really, I had not seen anything. I passed his car and walked to our van. Opening the doors at the back of the van, I hid from the men and their shattered window. After all, I reasoned, I had things to do. I reapplied sunscreen and filled my backpack with icy bottles of water from our cooler. As I drank some water and cooled down, I peered back at the two men from behind the van door. They were pacing around their car, visibly upset by the shattered window.

I sighed—why was I at this march, anyway?—and turned back to the men. *¿Quieren agua?* I tossed a couple of bottles of water to Jesús, who accepted them gratefully and passed one to his *compañero*. They were young, perhaps in their mid-twenties. There was silence as they guzzled water. Then

I listened. I listened as Jesús told me about how he had paid a man—*The security guard, you saw him, ¿no?*—to watch his car while they marched. I nodded. I had seen him. We, too, had been approached when we first parked: a man had walked up to our van just as we pulled in, peered inside, told us the cost of parking, and waited. At the time, we thanked him and assured that we would pay for our parking spot at the machine located at the front of the lot. The man quickly replied that *of course* we should pay the machine— definitely not him—he was not allowed to collect any money. We had also noted his companions, a group of men hanging out across the street who seemed to carefully eye each car and its passengers. So I had a pretty good idea of what had happened to the window of Jesús's sporty red car.

What should I do? Jesús asked. *I had money in there, five hundred dollars. It's gone. Stolen. What should I do? Should I call the police?*

I looked down at the ground, quiet this time because I wanted to help and knew the answer to his question, but I did not want to give it voice. Finally, I glanced up at him sideways, rubbing my forehead, and told him the truth: *I don't know if it's . . . safe . . . for you to talk to the police.*

Looking into his eyes, I saw that he understood what I was saying. I was hoping he would protest, hoping that my assumption about his immigration status had been wrong and he would tell me—not to worry—he had papers and all he needed was someone to interpret into English the details of the situation to a police officer. But he didn't. He was quiet. Resigned.

But I was angry. *Look,* I said, *I know someone we can talk to. We can ask if there is anything we can do. Maybe someone will be able to help.*

Together, Jesús and I walked back to the rally, leaving his friend to keep watch over the shattered window. We walked in search of one of the legal observers attending the march, who were decked out in neon-colored baseball caps and vests, a clear message to both police officers and marchers that they were on hand, monitoring. It was on the long, hot walk back to the capitol that I learned that my new acquaintance was named Jesús, that he had recently moved to Georgia from North Carolina, and that he was originally from Mexico.

Like many young Mexican men, Jesús had come to the United States seeking work to support his family back home. He had lived and worked in North Carolina for years without incident but had lost his construction job several months before the march in Atlanta. Since then, Jesús had been through difficult times, unable to find steady employment due to his lack of documentation. It seemed to him that North Carolina was becoming increasingly hostile to immigrants; police had begun to establish checkpoints and patrols outside predominantly Latinx neighborhoods, and *la migra*— Spanish slang for immigration enforcement—seemed to be working closely with police to apprehend unauthorized immigrants. A friend had told Jesús that he could find a job in Georgia, that the state was friendly to immigrants, and that he would not have to worry about *la migra*—at least not in Atlanta. Of course, this was before the passage of H.B. 87.

As we walked, I spotted Miguel Carpizo, the East Tennessee organizer for the Tennessee Immigrant and Refugee Rights Coalition. We filled Carpizo in on the details of Jesús's situation, and together the three of us set out in search of someone more familiar with Georgia's legal procedures.

It did not take long to spot one of the many lawyers who had volunteered their time as legal observers. Sporting a hot-pink baseball cap and high ponytail, she nodded again and again as Jesús slowly told his story in Spanish while Carpizo and I took turns interpreting into English. It was clear that she understood the situation. I was hopeful that she knew of a solution, that I had simply overreacted. After all, I reasoned, the police had given their word to organizers that they were not interested in the immigration status of marchers. And Jesús had done nothing wrong.

Her response, however, was not what we hoped for: *It's possible that the police will not ask for your status*, she said. *But they will make a report, and they will ask you a lot of questions. You'll have to give them your information. You might have to give them your driver's license.* She continued, *It's also possible that they might not ask these questions, but probably they won't be able to find the person who did this anyway, so you won't get your money back. In my opinion, a report made to the police could result in severe consequences for you. You could make a report, but—given the potential risks—I strongly caution against it.*

She went on to recommend that Jesús take pictures of the broken glass and damaged window and report the incident to his insurance company, if he had one. He nodded; he did not have insurance. As an undocumented immigrant, Jesús was prohibited from obtaining a driver's license in most states; this prevented him from purchasing car insurance from many insurance companies. I remember Jesús's eyes—stony, resigned—as the lawyer said, repeatedly, *I'm sorry, I'm sorry.* With great dignity, chin held high, Jesús thanked us, shook my hand, and headed back, alone, to the parking lot.

When I later returned to our van, Jesús's car was gone. Left behind were the broken shards of glass to serve as a reminder of our chance encounter on that sweltering Georgia afternoon.

Note

1. DREAMers are undocumented youth who would benefit from the DREAM Act, which would provide pathways to citizenship for those who grow up in the United States and fulfill certain requirements, including military service or higher education.

Immigrant Rights in
the Nuevo South

1

From Illegality to Resistance

WHEN I MET JESÚS in downtown Atlanta on that day in July, I recognized the tragedy of his immediate situation and that of people like him: individual immigrants, many of whom are struggling to survive, who are made vulnerable by other people and by enforcement policies and practices that make it impossible to report their victimization. I did not, at the time, appreciate the irony of the circumstances of Jesús's vulnerability. In the middle of a demonstration, as thousands of unauthorized immigrants openly declared their status and collectively confronted restrictionist practices, here was a solitary undocumented man who felt that he could not confront the crime that had been committed against him. As a group of thousands, unauthorized immigrants are protected from the prying questions of immigration agents and police officers deputized to enforce immigration law;[1] separately, they remain extremely vulnerable.

Every day, undocumented immigrants like Jesús are rendered vulnerable through policies and practices that illegalize them. That is, immigrants are *illegalized*, or actively made unauthorized, through discourses that determine who belongs within the boundaries of the United States, who does not, and under what conditions, as well as through the policies and practices that emerge from this ideology of belongingness and non-belongingness. Illegalization, then, is the hegemonic process by which unauthorized immigrants are socially constructed into dangerous criminals and taxpayer burdens who are undeserving of rights, dignity, and respect. It is also the legal process by which unauthorized immigrants become criminalized and subjected to heightened enforcement.

This book examines policies and practices that structure illegality for immigrants in the U.S. Southeast. I examine the Southeast as a new *frontera*, or border, within the interior of the United States that is constructed through racialized discourses and practices of belongingness and that marks people of Latin American ancestry and origin as different and "illegal" (Deeb-Sossa and Bickham Mendez 2008; Marrow 2011b, 2011c). In the Southeast, ideological foundations of illegality are weaponized through the proliferation of policies and practices that enforce non-belongingness. These weapons include collaboration programs between police and Immigration and Customs Enforcement (ICE) and bureaucratic enforcement policies, which enable state and local law enforcement agents, other public employees, and even community members to participate in immigration enforcement. Mechanisms such as these render the threat of enforcement omnipresent but never certain as they shape the everyday lives and experiences of immigrants in the *Nuevo* South. As Latinx people increasingly settle in this new *frontera*, states like Alabama, Georgia, and Tennessee have become important sites in the production of immigrant illegality.

This book also examines narratives that immigrant rights actors use to resist illegality and the complicated, sometimes contradictory, ways that resistance occurs. Just as thousands marched in Georgia to resist the state's "crimmigration" laws (Stumpf 2006),[2] unauthorized immigrants and allies across the Southeast are not silent in the face of increasingly restrictionist policies and practices. Immigrant rights actors voice resistance through narratives that challenge discourses and practices of illegality in order to shift dominant understandings of the "problem" of unauthorized immigrants and unauthorized immigration. There is irony here, too: even as immigrant rights actors resist characterizations of unauthorized immigrants as dangerous and undeserving, resistance counternarratives often reify broader structural foundations of illegality.

This book illuminates stories of enforcement, vulnerability, and resistance and how these stories intersect in ways that ultimately sustain a nation-state that is premised on "illegal" and otherwise exploitable bodies. This is a story of vulnerability in the midst of resistance, but it is also a story of resistance even in times of vulnerability. Above all, this is a story of struggle.

Borders and Belongingness

Immigrants exist because borders exist. Physical and ideological borders create the nation-state and the idea of national belongingness. Borders are conceptualized metaphorically as containers (Lakoff and Johnson 1980), geographically defining the entity of the nation (physical space contained within the border) and demarcating that which is not the nation (space outside the border). A literal understanding of borders suggests that one cannot exist simultaneously both inside and outside that which is established by the border. These borders may be clearly marked and visible to the eye, such as through signage that marks the crossing of state or national lines. Often, boundaries and the spaces they contain are fuzzy areas distinguishable only through GPS coordinates. Just so, no clear line differentiates the United States from Mexico in much of the Sonoran Desert.

Nation-states draw lines in the sand to bring imaginary boundaries into existence, and these spaces are then clearly defined in our maps of the world. In this way, borders appear firm and unmovable, historical and permanent. It seems that they have always existed and that they always will.

We know, however, that borders shift over time. The boundaries of the United States have expanded through conquest, occupation, and acquisition of lands contained within the boundaries of other nations. Just so, the U.S. invasion of northern Mexico during the Mexican-American War resulted in the Treaty of Guadalupe Hidalgo (1848), which reshaped the boundaries of Mexico and the United States and drew new borders around and between the two countries. Borders also expand and contract conceptually. Political geographers note that borders are "performed" (Wonders 2006), or enacted, in the interior spaces of a nation-state. In the United States, this performance has been established through enforcement practices that enable Border Patrol officers to operate anywhere within one hundred miles of the geographical border of the nation and ICE agents to operate throughout the interior, with or without the assistance of state and local law enforcement (Coleman 2007; Mountz 2011). Borders, and how they are established and performed, reflect broader social, political, and economic choices about nation building and boundary making.

Borders are also contested spaces, both political and politicized (Salter 2012). Nation-states assert the right to define their geographic boundaries, but vulnerable territories are negotiated and appropriated through colonization, war, and treaty. Many indigenous peoples, including those of Mexican indigenous heritage, dispute the legitimacy of U.S. sovereignty over the U.S. Southwest, not only in its dominion over the territories and people of the region but also by the nature of its creation (Dunbar-Ortiz 2015; Forbes 1973). Nation-states may also claim authority to define citizenship; to "control" and "secure" sovereign borders; and to authorize, deauthorize, and refuse authorization to noncitizens. Nonetheless, this authority is contested ideologically through frameworks that advocate expansive views of global citizenship and migration as a human right, and practically by unauthorized entrants and the employers who hire them.

Borders are not just geographical; they are also ideological (Pickering 2006). The United States is demarcated through discourses of "Americanness" that structure what it means to be "American" (Hing 2004; Ngai 2004; Zolberg 2006). These boundaries may be drawn around beliefs and symbols—manifest destiny, American exceptionalism, rugged individualism, the American dream, and the American flag (Lipset 1996)—but boundaries are also drawn around bodies. In the words of Gloria Anzaldúa, "Borders are set up to define the places that are safe and unsafe, to distinguish *us* from *them*" (1987: 25, emphasis in original).

We may seek to define our identities through geographical relationship to an imagined physical boundary—as Americans, for example, or southerners. However, boundaries of belongingness are not lines we draw around ourselves. In this way, the people who physically inhabit a bounded area are not always considered to belong to that area. This includes Native Americans who were massacred and forcibly removed from their territories, Africans and black Americans who were enslaved and legally excluded from the rights of full citizenship for much of the nation's history, U.S. citizens of Latin American ancestry who were deported during the Great Depression, and Japanese Americans who were interned during World War II.

Illegality is the manifestation of geographic and ideological boundaries of belongingness, a conceptual *borderland* (Anzaldúa 1987) that distinguishes those who belong from those who do not. It is a hegemonic story that categorizes the "legal" and the "illegal" and differentiates the included from the excluded (Coutin 2003). In this sense, the specter of illegality threatens any group that can be portrayed as other, though the primary targets explored in this book are unauthorized and marginally authorized immigrants who are marked by perceptions of foreignness through race, ethnic origin, language, socioeconomic class, and age (Ngai 2004).

Illegalizing Moves:[3] Enforcing Illegality

Illegality is enacted through federal, state, and local policies and practices that establish "illegal" status and enforce non-belongingness. Such policies and practices are naturalized alongside the geographical border and its ideological boundaries of belongingness. Unauthorized immigrants—noncitizens who are not authorized to be present in the United States—are said to be in violation of the law. "Illegal" is thereby reified as an objective category (De Genova 2004), something that exists unto itself, as in common phrases such as "What part of illegal [sic] don't you understand?" and "I'm not anti-immigrant. I'm anti–illegal [sic] immigrant."

Violation of the law is used to justify enforcement consequences. For example, the president of the Dustin Inman Society (a Georgia-based restrictionist group) notes, "Despite absurd claims to the contrary, no one is deported for a broken taillight or not having a driver's license. Violation of American immigration laws is the singular reason for removal" (King 2009).[4] This assertion—that unauthorized immigrants are never deported for a minor traffic violation—is technically correct but conceptually inadequate. People are deported because they are deportable. But what makes someone deportable?

Herein lies the importance of denaturalizing categories that seem objective. In reframing "illegal" immigrants as unauthorized, for example, we attend to the active role of nation-states in authorizing, deauthorizing, or refusing authorization to noncitizens. People are deported, then, not because they are "illegal" or because they are in violation of immigration laws but because the U.S. government actively denies them the ability to be present in the United States with authorization and then identifies deportation as an acceptable consequence for those who violate this denial.

Many scholars conceptualize illegality as a legal phenomenon (Calavita 1998; Chavez 2007; Coutin 2000a, 2003; De Genova 2002, 2004; Menjívar 2011; Menjívar and Abrego 2012; Willen 2007), and this is key to denaturalizing the status of "illegal." Legally, illegality is created through the implementation and administration of laws and policies, and it occurs as the by-product of restrictionist practices. Immigrant illegality is treated as the result of policy and legislation: immigrants become "illegal" because laws make them so. Unauthorized immigrants are not "illegal" (and therefore deportable) because they cross a human-made international boundary without proper authorization or because they overstay an expired visa.[5] Rather, they are *illegalized*—actively rendered "irregular" or unauthorized—through policies and practices that enforce boundaries of belongingness.

Unauthorized immigrants are not uniformly illegalized in day-to-day life. Since boundaries of belongingness are ideological, unauthorized immigrants are not equally perceived as "illegal." Nancy Wonders notes, for example, that "border agents and state bureaucrats play a critical role in determining where, how, and *on whose body* a border will be performed" (2006: 66, emphasis added). In the United States, all noncitizen residents are subject to enforcement through detention and removal, including authorized immigrants, who may be deauthorized for violating the terms of their visas.[6] However, it is telling that brown and black noncitizen bodies are disproportionately criminalized and deported (Aranda and Vaquera 2015; Golash-Boza 2015a; Morgan-Trostle, Zheng, and Lipscombe 2016). This disparity suggests that illegality, vis-à-vis the boundaries of belongingness, is largely a racial project (Chavez 2008; Omi and Winant 1994; Provine and Doty 2011).

Illegality is experienced through policies and practices that exclude unauthorized immigrants from full participation in public life. This includes programs that mandate or enable collaborative enforcement of immigration law between federal immigration authorities and state and local law enforcement agencies as well as state and local laws and policies that establish bureaucratic enforcement procedures. If illegality "entails a social relation to the state," as Nicholas De Genova (2002: 422) argues, it makes sense to contextualize the manifestations of illegality as phenomena of not just nation-states but also specific local contexts. Thus, immigrants who reside in jurisdictions that actively participate in enforcement are more likely to be illegalized than those who live in jurisdictions that do not participate in these practices. A minor traffic violation may serve as pretext for a traffic stop, particularly if a police officer is influenced by perceptions of the driver's non-belongingness, and set into motion a chain of events leading to detention or removal, especially if the arresting officer works in a jurisdiction that collaborates with immigration enforcement. In this way, a broken taillight may ultimately result in deportation.

Policies and practices of illegality have consequences for immigrants' embodied experiences of "being in the world" (Willen 2007). During periods of high enforcement, unauthorized immigrants report tension, anxiety, and concerns about being discovered, detained, deported, and separated from family (Dreby 2012, 2015; Marquardt et al. 2011; Roche et al. 2018). Responses to these fears include constant vigilance and defensive maneuvers as unauthorized immigrants become perpetually watchful of police officers and immigration agents and attempt to avoid interactions with anyone perceived to enforce immigration laws.

Although unauthorized immigrants are entitled to civil rights protections by law, many fear police and do not trust the legal system to protect their rights (Abrego 2011). Practically speaking, this translates into vulnerability for unauthorized immigrants, who are rendered so by perceptions of their non-belongingness, immigration laws and policies that enforce their illegality, and lack of recourse (real or perceived) if victimized. Illegality has therefore been likened to a physical and conceptual space of "nonexistence" (Coutin 2003). It is a place where unauthorized immigrants live shadowed lives as a condition of their status, avoiding the scrutiny of others, particularly those who seem determined to enforce immigration law.

Illegality is also a sociopolitical phenomenon (De Genova 2002), constructed in service of the nation-state as an imagined (bounded) entity. In this way, illegality is an active eradication of the underlying causes and consequences of international migration. Once in the United States, unauthorized immigrants are vulnerable because of boundaries of belongingness and policies and practices of illegality. However, it is precisely their vulnerability that renders them unauthorized in the first place. Proceedings that sustain policies and practices of exclusion (Coutin 1993)—such as restrictive policies on citizenship, immigration, and asylum and expansive practices of detention and removal—enforce illegality by denying authorization. And yet people are often forced into migration by social, political, economic, and environmental factors that undermine stability in their countries of origin—factors that are often influenced by U.S. policies. Importantly, all of these factors are rendered invisible. Despite (or, perhaps, because of) the reality that unauthorized immigrants are often labor migrants (Donato and Armenta 2011; Espenshade 1995; Hondagneu-Sotelo 2001; Massey 1999; Papadimitriou and Martin 1991), the politics of illegality obscure this fact and the vulnerabilities that impel international migration and maintain the status of "illegal." Structurally, illegality maintains a system that is dependent on perpetual re-creation of vulnerability.

Vulnerability, Resistance, Vulnerability

Vulnerability is embedded in the lives of those who are directly affected by the politics of illegality. In my work with undocumented people and their loved ones, I have met children and teenagers traumatized by constant worry that their parents will be picked up by *la migra* on the way to work or the grocery store and parents who are terrified of what would happen to their children if they were deported. I have commiserated with pregnant women and new mothers whose undocumented partners were detained. I have advised people of their rights, over the phone, as they hid in closets and bathrooms while immigration agents knocked on their doors. I have heard of workers who were physically threatened by employers when they sought payment for their labor, and I have heard from women who were refused orders of protection from abusive partners on the basis of their immigration status. I have heard from women who were coerced into sexual relationships by employers and police officers who threatened to reveal their status. I have heard of young girls who were sexually assaulted, whose parents were afraid to report these crimes to the police for fear that they, and not the abuser, would be taken into custody. Stories like these abound in the homes, workplaces, and communities of undocumented people.

Unauthorized immigrants endeavor to protect themselves and their families from the vulnerabilities of illegality (Marquardt et al. 2011; Menjívar 2006). Many seek to regularize their status. They consult with immigration attorneys, whose efficacy is constrained by restrictive pathways to authorized residency and criminalization of unauthorized entry. Immigrants pay hundreds or thousands of dollars to *notarios*—people who falsely represent themselves as immigration attorneys or qualified consultants— who take their money in exchange for false hopes or, worse, severe consequences for their immigration cases. Many prepare themselves for deportation, perhaps by making custodial arrangements for children and property. And many go underground during times of heightened enforcement, avoiding interactions with law enforcement—even as victims or witnesses of crime—to "stay out of trouble."

Unauthorized immigrants also resist the policies and practices that structure their daily lives, and resistance may occur even during times of great vulnerability. Leo Chavez (2007: 194) notes, "As nation-states narrow

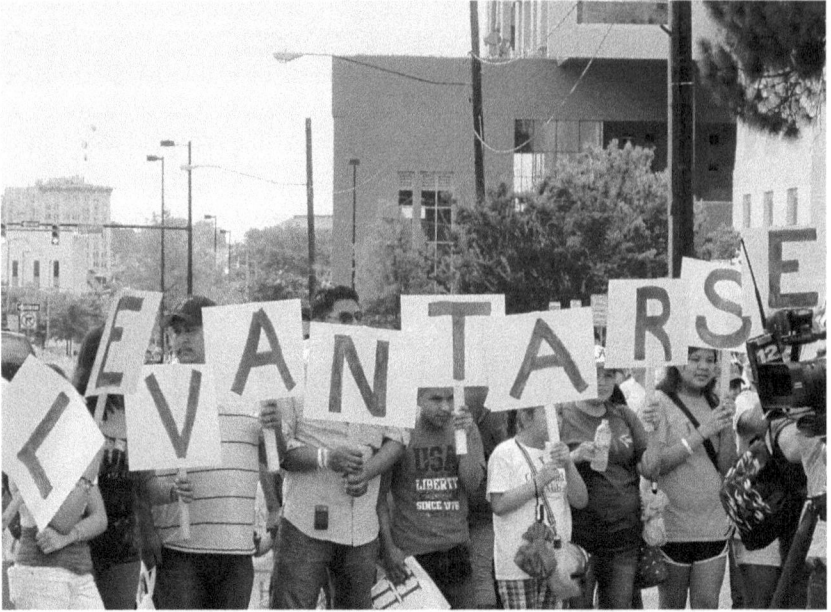

Demonstrators urge Montgomery to "rise up." (Author's collection)

the rights of immigrants and develop new techniques of control and surveillance, immigrant communities have responded by coming out of the shadows to engage civic debates on their presence (illegal), character (immoral; criminal), and motivations (threats to nation)." People may engage in active resistance when hardships—once perceived as personal problems—are reconstructed into collective grievances against the status quo and when they believe that the conditions that give rise to these grievances are both unjust and changeable (McAdam 1982; Piven and Cloward 1977; Snow et al. 1986). Of course, immigrant rights movements do not occur spontaneously but through the groundwork of emerging local, state, regional, and national organizations (Voss and Bloemraad 2011).

Noncitizens generally lack direct access to formal electoral participation regardless of their immigration status.[7] However, many noncitizens, including unauthorized immigrants, engage in political action by lobbying elected officials, campaigning on behalf of electoral candidates, and participating in demonstrations (P. Lewis and Ramakrishnan 2007; Marrow 2005). Protests and marches, such as the one described in the preface, are key demonstrations of collective resistance to restrictionist policies and practices. Unauthorized immigrants and their allies have turned out in droves for such protests (Bada, Fox, and Selee 2006; Voss and Bloemraad 2011), and they resist illegality through highly visible actions, ranging from rallies to civil disobedience, effectively coming out of the shadows to occupy physical space in public life.

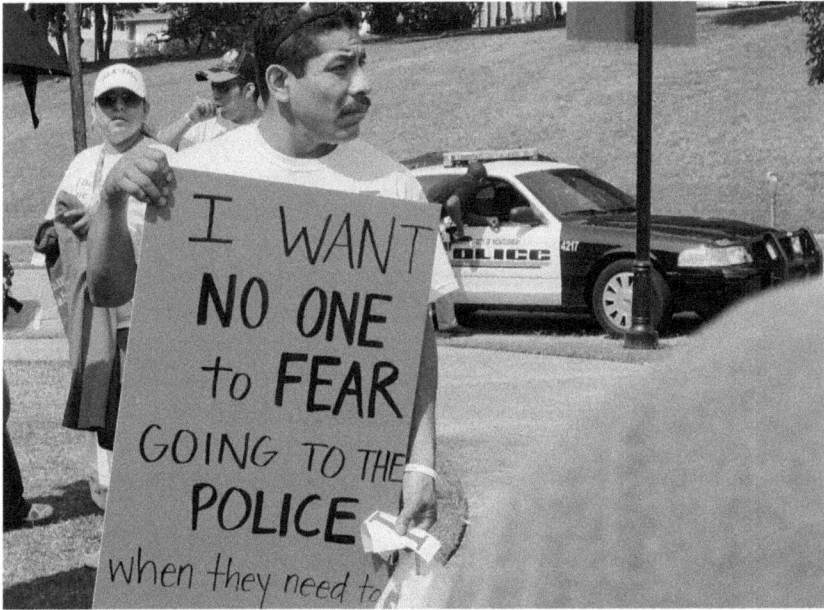

Chilling effects of police-ICE collaboration. (Author's collection)

Resistance occurs in ways that are less immediately visible, too. Immigrant rights actors, including undocumented people and their allies, challenge ideological spaces of non-belongingness through stories that contest the "natural" arrangements of illegality and provide conceptual space for organized resistance (Delgado 1989). These accounts highlight the voices, experiences, and histories of people who are directly affected by the politics of illegality through counternarratives of existence, deservingness, and (il) legitimacy. In this process of claims making, immigrant rights actors challenge taken-for-granted assumptions about the "problem" (Best 1987) of unauthorized immigrants and unauthorized immigration, offer competing narratives of harm and deservingness, and suggest alternative solutions.

Even as resistance occurs during times of vulnerability, the opposite is also true: vulnerability can be reproduced during times of resistance. The relationship is readily apparent in Jesús's story. Moments after leaving a march of thousands, Jesús was rendered vulnerable not only by a burglary but by his perceived inability to report his victimization. In this moment, Jesús was *illegalized* not by his immigration status but by enforcement policies and practices that exclude unauthorized immigrants from full participation in public life.

Unauthorized immigrants can be vulnerable regardless of whether they resist, and I am not suggesting that immigrant rights actors avoid challenging policies and practices of illegality. Indeed, resistance can result in positive change, including tangible reforms of federal, state, and local immigration policies as well as cognitive liberation for those who are directly affected. I raise the connection between vulnerability and resistance to show that illegality is insidious in its reproduction: as a structural condition, illegality recreates itself in service to the nation-state.

Unauthorized immigrants can be illegalized during physical acts of resistance to policies and practices of illegality, but they can also be illegalized through ideological forms of resistance. Many of the stories that immigrant rights actors use to challenge illegality, and to make visible its consequences, are constructed around existing boundaries of belongingness. Resistance narratives refute hegemonic accounts of immigrants as dangerous and undeserving by reframing immigrants as hardworking laborers, self-sacrificing mothers and fathers, and exemplary students. Narratives that highlight deservingness in these ways challenge illegality for some immigrants while upholding it for others. In doing so, immigrant rights actors may unintentionally sustain illegality, even as they seek to resist it.

Activist Research for Immigrant Rights

This book comprises more than three years of ethnographic fieldwork with those who experience and resist illegality in the Southeastern United States. However, my interest and involvement in the rights of undocumented people began long before I started researching and writing this book. Early in my career, I worked in social services, including for an emergency domestic violence shelter and a child abuse prevention program. I worked with immigrant women, all of whom were undocumented, most of whom spoke little to no English. I was appalled by the barriers these women confronted in leaving abusive partners, navigating the criminal justice and child welfare systems, gaining community support, and building new lives.

One incident stands out in my memory. A woman had fled her home after her husband shoved her against a wall. She was cradling their infant in her arms when it happened—the breaking point in a history of abuse. The shelter's policy was to report any incidents of violence that involved children, or incidents that occurred in the presence of children, to Child Protective Services, and so the woman and I together called to make the report. When an investigator arrived to document the incident, he asked the woman if she was "illegal" and scolded her that the abusive husband had a right to know his child's whereabouts. Infuriated, I ended the interview and contacted the investigator's supervisor, but the damage was already done: the woman left the shelter with her infant the following morning, and they never returned.

Notwithstanding incidents such as this one, I loved my work. It was meaningful and fulfilling, and I know that social welfare programs provide critical material and psychological supports to people in vulnerable situations. As a caseworker, though, I was supposed to tackle these issues as the concerns of individual people with individual problems. For an undocumented woman with an abusive partner, the solution was to leave the husband and, if possible, work with an immigration attorney to regularize her status.

However, problems like these are anything but individual, and their solutions are anything but straightforward. Just as ending violence against women requires more than helping individual women leave their abusers, ending illegality requires more than providing authorization to individual undocumented people. This is because illegality is about more than being unauthorized. Providing authorization to one undocumented person—or even to eleven million undocumented people—would certainly lessen the vulnerabilities of those individuals, especially in the context of heightened immigration enforcement, but it would not address the structural causes of illegality. To address illegality, we must tackle political, economic, and social policies and the ideological constructions of borders, immigrants, and immigration that reproduce structural inequalities for those outside the boundaries of belongingness. It is precisely this disconnect between individual solutions and structural problems that led me to immigrant rights activism.

For some of my research, I had the benefit of traveling with Miguel Carpizo of the Tennessee Immigrant and Refugee Rights Coalition (TIRRC). We became friends after attending a retreat in Arlington, Virginia, that was hosted by the National Day Laborer Organizing Network. The theme of the conference, "Turning the Tide from Hate to Human Rights," centered on strategizing responses to the criminalization of immigrants, especially in the wake of Arizona's S.B. 1070 law. It was at this conference that I promised Georgia organizers that I would mobilize a protest group from Knoxville if their Arizona copycat bill became law. Carpizo and I had met once or twice before—he had recently been hired as TIRRC's East Tennessee organizer—but we had not spoken much. At the Virginia conference, we conspired to sneak away for a decent cup of coffee, and thereafter we continued meeting for coffee and strategy sessions until he moved out of the state.

Miguel Carpizo introduced me to the broader regional community of immigrant rights actors. He often invited me to accompany him when he traveled to workshops across the region, and I tagged along whenever I could. Given my status as a U.S. citizen with a driver's license, he sometimes volunteered me to drive undocumented people to these events, and I relished the opportunity.

Between 2009 and 2013, I participated in organizing meetings, workshops, demonstrations, and public hearings in cities and rural areas across Alabama, Georgia, and Tennessee and, to a lesser extent, North Carolina, Mississippi, and Virginia. These events were often convergence spaces for immigrant rights groups and *comités populares* (people's committees) from across the Southeast. I met undocumented people and allies from rural

Children are a regular presence in organizing spaces. (Author's collection)

towns in Alabama, farming communities in Georgia, cities in South Carolina, and elsewhere across the region. Many of the same people showed up to workshops and demonstrations across the Southeast. Some were employed as organizers, and their work enabled them to travel and participate in these events. The vast majority, however, were unpaid organizers and community members who were directly affected by the politics of illegality. Some of these people might describe themselves as activists, organizers, and rabble-rousers. In my experience, though, most thought of themselves as mothers and fathers, students, children of undocumented parents—labels more central to their identities. People told me that they were regular people doing what needed to be done to protect their families and communities.

"Showing up" is an important aspect of fieldwork, particularly for those studying social movements (Pollner and Emerson 1983; Thorne 1979), and my experience was no different. As I showed up, again and again, to events across the region, people started recognizing me: the activist-academic, that person doing research. And people wanted to hear about my research and findings: Had I finished yet? Was I still doing interviews? Would I like to interview them?

In my fieldwork, I was both participant and researcher, trying desperately to maintain a delicate balance between what Barrie Thorne (1979: 73) refers to as "an insider, a participant in the world one studies, and an outsider, observing and reporting on that world." In a very real sense, I was an outsider, and I still am: I am a white, non-Latina, U.S.-born citizen in a time when many of the people involved in immigrant rights organizing—and certainly many who experience illegality—are Latinx noncitizens of varying immigration statuses. Conscious of these status privileges, I constantly fretted over my role in organizing spaces. Should I be speaking from my personal experience or my academic background? Should I be speaking at all?

Ethnographers are often self-conscious about their identities during fieldwork (Snow 1980). I worried that I would be exposed as an interloper—a researcher rather than an *activist* researcher—and I was always vigilant for signs that my researcher self was unwelcome. Thus, I was particularly distressed when an undocumented poet joked, during a celebratory festival hailing a recent successful action, that U.S. citizens "steal everything" from immigrants. Even as I laughed at the joke, I wondered: Is that me? Am I stealing the stories of their experiences with illegality? Am I stealing their stories of resistance? I never asked what he meant. At the time, I thought it would be selfish to ask, and I did not want to be coddled. Looking back, I wonder if part of the reason I did not ask was because I was afraid of what his response might be.

Discomfort with "stealing" people's experiences has motivated me to work carefully with those whose stories appear throughout this book, to share with them their narratives and the context in which they appear, and to adjust my retelling as needed. I have been humbled by the people who spent precious time, during periods of unrelenting crisis for immigrant rights activism, critiquing my narrative and analysis. I have been overwhelmed beyond joy by those who told me that they heard their voices clearly in the text.

In the field, I found myself assuring those with whom I interacted that my research stemmed from a deep commitment to justice and that I had been involved in immigrant rights issues long before the start of my project. This explanation came at lightning speed, without pause, following any questions about myself or my work. I think my uneasiness had more to do with internal struggles than with participants' responses. Despite my nervousness, most people were excited by my research and thrilled that a *U.S. citizen* was committed to immigrant rights. This excitement did little to ease my discomfort; to the contrary, it made me even more anxious, because I experienced this response as their othering of themselves: Why would a U.S.-born citizen *not* care about the rights of immigrants?

Undocumented youth were most likely to press me on my work. *But is your research going to help the movement?* they asked. I agonized over this question. I wanted to give back to the movement, but I had only the vague idea that my work would, in some way, contribute "analysis." After all, that is what I had heard over and again at workshops and trainings: *We need more analysis. We need a deeper understanding.* But the people who said this were as vague in their meanings as I was in mine. What analysis did we need, specifically? What understanding did we lack? Most of the trainings and meetings I attended seemed embedded in analysis—organizers and participants drew connections between immigrant rights and racial justice, brainstormed relationships between restrictionist legislation and private prisons, and identified parallels with women's rights, civil rights, and LGBTQ liberation.

At the same time, I took on more organizing responsibilities in Knoxville. In 2012, Allies of Knoxville's Immigrant Neighbors (AKIN), an organization I cofounded, launched a campaign against the county sheriff's application for a 287(g) program; if approved, this program would deputize officers in the county jail to enforce immigration law. Through AKIN, I helped support local grassroots mobilizations of undocumented people and TIRRC's organizing work in East Tennessee. I consulted with local undocumented youth as they developed storytelling methods in support of campaigns against deportation and for tuition equality. I was appointed to the steering committee of the Southeast Immigrant Rights Network. Although I was giving back through this work, I was not satisfied that my contributions fulfilled the promises I had made.

Originally, I intended to study how immigrant rights groups in the Southeast developed infrastructure to resist restrictionist policies and practices. However, in the course of my research, I was increasingly drawn to how policies and practices functioned to shape the lives of unauthorized immigrants in the Southeast, and I thought that activists might benefit from an accounting of this process. I also noticed that narratives of resistance used by immigrant rights actors—myself included—unintentionally supported illegality. This unnerving realization forced me to rethink how I spoke and wrote about immigrants and immigration, and it continues to challenge me to this day.

Now, years later, I confess that I am still not entirely comfortable critiquing a movement that I care deeply about. I struggle with how to talk about the narrative contradictions abundant in the immigrant rights movement. Who am I to ask an undocumented man—someone who lives illegality—to modify the story he tells about why he should not be deported? I have no right to his story or how he tells it. Instead, I have focused on challenging allies on the stories we tell about unauthorized immigrants and unauthorized immigration, encouraging us to think beyond "deserving" immigrants when we consider enforcement, and affirming that immigrants are worthy of dignity not because of their spotless record or exemplary achievements but because of their humanity. I believe this work is my most important contribution to the people and groups across the Southeast that have come to mean so much to me. I hope that those who read this book will take the analysis I offer in the spirit that it is intended—respectfully, lovingly, and with a great deal of admiration for all the organizers, activists, and advocates who appear in this project, whether named or unnamed, and for all those who struggle against illegality. We have made mistakes, and we will continue to do so. But the struggle against illegality, and for dignity, is one worth having.

Notes

1. Immigration and Customs Enforcement restricts—though it does not entirely prohibit—enforcement activity in "sensitive locations," including sites of public demonstrations.

2. *Crimmigration* is the convergence of criminal and immigration law, such as through laws that criminalize unauthorized status or its consequences.

3. The phrase "illegalizing moves" is a variation on the title of Susan Bibler Coutin's (2000b) *Legalizing Moves*.

4. The Southern Poverty Law Center refers to the Dustin Inman Society as a "nativist extremist" organization that actively targets individual immigrants.

5. Federal laws restricting entry into the United States were enacted under the Page Act of 1875; sanctions for unauthorized entry were codified in 1980.

6. Naturalized citizens may also be denaturalized if they commit fraud in their naturalization petitions.

7. There are limited exceptions to restrictions on formal electoral participation. Chicago, for example, allows all residents, including noncitizens, to vote in school board elections.

2

New Destination Borderlands

I MOVED TO TENNESSEE in the summer of 2006, just months after immigrants across the nation took to the streets in protest against the threat of increasingly punitive federal immigration policies. At the close of the 2005 legislative session, the U.S. House of Representatives passed H.R. 4437, the Border Protection, Anti-Terrorism and Illegal Immigration Control Act, which proposed to curb unauthorized migration by criminalizing unauthorized residents of the United States. H.R. 4437 (often referred to as the Sensenbrenner Bill for its main sponsor, Wisconsin Republican Jim Sensenbrenner) threatened criminal penalties for immigrants whose presence in the United States was not authorized by the Department of Homeland Security. In addition, the Sensenbrenner Bill proposed to authorize the construction of seven hundred miles of fencing along the U.S.-Mexico border and to levy fines and criminal penalties against people, organizations, and businesses that knowingly employ or aid unauthorized migrants.

By the end of 2005, the Senate failed to pass a bill corresponding to H.R. 4437, thereby ending the bill's short tenure in the legislature. Although the criminalization provisions of the Sensenbrenner Bill were not enacted into law, the ideas behind the bill had not lost momentum—indeed, we continue to see their descendants today. In the early months of 2006, Senate Majority Leader Bill Frist, Republican from Tennessee, introduced S.B. 2454, the Securing America's Borders Act, which emphasized the criminalization, or illegalization, of unauthorized presence in the United States as well as enforcement-only measures to address the resident unauthorized population.

Legislative focus on the illegalization and removal of the nation's estimated eleven million unauthorized migrants sparked a wave of protests that reverberated across the nation in the spring of 2006. Provoked by these harsh approaches, immigrants, religious institutions, civil and immigrant rights groups, unions, and humanitarian organizations mobilized massive demonstrations in opposition. The Sensenbrenner and Frist proposals offered no opportunities for unauthorized immigrants to adjust their status and become authorized, and protestors were incensed by the enforcement-only approach to immigration policy reform. Faith leaders and social workers were outraged by their potential culpability under the proposed laws, because the broad wording of these bills made it possible that service providers could be held criminally liable for providing assistance to unauthorized migrants.

Between February and May, protests erupted in cities across the nation as millions of protestors marched in the streets (Bada, Fox, and Selee 2006; Wang and Winn 2006). The majority of demonstrators were people of Latin American origin and ancestry, and many were immigrants of Mexican origin. By all accounts, the scale and duration of these protests were unprecedented in the history of immigrant rights demonstrations in the United States (Johnson and Hing 2007). As U.S.- and foreign-born Latinx people filled the streets, chanting, "*Hoy marchamos, mañana votamos*" (Today we march, tomorrow we vote), commentators, organizers, and scholars noted the burgeoning political strength of the nation's largest minority group, a "sleeping giant" that had remained largely silent in the face of previous threats.[1]

To understand why the Sensenbrenner Bill provoked such outrage, we must first examine assumptions surrounding unlawful presence. After all, it is common to hear unauthorized migrants referred to as "illegal" immigrants, a broadly accepted term that passively implicates the unauthorized in criminal activity, often used to justify the denial of civil rights. Despite the implicit transgression conveyed by the word *illegal*, never in the history of the United States has unauthorized presence been codified as a criminal violation. Removal (banishment) was once considered a punishment suitable for citizens and noncitizens alike until the late nineteenth century, when the Supreme Court ruled that neither exclusion nor deportation constituted criminal proceedings (Markowitz 2011).[2] But at the time of the Sensenbrenner Bill's introduction (and still today), unauthorized presence was considered a violation of civil immigration law rather than criminal law.

This distinction, though technical, is no small difference for those who may be impacted. People facing civil proceedings are not guaranteed the same constitutional protections under the Sixth Amendment as those facing criminal proceedings. Immigrants in removal (deportation) proceedings, which are civil matters, do not have a right to legal representation in courts of law. The U.S. Code, which codifies the nation's laws, notes that immigrants in such proceedings "shall have the privilege of being represented, at no expense to the Government, by counsel of the alien's [sic] choosing."[3] Of course, defendants in removal proceedings may hire their own attorneys, but the court is not required to provide counsel free of charge—a determination that has been upheld consistently, even for very young children.[4] This means that ability to pay is a barrier to legal representation for many immigrants (Stave et al. 2017).

The severity of consequences implied by the distinction between civil and criminal violations is not as straightforward as we might assume. Unauthorized migrants may face civil penalties (such as detention, removal, and restrictions on or exclusion from future admissibility) for their unauthorized presence in the United States, but these are hardly minor outcomes (Markowitz 2011). Indeed, detention, removal, and bars on admissibility result in family separation, as children may be left behind with relatives or placed in foster care when parents are detained or deported (Wessler 2011). For those who migrated to escape violence and political instability, deportation can be dangerous—even lethal (Brodzinsky and Pilkington 2015; Stillman 2018).

To complicate matters, some immigration violations are prosecuted as crimes. Operation Streamline, initiated in 2005, enables criminal prosecution of unauthorized border crossers, including first-time entrants, who are apprehended in specific geographic regions or sectors. Unauthorized entrants may therefore face criminal penalties if they are apprehended by the Border Patrol while crossing the border without inspection,[5] and these penalties increase with multiple violations.[6] First-time offenders may be prosecuted for misdemeanor illegal entry, while repeat offenders (those who are removed and later re-apprehended, including in the interior of the country) may be charged with felony reentry (Lydgate 2010). In 2018, the Trump administration initiated a zero-tolerance policy that mandated criminal prosecution of all unauthorized entrants, provoking widespread outrage and international condemnation as it resulted in the forcible separation and detention of migrant parents and children who were apprehended together.

Of course, unauthorized residents may also face criminal penalties if they are convicted of misdemeanors or felonies while in the United States, and many (cf. De Genova 2004; Stumpf 2006) have pointed to the expanded use of state and federal nonimmigration crimes (such as identity theft) to criminalize immigrants—a point I return to in chapter 3. However, an unauthorized immigrant's mere presence in the United States is not in itself a violation of criminal law and thus is not subject to criminal penalties.

Had the Sensenbrenner Bill become law, unauthorized residents would become arrestable for their presence, criminalized for the sheer fact of being in the United States without authorization. They would be subjected to hefty fines, criminal penalties, and removal. That Congress ultimately did not enact the punitive enforcement mechanisms of the Sensenbrenner Bill offered little consolation to protestors, who also decried legislators for their collective failure to effect proactive and humanitarian reforms to immigration policy. The most recent legalization measures had been implemented two decades earlier, in 1986, through the Immigration Reform and Control Act (IRCA), which regularized the status of two million to three million previously unauthorized immigrants. Twenty years later, immigrant rights advocates demanded that Congress reform U.S. immigration policy once again. As evidenced by the 2006 mass mobilizations, enforcement-centric legislation that sought only to criminalize unauthorized immigrants was unacceptable. Advocates were further troubled by the fact that H.R. 4437 would exacerbate the vulnerability of unauthorized immigrants. Cardinal Roger Mahony (2006), archbishop of Los Angeles, noted in an open letter to President George W. Bush that the law's provisions would require service providers to become "quasi-immigration enforcement officials"; he further criticized the United States for turning a "blind eye" to the suffering of unauthorized immigrant workers, who were often exploited by their employers.

The Sensenbrenner Bill blatantly ignored the nation's failure to address systemic inequalities in the immigration system. Centuries of racialized preference systems, class biases, and national origin quotas, combined with contemporary "colorblind" immigration policies and inadequate allotment of visas, have produced relatively few pathways to authorized migration for those from high immigrant-sending countries such as Mexico and the Philippines (Golash-Boza 2012; Ngai 2004; Ogletree 2000). In early 2006, the Leadership Conference on Civil Rights (2006) issued a press statement articulating, "The entire history of the civil rights movement has been based on the recognition that there can be no such thing as second-class Americans. . . . Yet for too long, our immigration laws have created a two-tiered society and have perpetuated racial and ethnic discrimination." The Leadership Conference on Civil Rights, a coalition of civil, immigrant, and labor rights organizations, called on Congress to enact reforms focused on five criteria: a path to permanent residency for unauthorized residents; fair enforcement of immigration laws; restoration of due process for migrants in detention or removal proceedings; family reunification; and a reasonable approach to the flow of immigrant workers. In short, advocates marched in demand of comprehensive reforms that would recognize the conditions and consequences of unauthorized status.

The largest marches—*las mega marchas*—occurred in cities such as Chicago, Los Angeles, and New York (Bada, Fox, and Selee 2006). In Chicago, more than 100,000 marchers emerged on March 10, 2006, to protest criminalization of unauthorized immigrants and lack of comprehensive reform. Half a million protestors marched in the streets of Los Angeles on March 29. These cities sustained large marches throughout the spring, culminating in a nationwide May Day protest. On May 1, 2006, more than 400,000 people marched in Chicago, and another 650,000 marched in Los Angeles. Alternately referred to by protestors and Spanish-language media as *"Un Día Sin Inmigrantes"* (A Day Without Immigrants), *"El Gran Paro Estadounidense"* (The Great United States Strike), or simply *"El Gran Paro,"* protestors—predominantly Latinx immigrants—closed their stores, left work and school, boycotted businesses, and rallied to express their frustration at Congress's singular focus on criminalization.

Aside from the fact that cities like Chicago, Los Angeles, and New York experienced some of the largest and most sustained protests against H.R. 4437 and similar bills, these places also share in common their positions as large metropolitan areas with extensive histories of Latinx settlement and sizable immigrant populations. Known as established destinations for U.S.- and foreign-born people of Latin American ancestry, Los Angeles, New York, and Chicago are the three metropolitan areas in the United States with the largest Latinx populations (Suro and Singer 2002). In addition, these places are among the major contemporary immigrant-receiving gateways, meaning that they are primary entry and settlement points for all migrants to the United States, including those from Latin America (Singer 2004). In hindsight, it is not particularly astonishing that these areas witnessed substantial and prolonged protests in 2006, especially given the mobilizing roles of Spanish-language radio stations, churches, and neighborhood associations in these places (Voss and Bloemraad 2011).

Perhaps more surprising is that large-scale protests with significant Latinx turnout occurred in places that are not customarily thought to have sizable Latinx or immigrant populations. Even though established immigrant destinations claimed the largest demonstrations, marches also occurred in Southeastern and Midwestern cities with smaller Latinx populations and more recent patterns of immigrant settlement (Bada, Fox, and Selee 2006). In Charlotte, North Carolina, three thousand protestors demonstrated against harsh immigration laws on March 25. Days later, nine thousand people marched in Nashville, Tennessee. On April 9, four thousand people marched in Birmingham, Alabama, while more than thirty thousand marched in St. Paul, Minnesota. In Omaha, Nebraska, as many as ten thousand demonstrators marched on April 10. Incredibly, an estimated eighty thousand protestors marched in Atlanta, Georgia, on March 24. The sleeping giant had awoken, and not just in traditional immigrant destinations.

The Rise of New Immigrant Destinations

It is significant that massive protests erupted in unexpected places like Alabama and Tennessee. Large-scale turnout of Latinx and immigrant protestors in such destinations reveals shifts in immigrant settlement patterns that have emerged since the 1980s. Immigrant settlement patterns are influenced by preexisting networks of established immigrants. Recent immigrants tend to group in places with large, well-defined co-ethnic populations (Massey 1987; Portes and Rumbaut 1996; Zhou 1992). Network-driven settlement has practical foundations: by settling among established co-ethnic residents, incoming migrants may benefit from access to the community's accumulated knowledge, social capital, and resources (Hernández-León and Zúñiga 2003; Portes and Rumbaut 1996; Portes and Stepick 1993; Zhou 1992; see also Conley and Bohon 2010 and Hagan 1998 for gendered access to migrant social networks). Well-established co-ethnic communities may bolster the ability of immigrant groups to respond to potential threats during politically opportune moments, enabling grassroots mobilization for political protest and social change (cf. Fujiwara 2005; Horton 1995; Martinez 2008; Pardo 1990, 1995; Portes and Stepick 1993; J. Wong 2007; Zlolniski 2006).

The benefits of settling among established co-ethnic populations helps explain the spatial concentration of immigrants. Prior to the 1980s, 90 percent of all Mexican migrants—currently the largest population of immigrants in the United States—resided in just five states (Durand, Massey, and Charvet 2000). In 2000, two-thirds of all immigrants resided in six states— California, Florida, Illinois, New Jersey, New York, and Texas. Remarkably, more than half of all U.S. immigrants in the 1990s resided in just five metropolitan areas—Chicago, Los Angeles, Miami, New York City, and Orange County (Singer 2004).

Migration streams have changed dramatically in recent decades. Since the 1980s, Latinx immigrants have dispersed throughout the country to new destinations, particularly in the Southeast and Midwest. Audrey Singer (2004) documents six types of immigrant gateways—former, continuous, post–World War II, emerging, reemerging, and preemerging—based on census data of the absolute size and growth of immigrant populations in metropolitan areas compared to national averages and historical trends. In this typology, destinations considered to be established (including former, continuous, and post–World War II gateways) have historically higher-than-average rates of immigrant population growth and an overall large immigrant population in absolute numbers. Established gateways include Detroit and Philadelphia (former), Chicago, New York, and San Francisco (continuous), and Houston, Los Angeles, and Miami (post–World War II).

Emerging gateways, often referred to as new immigrant destinations, had a small percentage of foreign-born persons until 1970 as well as a relatively small foreign-born population in absolute numbers, followed by exponential increases in both the percentage and absolute number of immigrants after 1980. In Singer's typology, Atlanta and Washington, DC, are emerging gateways, or new destinations for immigrants. Preemerging gateways, which are places with a relatively small percentage increase in the immigrant population and a small immigrant population in absolute numbers, include Charlotte and Raleigh-Durham.

Patterns of Dispersal: The Push and Pull of Immigrants to New Destinations

Immigrants settle in particular areas for practical reasons, not the least of which is the presence of co-ethnic kinship or friendship networks, which often provide access to tangible and intangible supports (Hagan 1998; Portes 1998; Portes and Rumbaut 1996; Portes and Stepick 1993; Zhou 1992). True to these considerations, a large percentage of immigrants in the United States settle in established destinations, and these areas continue to receive the bulk of recent immigrants and maintain high overall immigrant populations in absolute numbers (Singer 2004). Additionally, Latinx people overwhelmingly reside in established Latino metros (Suro and Singer 2002) such as Los Angeles, Chicago, Miami, and New York.

However, immigrants and U.S.-born people of Latin American ancestry are increasingly dispersing to destinations with historically small populations of either group. By definition, new destinations lack a well-established co-ethnic community—a factor that should make these destinations less attractive than established destinations. The Latinx population in new destinations is small and mostly comprises new immigrants, which may correlate to a host of challenges for recent arrivals, including struggles with support services, integration, and reception context (Atiles and Bohon 2002; Gouveia, Carranza, and Cogua 2004; Kochar, Suro, and Tafoya 2005; Millard and Chapa 2004). Marie Price and Audrey Singer (2008) note, for example, that schools in emerging destinations face new pressures on educational resources in response to rapidly growing numbers of students with limited English proficiency, and Timothy Dunn, Ana Maria Aragones, and George Shivers (2005) note that health care facilities in these places often lack adequate interpretation services or Spanish-speaking staff to serve the needs of a growing Latinx population. New destinations may also lack capacity and infrastructure for immigrant-led political activity to address these challenges, especially compared with infrastructure developed over time in established destinations such as Los Angeles (Horton 1995) and Miami (Portes and Stepick 1993). At the same time, religious institutions, and especially immigrant-dominant congregations, often play an important role in mobilizing resources in support of immigrant communities in new destinations (Crane and Millard 2004), just as they have in established destinations (Heredia 2011; Yukich 2013).

Despite these challenges, immigrants are increasingly dispersing to new destinations. These recent changes are attributed to interrelated factors, some of which have pushed immigrants out of their countries of origin and established destinations and gateway cities and some of which have pulled them to new destinations throughout the United States. International migration is influenced by complex factors, including globalization, economic and political contexts of sending and receiving countries, labor markets and wage differentials, elaboration of transnational migrant social networks, social capital and funds of knowledge of individual migrants and their networks, and cultural and community expectations of migration as a rite of passage (Goss and Lindquist 1995; Massey 1987, 1999; Pessar 1999; Portes and Bach 1985). As Douglas Massey (1999) argues, international migration results from a synthesis of these factors; any one element is insufficient to explain the push and pull of migrants between countries.

The decision (or draw) of immigrants to settle in particular locations— whether established or new—is similarly influenced by multiple factors. Local, state, and international factors, and their impacts on the push and pull of immigrants to particular destinations, are interrelated rather than competing in explanatory power. Push factors include IRCA's amnesty of previously unauthorized immigrants; saturation of low-wage labor markets in high-density immigrant destinations; militarization of the border; and legislative targeting of unauthorized immigrants in established destinations. Pull factors include employment opportunities in new destinations, particularly in the Midwest and Southeast; perceived safety, aesthetics, and affordability of these regions in comparison to costlier and often dilapidated central cities in established destinations; and rapid creation of network migration patterns linking Latin American sister cities to new destinations.

The Immigration Reform and Control Act of 1986 addressed the burgeoning population of unauthorized immigrants—estimated at the time to comprise between three million and five million people—by providing pathways to citizenship for unauthorized immigrants who could prove that they had lived and worked in the United States for at least five consecutive years. IRCA also created pathways for temporary migration to fill industry labor shortages and required employers to obtain official work documentation for all employees. In consequence, IRCA provided both the impetus and possibility for many newly authorized immigrants to leave agricultural work and other jobs in established destinations in search of better economic opportunities elsewhere in the United States (Durand, Massey, and Capoferro 2005; Gouveia and Saenz 2000).

The sudden authorization of an estimated 2.3 million previously unauthorized Mexican migrant agricultural workers saturated local labor markets in California with newly upwardly mobile immigrant workers. This expanded labor pool, combined with the threat of employer sanctions for hiring undocumented workers, exerted downward pressure on wages as low-wage work was subcontracted to avoid economic penalties (Durand, Massey, and Charvet 2000; Phillips and Massey 1999). The Seasonal Agricultural Worker program, a provision of IRCA, regularized the status of agricultural workers who could prove continuous employment in agricultural work and thus enabled newly authorized workers to seek work with better compensation in the nation's interior (Gouveia and Saenz 2000). Moreover, IRCA's revision and expansion of the guest worker program into H2A and H2B visas pulled immigrants to new destinations to serve in seasonal or temporary positions with severe labor shortages, such as tree planting and agricultural work (McDaniel and Casanova 2003).

Beyond amnesty, IRCA increased funding for border security, instigating the militarization of the U.S.-Mexico border. Since 1986, congressional action on immigration has focused almost exclusively on expanding and funding border and interior enforcement, stipulating civil and criminal penalties for unauthorized immigration and imposing restrictions on access to federal social welfare programs for both authorized and unauthorized immigrants (Zolberg 2006). In the early 1990s, the U.S. Border Patrol shifted to a strategy of entry prevention marked by dual tactics of "prevention through deterrence" and "targeted enforcement" (Nevins 2002). Evidenced by programs such as Operation Hold-the-Line in 1993 and Operation Gatekeeper in 1994, these strategies deployed high concentrations of Border Patrol agents along the heavily trafficked migrant corridors of El Paso and San Diego. The Immigration and Naturalization Service, which has since been reorganized under the Department of Homeland Security (DHS), presumed that the presence of a robust and concentrated population of visible Border Patrol agents along established points of entry would deter unauthorized immigrants and better enable agents to apprehend those who did attempt to enter without inspection. Testifying before Congress on this border enforcement strategy, U.S. representative from Arizona Ed Pastor (1996) observed that the "overarching goal of the strategy is to make it so difficult and so costly to enter this county [sic] illegally that fewer individuals even try." Indeed, proponents of this strategy, including Doris Meissner, commissioner of the Immigration and Naturalization Service, noted, "We did believe that geography would be an ally to us. . . . It was our sense that the number of people crossing the border through Arizona would go down to a trickle once people realized what [it's] like" (quoted in Borden 2000).

Paradoxically, the militarization of the border through IRCA and subsequent policies contributed to an increase in the resident unauthorized population, even as border enforcement practices have made it more difficult for unauthorized migrants to enter without inspection (Cornelius 2001; Massey 2005; Massey, Durand, and Pren 2016). Prior to IRCA, unauthorized Latinx immigrants, primarily from Mexico, might cross the U.S.-Mexico border multiple times over the course of a lifetime, coming to work for a short period of time, migrating back across the border to reunite with family after achieving a discrete financial goal, and repeating as necessary (Gentsch and Massey 2011; Massey 1987). Militarization of the U.S.-Mexico border disrupted these cyclical migration patterns by intensifying the personal risks and costs associated with unauthorized entry (Massey, Durand, and Malone 2002).

Critics of border militarization argue that this strategy has had dangerous, even deadly, consequences for migrants (Cornelius 2001; Nevins 2002). Despite the federal government's assumption that geography would discourage migration, unauthorized entrants have undertaken longer and more dangerous journeys through remote desert lands of New Mexico and Arizona to avoid routes that were heavily monitored by Border Patrol agents. This adaptive practice has resulted in a precipitous increase in migrant deaths at the border (Hellman 2008; for narrative accounts, see Regan 2010 and Urrea 2004).

Massey and his colleagues (2016) note that unauthorized entrants must increasingly rely on professional *coyotes*, or guides, to cope with the manufactured dangers associated with contemporary border crossings. Relatedly, the price of border crossing with a *coyote* has increased alongside border militarization. Expenses associated with hiring a *coyote* easily total thousands of dollars, meaning that immigrants must remain in the United States for longer periods to recoup the costs of migration. Unauthorized immigrants are now more likely to stay in the United States, settling with their families in neighborhoods and communities across the nation (Massey 2005; Massey, Durand, and Malone 2002).

Over time, these border militarization practices, combined with insufficient and highly restricted pathways to authorized entry and residency, have resulted in a significant increase in the resident unauthorized population, particularly in established destinations (Massey, Durand, and Malone 2002; Massey and Riosmena 2010; Riosmena 2004). The resident unauthorized population stands at more than eleven million people, the vast majority of whom originate from Latin America.

Border militarization practices set in motion by IRCA, and later expanded by the 1996 Illegal Immigration Reform and Immigrant Responsibility Act, have also indirectly contributed to the dispersal of the resident unauthorized population. Border Patrol operations influenced the out-migration of immigrants from heavily patrolled border states, which were perceived as increasingly risky places of settlement for unauthorized residents (Durand, Massey, and Charvet 2000). The Border Patrol has established interior immigration checkpoints—some permanent—on major thoroughfares throughout the Southwest United States, where agents may interrogate travelers about their immigration and citizenship status and detain those suspected of being in the country without authorization. Although the Border Patrol is authorized to operate within one hundred miles of any border—and approximately two-thirds of the U.S. population lives within this range—the presence of interior checkpoints is most apparent in the Southwest.

Restrictionist legislation and rising hostility toward immigrants in some established destinations, perhaps a by-product of the increase in unauthorized residents (Espenshade and Calhoun 1993), helped push immigrants out of those states (Durand, Massey, and Capoferro 2005). In California, for example, during the economic downturn of the 1980s and 1990s, voters passed several ballot initiatives intended to curtail rights and services for unauthorized immigrants in response to outrage over IRCA's "amnesty" provisions, awareness of increasing numbers of newcomers perceived to be unauthorized, and suspicions that immigrants abuse social welfare programs at taxpayer expense (Barkan 2003; Newton 2008; P. Wilson 1994). Proposition 187 (also known as "Save Our State") denied unauthorized immigrants access to public K–12 education and state-funded nonemergency health services, while Proposition 227 banned bilingual education in public schools. As written, the ballot measures did not explicitly target any one ethnicity or language group; however, the implicit message was that Latinx— and specifically Mexican—immigrants posed significant threats and costs to the United States (Santa Ana 2002). Latinx residents of California perceived these measures as anti-Mexican in intent (Bedolla 2003).

Robin Dale Jacobson (2008) describes how California's unauthorized immigrant population was conflated with Mexican immigrants and, further, how "Mexicanness" became symbolic of invasion and criminality. Jacobson notes that supporters of Proposition 187 commonly used the words *Hispanic, Latino, Mexican, immigrant,* and *illegal* interchangeably, suggesting that these words were viewed as coterminous. Those from south of the U.S.- Mexico border were labeled as Mexicans, the placeholder ethnicity for nationals of all Latin American countries. No visible markers distinguish citizens and authorized immigrants from the unauthorized, and Mexicans in California and many Mexican Americans were presumed to be unauthorized (Ono and Sloop 2002).

The rhetoric used to mobilize support for Proposition 187 framed unauthorized immigrants as a criminal element in violation of not just immigration policies but also laws that ensure the safety and security of U.S. citizens. California governor Pete Wilson, a proponent of restrictionism, stated that unauthorized immigrants were "endangering . . . the safety of too many California neighborhoods" and creating a "public safety hazard" (quoted in Jacobson 2008: 55). Supporters of Proposition 187 distributed pamphlets asserting that Californians were "victimized by the nearly 18,000 illegal alien [*sic*] felons now in prison (with tens of thousands more on our streets)" (quoted in Jacobson 2008: 55). Perceptions such as these fueled restrictionist legislation and a climate of hostility against Latinx people, which in turn made established destinations much less attractive to immigrant newcomers, particularly the unauthorized.

If IRCA provided the possibility for newly authorized immigrants to move freely throughout the United States, the expansion of economic opportunities in the Southeast and Midwest provided the incentive for immigrants to migrate to these new destinations. California's high taxes and labor market saturation made the state less economically viable for many immigrants. The deindustrialization of the Northeast, combined with the influx of factories into the Southeast and Midwest, contributed to high unemployment in established destinations while expanding economic opportunities in new destinations (Kandel and Parrado 2005; Zúñiga and Hernández-León 2005). Meat and poultry processing industries were particularly attracted to the Southeast and Midwest due to regional histories of business-friendly practices; compared especially with the more unionized Northeast, the Southeast and Midwest had lower property taxes, lower rates of unionization, and relatively stagnant and depressed wages for so-called low-skill workers (Fink 2003; Griffith 2005; Guthey 2001; Kandel and Parrado 2004, 2005; Striffler 2005). Moreover, the overall economic expansion of the 1990s allowed many U.S.-born workers to leave less desirable, low-paying and physically demanding jobs in search of opportunities in the service sector, thereby creating key labor shortages in Southeastern carpet and poultry factories and the agricultural industry (Hernández-León and Zúñiga 2003).

As industries were drawn to the Southeast and elsewhere, immigrants seeking new and expanded job opportunities felt the pull as well (Johnson-Webb 2002; Kandel and Parrado 2004). Immigrants and their descendants already living in the United States were attracted to new destinations by economic prospects, and immigrants in sending countries were drawn both by other immigrants who had already established themselves as well as by employers. New destination employers used formal and informal strategies to recruit new employees, including posting job advertisements in sending communities and using preexisting network ties of immigrant employees to their origin communities and to other migrants throughout the United States (Donato, Stainback, and Bankston 2005; Grey 1999; Griffith 2005; Johnson-Webb 2002; Striffler 2009).

Just as factories targeted the Southeast and Midwest for relatively low costs to business, immigrants were attracted to these regions for their comparatively lower costs of living and perceived better quality of life (Marrow 2005). Ivan Light and Michael Francis Johnston (2009) argue that immigrants were pushed out of established destinations not just because of falling wages but also due to declining rent-to-wage ratios; as immigrants saturated the labor market and the low-cost housing market, the decreasing affordability and acceptability of housing in established destinations encouraged immigrants to explore options in the interior of the United States. Although some research indicates that immigrants are drawn to new destinations for the lower cost of housing (Datel and Dingemans 2008; Furuseth and Smith 2006; Price and Singer 2008; Skop and Buentello 2008), it is increasingly evident that new destinations lack sufficient affordable housing to accommodate low-wage workers (Atiles and Bohon 2002, 2003). Still, new destinations may attract immigrants for other reasons, such as perceptions of good schools and safe communities (Atiles and Bohon 2002).

Immigrants are also drawn to new destinations by perceptions of better security. Unauthorized immigrants may believe, for example, that destinations with smaller immigrant populations are less risky than border states, especially states in the Southwest. In border states, strict border enforcement practices and constant Border Patrol operations present significant obstacles for those who lack authorization (Durand, Massey, and Capoferro 2005). ICE agents as well as civilian vigilante groups such as the Minutemen tend to operate more actively in states like California than in new destinations, where unauthorized immigration has been largely viewed as a minor issue until recently (Dove 2010; Mariscal 2005). Increasingly, however, immigration enforcement is active even in places with small immigrant populations, and immigrants in emerging destinations such as Georgia and North Carolina often feel singled out and targeted for discrimination as a result of their ethnic origins (Atiles and Bohon 2002; Southern Poverty Law Center 2009; Torres, Popke, and Hapke 2006). This is especially true as enforcement devolves to state and local authorities and as new destination states implement restrictionist crimmigration policies.

As immigrants disperse to new destinations, network migration chains have created new "sister city" links in other countries to specific cities in the United States. Cases of single-stream migration between sending communities abroad and receiving communities in the United States—such as the established links between Villachuato, Mexico, and Marshalltown, Iowa (Grey and Woodrick 2002)—indicate that migrants are pulled to new destinations just as they are pulled to established destinations. Once transnational communities are linked, practical migration strategies, such as network-facilitated migration and hiring practices, boost immigrant settlement in new destinations (Zúñiga and Hernández-León 2005). Network ties between immigrants in sending and receiving communities facilitate the availability of resources for recent arrivals, thereby decreasing costs and stressors associated with migration (Massey 1999). Thus, established networks in new destinations—even though they might be quite small—can facilitate network migration through social and tangible supports such as housing, start-up capital, and funds of knowledge (Donato, Stainbeck, and Bankston 2005).

Latinx immigrants have increasingly dispersed to new destinations across the United States despite the fact that these new places may lack the larger co-ethnic support networks characteristic of established destinations. Push factors related to policies such as IRCA and the Illegal Immigration Reform and Immigrant Responsibility Act, combined with economic factors such as the saturation of the low-wage labor market and high housing prices as well as anti-immigrant hostility, increasingly restrictive local legislation, and border militarization practices, have encouraged immigrants to explore settlement options outside established destinations. At the same time, pull factors such as job opportunities, cost of living, perceived security, and network migration have steadily encouraged immigrants to settle in new destinations, thereby increasing the size of immigrant populations. As a result, when massive immigrant rights protests erupted across the nation in response to the Sensenbrenner Bill, new destinations were not left out: immigrants in the Southeast, too, had a stake in resisting the policies and practices of illegality.

The Southeast as Border and Borderland

The Southeast is not just a new destination for Latinx immigrants; it is also a border within the United States—a *frontera* within a *frontera*. Regionally, culturally, and demographically distinct from traditional immigrant and Latinx settlement spaces (Marrow 2011a; McConnell 2011), the Southeast is a new site of exclusion in the creation of immigrant illegality. This is true even as the tools of exclusion—the borderlands of illegality or the spaces of nonexistence (Coutin 2003)—resemble those that have long been manufactured and sustained elsewhere.

Regardless of immigration and citizenship status, Latinx people in the Southeast are often perceived and portrayed as distinct others from the established resident population by a number of differences, not the least of which are racial and ethnic markers. In a region long characterized by a color line that has been drawn along a binary of black and white (Marrow 2009; Stuesse 2016), brownness complicates racialized understandings of belongingness. Latinx immigrants, in particular, experience this "*Nuevo New South*" (Mohl 2003) through the responses of their receiving communities, which are structured by racialized discourses of difference and belongingness (Furuseth and Smith 2006; Lippard and Gallagher 2011).

The Southeast is not unfamiliar with overt racial tensions, and politicians have long cultivated the hostilities of white southerners against black residents as an institutional political strategy (Bass and De Vries 1995; Black and Black 2003; Roemer, Lee, and Van der Straeten 2007). When I moved to Tennessee in the summer of 2006, shortly after immigrant rights protests swept the nation in outrage over the Sensenbrenner Bill, the state was in the middle of a contentious U.S. Senate campaign. Republican nominee Bob Corker and Democratic challenger Harold Ford Jr. both embraced racialized political advertisements as they vied for the seat soon to be vacated by Bill Frist. If elected, Ford would become the first black U.S. senator from the South since Reconstruction, and it was clear from the campaign ads that this was no small issue. Described by pundits as one of the "most competitive and nasty U.S. Senate races in the nation" (*CBS News*, 2009), the race gained widespread notoriety for racialized propaganda.

In what has been referred to as the "Southern strategy," the Republican Party has historically used racially coded messaging to win over white Southern voters in the backlash against the civil rights movement (Lamis 1999). Such messages may be covert, as with Ronald Reagan's oblique references to "welfare queens," "states' rights," and the "war on drugs," which intend to obscure racial stories through parables of morality, justice, and responsibility. Messages may also be more overt, depicting black people as untrustworthy, suspicious, or threatening, as with the infamous Willie Horton commercial in George H. W. Bush's 1988 presidential campaign. Black men, in particular, are portrayed as dangerous, especially to white women and families (Mayer 2002).

It was clear that the Republican National Committee and partisan political action committees relied on this strategy in political ads for the 2006 Tennessee election. In one pro-Corker commercial, paid for by the Republican National Committee, a blonde-haired, ivory-skinned woman wiggled her bare shoulders and cooed, "I met Harold at the Playboy Party!" Later in the commercial, the woman winked at the camera as she whispered, "Harold, call me." On the surface, the ad appeared to underscore Ford's apparent untrustworthiness, to identify him as a man with dubious ethical practices, undeserving of the U.S. Senate. More profoundly, NAACP Washington bureau director Hilary Shelton noted the commercial's "powerful innuendo that plays to pre-existing prejudices about African-American men and white women" (quoted in Wallsten 2006). The ad's reference to interracial sexuality—and the perceived threat that this implied—combined with the added danger posed by the light-skinned Ford's potential to pass as white, was unambiguous: Ford constituted a racial threat to white political, social, and economic power in Tennessee.

Shortly after its launch, the Republican National Committee's commercial was broadly condemned as race baiting. Even Corker criticized the ad as "over the top" (Wallsten 2006) in an attempt to distance his campaign from the national Republican organization. Still, racialized messaging continued throughout the Tennessee Senate race. Another pro-Corker ad, paid for by Tennesseans for Truth, contended that Ford "represents the interests of black people above all others." Yet another campaign ad, paid for by Corker for Senate and endorsed by Corker, obliquely referenced Ford's racial otherness through its musical sound track. The radio ad paired Corker's name and accomplishments to a soaring patriotic orchestra; in juxtaposition, Ford's name was accompanied by sounds broadly interpreted as "jungle drums."

The national press was not kind in its coverage, eventually prompting Corker's campaign to disavow such tactics. At the same time, other ads with equally racialized messages—albeit targeting Latinx immigrants—received little national attention. Both campaigns proclaimed their candidate as "tough" on the border, and their ads incorporated threatening messages of Latinx "invasion" to convey urgency and moral panic. One commercial, sponsored by the Ford campaign, presented an exposé of Corker's inclination to hire "illegals" [sic] at his construction sites: "Bob Corker likes to talk tough about illegal [sic] immigration. What Bob Corker doesn't tell you is when he was building these apartments, INS [Immigration and Naturalization Service] agents warned him twice about illegals [sic] on his worksite. . . . He looked the other way for cheap labor, and we're paying the price" (emphasis added).

Ford's accusation—that Corker employed unauthorized immigrants even as he "talk[ed] tough" about "illegal [sic] immigration"—was not an accounting of the candidate's hypocrisy in profiting from the dislocation of vulnerable migrants or the exploitation of low-wage labor, immigrant or otherwise. Nor was it merely a story of Corker's complacency—or even culpability—around unauthorized migration. Instead, the commercial communicated the danger, or threat, of unauthorized immigrants to U.S. citizens. Complementing the commercial's voice-over was imagery depicting dark-skinned, steely-faced Latino-looking men, clad in dark jeans and jackets, stepping through wire fencing, ambiguous terrain in the background. According to this narrative, unauthorized migrants not only provide "cheap labor," thereby displacing jobs and benefits from U.S. citizens; they also violate what should be inviolable, the borders of the United States. The commercial implies that unauthorized migrants, racialized as Latinx figures, have also breached the Southeastern state of Tennessee.

Complicating historical racial tensions of the black-white color line, then, was the newly emerging—though, for much of the Southeast, small in absolute numbers—Latinx population (Kochar, Suro, and Tafoya 2005; Lee and Bean 2007; Marrow 2009). As someone newly transposed to the cultural South from a state more heavily populated by both immigrants and U.S.-born people of Latin American ancestry, I wondered whether Tennesseans were really concerned about border enforcement or Latinx in-migration. After all, the U.S.-Mexico border seemed so distant, so abstract, and the Latinx population seemed minuscule. In 2000, fewer than 124,000 Latinx people—2.2 percent of Tennessee's population—resided in the entire state; by 2010, the number had more than doubled to 290,000, a significant increase to be sure but still just 4.6 percent of the state's population (Ennis,

Ríos Vargas, and Albert 2011); the vast majority of these people were U.S.-born citizens.

Some research suggests that new receiving destinations are largely ambivalent to immigrant settlement (De Jong and Tran 2001; J. Johnson, Johnson-Webb, and Farrell 1999; Mohl 2003; Studstill and Nieto-Studstill 2001). Latinx immigrants may be interpreted as beneficial to the community based on perceptions of strong family ties, moral values and religiosity, and work ethic (Padin 2005). U.S.-born residents in new destinations may also value the multicultural diversity or cultural novelty of immigrants, as localities institutionalize the celebration of cultural festivities such as Cinco de Mayo (Shutika 2008) or Hispanic Heritage Month. Reception context has implications for the willingness of communities to reach out to immigrant newcomers as well as for the ability of recent arrivals to access community resources. When immigrants appear to fit in or contribute to the community, they are often welcomed (Naples 2007; Padin 2005).

At the same time, attitudes toward immigrants vary depending on the region or rurality of settlement destinations. For example, new destinations in the Midwest may be more receptive to immigrants than new destinations in the Southeast, and metropolitan areas may be more receptive than rural areas (De Jong and Tran 2001; Marrow 2005). A sudden, rapid increase of immigrants—especially immigrants who are easily distinguished linguistically and racially from U.S.-born residents of the area—may be interpreted as threats to the "normalcy" of a community's way of life (Neal and Bohon 2003) or, more pointedly, to the racial hierarchy (Jackson 2011; McConnell 2011).

The racialized ads in the 2006 Tennessee U.S. Senate race, which was ultimately won by Bob Corker, both reflected and marketed a new anxiety felt by many in the Southeast related to the changing demographic structure of the local population. White residents of new destinations often feel threatened by rapid demographic changes. They may perceive that immigrants challenge the foundations of their communities either by shifting the racial composition—an increase in brown immigrants in a destination that previously was thought of as black and non-Latino white—or by defying deeply held impressions of racial belongingness (Lippard and Gallagher 2011; Mohl 2003; Naples 2007). This fear is exacerbated by electoral strategies that portray immigrants as criminals (Jacobson 2008), as burdens on taxpayer resources (Neal and Bohon 2003), or as fundamentally unassimilable or un-American (Padin 2005). Since new destinations are often unprepared to meet the needs of a rapid population surge, immigrants' use of, or demand for, any resources may be perceived negatively by others (Gouveia, Carranza, and Cogua 2005; Lacy 2011; McClain 2006), thereby reinforcing established residents' racialized fears of newcomers.

Perhaps these racialized political ads were a response to the wave of protests that had erupted even in the Southeast, a *nuevo* Southern strategy intended to exploit fears of the changing demographic composition of Tennessee and the southern states more generally. In the Southeast and elsewhere, Latinx migrants are constructed as political scapegoats of systemic problems. This is not the least in part because Latinx newcomers—who are largely perceived as both foreign-born and unauthorized (Bohon and Macpherson Parrott 2011)—can be portrayed as threatening to white and black southerners alike (Mindiola, Niemann, and Rodriguez 2002), even as policies surrounding this rhetoric ultimately sustain white institutional and economic power (Jackson 2011).

In this sense, the campaign season's political ads were not solely about fortifying the U.S.-Mexico border against the arrival of unauthorized entrants into the United States; they were also a metaphor for protecting the *frontera* of the U.S. Southeast from the Latinx migrant. Structured by racialized and cultural discourses of otherness, the Southeast has positioned itself as a space of non-belongingness for Latinx immigrants, a new borderland ripe for producing immigrant illegality.

Notes

1. Miami's Cuban enclave—with its significant political strength, cohesion, and economic capital—is one exception (Garcia 1996; Portes and Stepick 1993).

2. *Chae Chan Ping v. United States*, 1889, and *Fong Yue Ting v. United States*, 1893.

3. 8 U.S. Code § 1229a.

4. *C.J.L.G. v, Sessions*, 2018.

5. Noncitizens who enter the United States must obtain prior approval from U.S. Citizenship and Immigration Services or U.S. Customs and Border Protection. On entering, noncitizens must present documents (i.e., visas) for inspection by a Border Patrol officer; on approval, these individuals are authorized to remain for a specified duration of time or for a particular purpose as long as they comply with the visa terms, which may include restrictions on work and travel. Those who enter without engaging this process are said to have entered "without inspection." Entry without inspection is only one of many actions that can result in unauthorized status.

6. Criminal prosecutions for illegal entry and reentry increased under the Obama administration. In 2018, the Trump administration announced a zero-tolerance policy on illegal entry and reentry and vowed to prosecute all unauthorized entrants.

3

Multiplying Forces in the Homeland Security State

AN ADVERTISEMENT for U.S. senator John McCain's 2010 reelection campaign opens on a bare stretch of dusty road in the Arizona border town of Nogales. Zooming in, we see Senator McCain and Paul Babeu, the sheriff of Pinal County, walking together alongside the skeleton of a border fence. As they walk the dusty road, we seem to eavesdrop on their conversation:

> McCAIN: Drug and human smuggling, home invasions, murder.
> BABEU: We're outmanned. Of all the illegals [*sic*] in America, more than half come through Arizona.
> McCAIN: Have we got the right plan?
> BABEU: Plan's perfect. You bring troops, state, county, and local law enforcement together . . .
> McCAIN: . . . and complete the danged fence.
> BABEU: It'll work this time. Senator, you're one of us.

Political campaigns trade in fears of the unauthorized, particularly the "Latino threat" (Chavez 2008) from south of the U.S.-Mexico border (Lugo-Lugo and Bloodsworth-Lugo 2010; Mariscal 2005). Indeed, Latinx migration is often characterized through imagery reminiscent of invasion, and discourse surrounding the border suggests crisis and anarchy (Chavez 2001). In this regard, McCain is unexceptional in his characterization of the border as the epicenter of violent criminality and his support for the "danged fence" as a necessary tool to protect U.S. citizens from villainous immigrants; his rhetoric might even be considered tame by today's standards. After all, in 2015, Donald Trump announced his presidential campaign by excoriating Mexican immigrants as criminals, rapists, and "bad hombres." Trump's signature campaign pledge was to build a wall and make Mexico pay for it.

Fortification of the nation's southern border has long occupied the political and popular imagination, articulating a combination of both real and fictional stories of unauthorized migration. It is certainly true that many unauthorized immigrants enter the United States through Mexico; however, unauthorized entry is on the decline and has been for some time. In the 1990s and mid-2000s, Border Patrol agents apprehended an average of more than one million unauthorized entrants per year, the overwhelming majority of whom were caught along the U.S.-Mexico border. Since 2006, border apprehensions have steadily decreased, dropping sharply to 340,000 in 2011 (U.S. Customs and Border Protection 2017d). This decrease is considered to reflect a decline in unauthorized entry (Passel, Cohn, and Gonzalez-Barrera 2012; Sapp 2011), which is largely attributed to global economic conditions that influence the decision structure surrounding migration. Since 2011, apprehensions have increased intermittently, corresponding to an increase in migrants from El Salvador, Guatemala, and Honduras who are fleeing the impacts of violence and climate change. In 2017, however, apprehensions fell to 310,500, substantially fewer than any year since 1971, reflecting an overall downward trend in unauthorized entry (U.S. Customs and Border Protection 2017a, 2017d).

The decrease in unauthorized entrants has not been accompanied by a decrease in resources for measures that are uncritically referred to as "border security." Since the early 1990s, the Border Patrol's budget has grown exponentially, from $326 million in 1992 to more than $3.6 billion in 2016 (U.S Customs and Border Protection 2017b). The border and border communities were heavily militarized during this period, both in terms of the number of personnel who police the boundary and the technology they use to do so. In 1992, prior to intensification of border controls through Operation Hold-the-Line and Operation Gatekeeper, the Border Patrol employed roughly 4,100 agents, 85 percent of whom patrolled the nearly two thousand-mile border region between the United States and Mexico. By 2016, the number of agents had grown to twenty thousand, an increase of nearly 400 percent; seventeen thousand of these agents monitored the Southwest border (U.S Customs and Border Protection 2017c).[1]

Those who romanticize the Border Patrol as agents who travel the border on horseback, sign-cutting through the desert in search of unauthorized entrants, are disconnected from present-day reality.[2] The modern Border Patrol engages sophisticated surveillance technology—including infrared night-vision scopes, remote-controlled drones and video cameras, motion sensors, and even a crowd-sourcing system[3]—to aid in the detection and apprehension of unauthorized entrants (Heyman 2014; Koslowski 2011). Though the "danged fence" looms large in people's imagination, it is only one tool of many intended to secure the border and deter unauthorized migration.

Although the rhetoric may not be exceptional, what have changed are the strategies and tools used by the United States to mobilize immigration enforcement powers. In the aftermath of the 2001 attacks on the World Trade Center, immigration enforcement has become a growth industry, expanding beyond the exclusive role of the federal government to emphasize a collaborative approach between federal, state, and local agencies (Coleman 2012; Mittelstadt et al. 2011; Waslin 2010). This strategy, articulated by Sheriff Babeu in McCain's campaign ad, is to bring together "troops, state, county, and local law enforcement" in service of homeland security, creating a formidable, and critically entangled, immigration enforcement regime (Coleman and Kocher 2011)—a regime that operates not only along the border but within the nation's interior as well.

Sheriff Babeu's proposal may seem unremarkable today, as immigration enforcement is pervasive throughout the country, and enforcement actions large and small are chronicled weekly in every major news outlet. As the resident unauthorized population has risen over the last few decades—in no small part a consequence of border militarization—interior enforcement has emerged as a central effort in protecting and defending the homeland (Capps et al. 2011; Coleman 2008; Waslin 2010; T. Wong 2012). The modern enforcement regime of the "homeland security state" (De Genova 2007) expands the strategy of "prevention through deterrence"[4] as articulated by the Border Patrol of the 1990s to one of enforcement through attrition and criminalization of even the most mundane activities of daily life. By linking federal immigration authorities with state and local law enforcement agencies, the modern enforcement regime enables a universal approach to deportation, expanding potential targets to include the nation's entire resident unauthorized population. In this way, enforcement policies and practices may illegalize unauthorized immigrants not just when they are apprehended along the border but anytime and anywhere in the United States.

Immigration Enforcement Meets Homeland Security

In the aftermath of two national disasters—the 2001 attacks on the World Trade Center in New York City and the 2004 post–Hurricane Katrina flooding of New Orleans—Congress and the George W. Bush administration commissioned reports to examine weaknesses and failures of U.S. institutions to prevent and respond to catastrophes (cf. Executive Office of the President 2006; National Commission on Terrorist Attacks 2004). Analyses indicated that the intelligence community and emergency responders had been hindered by insufficient communications infrastructure and inadequate coordination across federal, state, and local agencies. The reports also acknowledged a breakdown in agencies' capacities to respond to a new era of risk and specifically implicated deficiencies in shared radio frequencies, access to medical records between state and local agencies, and intelligence-sharing across government agencies at all levels. As dangers to the nation's security broadened, the reviewers argued that the nation's interagency coordination procedures and communications infrastructure must adapt to the changing nature of threats.

The reports also recommended that the federal government spearhead an "information sharing revolution" across governmental agencies at all levels as a tool of emergency preparedness. It was thought that efficient access to information would improve the efficacy of public safety organizations in the event of another national emergency. In theory, widespread information sharing would also strengthen the capacity of federal agencies to identify and assess potential threats to national security, enabling the United States to prevent catastrophes before they happen.

In practice, information sharing functions as *interoperability*. This term has come to be used by the federal government to articulate cooperative partnerships between federal agencies and state and local public health and safety departments through the implementation of extensive information-sharing networks and interagency communication. Many community-based first responders, including law enforcement, fire fighters, and emergency medical providers, view interoperability as logical and beneficial. According to their reasoning, agencies that are interoperable, or able to collaborate with one another, are better equipped to strategically organize and deploy services, especially during times of crisis. Ideally, interoperability promotes a rapid and effective response to community safety concerns.

The origins of interoperability are instructive for understanding the contemporary manifestation of immigration enforcement in the United States. By 2003, the investigative functions of the Immigration and Naturalization Service—the federal agency formerly tasked with the administration of immigration policy—and the enforcement arm of the U.S. Customs Service—the federal agency formerly tasked with processing goods and people at ports of entry—had been largely reorganized as Immigration and Customs Enforcement under the Department of Homeland Security, a massive institution dedicated to preventing and responding to terrorist attacks and other threats to the United States by reducing the nation's vulnerabilities, especially in terms of immigration-related security. The momentum for interoperability arose in coordination with federal departmental changes, and the now ubiquitous nature of police-ICE collaboration—a relatively new phenomenon—was inspired by the repercussions of the 2001 attacks on the World Trade Center.

Empowered to address national security threats, ICE appeared to take seriously the "importance of intelligence analysis that can draw on all relevant sources of information," as articulated in the *9/11 Commission Report* (National Commission on Terrorist Attacks 2004: 416). Previously untapped sources of information included state and local law enforcement agencies. Institutionalization of cooperative partnerships—under the label of ICE ACCESS (Agreements of Cooperation in Communities to Enhance Safety and Security) programs—would allow local jurisdictions to "combat specific challenges in their communities" (U.S. Immigration and Customs Enforcement 2010a: 1) and assist the federal government in identifying national security threats. According to ICE: "Terrorism and criminal activity are most effectively combated through a multi-agency/multi-authority approach that encompasses federal, state and local resources, skills and expertise. State and local law enforcement play a critical role in protecting our homeland because they are often the first responders on the scene when there is an incident or attack against the United States. *During the course of daily duties, they will often encounter foreign-born criminals and immigration violators who pose a threat to national security or public safety*" (U.S. Immigration and Customs Enforcement 2010a: 1; emphasis added).

The restructuring of immigration matters under the Department of Homeland Security and the institutionalization of police-ICE collaboration are motivated in part by two assumptions. First, local law enforcement officers are more likely than ICE agents to have routine interactions with immigrants, including those who are unauthorized. This assumption is reasonable given the sheer quantity of police officers (compared with the smaller number of ICE agents), their presence in communities, and the routine tasks embedded in their positions. When measured as the capacity to identify and apprehend unauthorized immigrants, involvement of state and local law enforcement agencies in immigration enforcement increases the overall efficiency of the Department of Homeland Security.

In this sense, local law enforcement serves as a *force multiplier* for DHS. Force multiplication, an expression derived from military terminology, is the process of increasing an entity's capabilities—such as through the additional use of technology or tactics—to increase the entity's effectiveness at completing its mission. As articulated in McCain's campaign advertisement described at the beginning of this chapter, state and local law enforcement agencies—even federal agencies generally unrelated to immigration matters—are force multipliers aiding the Border Patrol and Immigration and Customs Enforcement in the enforcement of federal immigration law for the protection of the homeland. If the mission of federal immigration authorities is to identify and remove all unauthorized immigrants from the country, partnership with these other agencies increases capacity to accomplish this goal.

Perhaps more important to understanding fundamental changes in enforcement activity, however, is the second assumption: the idea that immigrants, particularly those who are unauthorized, pose a distinct risk to national security. Grounded in the conflation of unauthorized migration with terrorism—or criminal activity more generally—this assumption underlies the transfer of immigration matters to the Department of Homeland Security and inspires the apparent need for involvement of multiple levels of law enforcement in matters of immigration enforcement. In this rationale, individuals who violate immigration laws will inevitably violate non-immigration-related criminal laws, justifying the role of state and local law enforcement in immigration enforcement to prevent community harms. Police-ICE collaboration is, therefore, a "common sense" tool for protecting the homeland. Thomas Homan, former acting director of ICE, articulated this precisely: "By partnering with ICE . . . counties will be able to identify criminal aliens [*sic*] in their jails and turn them over to ICE. . . . *It is common sense partnerships like these that help law enforcement achieve our mutual goals*, and I'm encouraged by the increased interest from law enforcement professionals who seek to join this program and protect public safety" (U.S. Immigration and Customs Enforcement 2017b; emphasis added).[5] Police-ICE collaboration is therefore marshalled in service of "mutual goals," conceived here as the protection of public safety. The belief that such collaboration is necessary and desirable is only common sense if we assume that unauthorized immigrants—"criminal" or otherwise—constitute a threat to the homeland.

The logic that defines unauthorized immigrants as "criminal aliens" is validated through the implementation of laws that prohibit unauthorized immigrants from engaging in mundane activities such as driving and working and that further criminalize those who participate in these activities. In the United States, it is illegal to drive without a license, and many unauthorized immigrants experience a chain reaction of immigration enforcement consequences when they are arrested on this charge. Just so, in 2018, I was contacted by a man whose father had been arrested for driving without a license and then processed for removal after a police officer witnessed another driver rear-end the father's car. The police report of the incident confirms the son's story, but it reveals nothing about the fact that the father had lived in Knoxville for more than a decade prior to this arrest, quietly building a life to sustain his family.

It is worth noting that the proximate cause of this man's arrest—driving without a license—is itself a consequence of policy decisions by the Tennessee legislature. Like many states, Tennessee denies driver's licenses to unauthorized immigrants. This was not always the case: from 2001 until 2004, the state issued driver's licenses regardless of immigration and citizenship status, thanks in part to a dedicated campaign by immigrants and advocates (Ansley 2010). However, state implementation of federal standards invoked in the REAL ID Act—which mandates that state agencies verify an applicant's immigration and citizenship status prior to issuing driver's licenses and nondriver identification—prohibits those who cannot prove authorized residence from obtaining federally approved documents. States may issue separate identification documents to unauthorized immigrants, including driving certificates, but these must be specially marked as invalid for federal identification purposes (such as for voting, obtaining public benefits, or boarding a plane); only a handful of states do this. Tennessee initially complied with this two-tier system; however, the legislature eliminated this option in 2007. Today, in the majority of states, including Tennessee, unauthorized immigrants are criminalized by the routine act of driving, even as broader policy decisions (around mass transportation, for example) shape the extent to which driving is necessary to accomplish daily tasks of life, especially in the "car-based economy" of the New South (Stuesse and Coleman 2014).

Similarly, unauthorized migrants may be charged with identity theft or criminal impersonation for soliciting employment with falsified documents. Since unauthorized immigrants are legally prohibited from entering into formal employment relationships, they must often use a false name and false social security number to solicit employment. This situation is exacerbated by universal implementation of employment eligibility verification documents (Form I-9) as well as widespread implementation of E-Verify, an electronic verification program that confirms the identity and employment eligibility of newly hired employees. As a sociopolitical condition, there is nothing inherent to unauthorized status that requires the denial of driver's licenses or work authorization. Instead, laws are deployed to create and justify the condition of illegality, and some have documented the perverse ways that the introduction of immigration enforcement into the workplace and routine traffic stops can produce exploitation and racial profiling (Smith, Avendaño, and Martínez Ortega 2009; Stuesse 2016). If legal permission to drive and work is unavailable to unauthorized immigrants, then the unauthorized must, as Susan Bibler Coutin (2003) argues, engage in unlawful practices as a condition of survival. In this way, criminalization of the circumstances and actions required to survive naturalizes the involvement of state and local law enforcement agencies in easing the detection, apprehension, and removal of unauthorized immigrants. It is therefore "common sense" to involve state and local police in the identification of unauthorized immigrants, who will necessarily become criminals.

As "homeland security" has become tantamount not just to border security but also to interior enforcement, the collaboration (or interoperability) of law enforcement agencies and federal immigration authorities is naturalized as a reasonable solution to the manufactured threat of unauthorized immigrants. With regard to immigration enforcement, interoperability refers to cross-agency cooperation between DHS, ICE, and federal, state, and local law enforcement agencies. Cooperative mechanisms present in various ways, from delegation of immigration authority to routine sharing of biometric data across local, state, and federal agencies. The following sections highlight two programs—287(g) and Secure Communities—that play starring roles in collaborative immigration enforcement partnerships.

287(g) Delegation of Immigration Authority: The Story of Juana Villegas

On July 3, 2008, Juana Villegas was driving home from a doctor's appointment when she was stopped by a police officer for careless driving. According to the officer, Villegas failed to come to a complete stop before continuing through an intersection. The officer soon discovered that Villegas lacked a valid driver's license, registration, and car insurance and further suspected that she was undocumented. Juana Villegas, nearly nine months pregnant at the time of the stop, was arrested and taken to jail. Because she was stopped in Davidson County, Tennessee, a jurisdiction that deputized corrections officers to function as immigration agents through participation in the 287(g) program, the jail was able to determine that Villegas was, indeed, undocumented and moreover that she had ignored a prior order of removal from 1996—a felony immigration violation; Villegas was held in custody and processed for ICE.

"I was in jail when my water broke," Juana Villegas later shared in an interview with a global women's rights organization. "They took me in an ambulance and cuffed my hands and feet. When we got to the hospital, they moved me to the bed and cuffed [my] hand and foot to the bed" (quoted in Breakthrough 2009). Villegas remained handcuffed to the bed throughout her labor, a common practice for incarcerated women regardless of immigration status; her handcuffs were temporarily removed while she gave birth. After the birth, she was once again handcuffed to the bed, making it difficult to hold and nurse her newborn son. Three days later, her infant was taken from her, and Villegas was transported back to the county jail to await further processing by immigration officials. She was given no information about her newborn's whereabouts, nor was she permitted to contact her husband and family. Unable to nurse her child and denied access to adequate medical care—such as a breast pump, cold compresses, and anti-inflammatory medications—Villegas developed a painful breast infection.

Delegation of authority under 287(g) enables state and local law enforcement agencies to collaborate with federal immigration authorities to enforce federal immigration laws. Commonly referred to by its section number in the Immigration and Nationality Act, 287(g) was codified as an amendment to the legislation through the 1996 Illegal Immigration Reform and Immigrant Responsibility Act. The amendment states:

> The Attorney General may enter into a written agreement with a State, or any political subdivision of a State, pursuant to which an officer or employee of the State or subdivision, who is determined by the Attorney General to be qualified to perform a function of an immigration officer in relation to the investigation, apprehension or

detention of aliens in the United States (including the transportation of such aliens across State lines to detention centers), may carry out such function at the expense of the State or political subdivision and to the extent consistent with State and local law. (Sec. 287(g)(1) [8 U.S.C. 1357])

Under 287(g), Immigration and Customs Enforcement may enter into memoranda of agreement with state and local law enforcement agencies to confer enforcement authority for certain provisions of federal immigration law. Specifically, the 287(g) program deputizes specially trained law enforcement officers, including police officers, correctional facilities staff, and state troopers, to perform the duties of immigration officials. These duties may include identifying and interrogating unauthorized immigrants or "criminal aliens," serving immigration arrest warrants, detaining immigrants for civil immigration violations, and initiating removal proceedings. Deputized officers are trained and supervised by ICE, but they are employed and salaried by state and local jurisdictions. Signed agreements last for two years and may be renewed.

The 287(g) program was originally conceptualized as three programmatic models: task force, jail enforcement, and hybrid. In the task force model, designated officers may interrogate people about their immigration status during the course of regular law enforcement duties, such as stops for minor traffic violations, and make arrests based on immigration status. In the jail enforcement model, designated officers in state and local correctional facilities may interrogate people about their immigration status once they are arrested and booked on criminal charges, regardless of the severity of charges, and they may detain those determined to be in violation of civil immigration laws above and beyond the time allowed to process criminal charges. Correctional facilities officers may also prepare charging documents, such as the Notice to Appear, to initiate the process of removal, more commonly referred to as deportation. The hybrid model permits designated officers to perform both functions, serving as immigration officers in the streets and in jails.

Even though 287(g) was organized as three distinct models, powers designated specifically for officers operating under the task force model often creep into jail enforcement jurisdictions (Kee 2012; Nguyen and Gill 2010). In other words, jurisdictions with jail enforcement authority may nevertheless see law enforcement officers within that jurisdiction, or in associated jurisdictions, patrolling differently in the streets, despite the fact that those officers have no legal authority to enforce immigration laws. Just so, when Juana Villegas was arrested, the arresting officer had no immigration enforcement powers. Yet, as Amada Armenta (2017) makes clear in her examination of Juana Villegas's 2008 traffic stop by a Berry Hill police officer,

Villegas was arrested not because she lacked a driver's license (even though that was the official charge on the arrest report) but because she was undocumented. In dashboard camera footage of the incident, the officer is overheard explaining the arrest to Villegas's brother-in-law, who arrived at the scene of the traffic stop to collect Villegas's three young U.S.-born children, who were in the car at the time: "Nashville has an ICE office. . . . She's [Villegas] got to show me . . . something that says she's here legally. If she can't show me that, then she goes to jail. They'll interview her down there. If she's here illegally, I can promise you, she's going back to Mexico" (quoted in Armenta 2017: 139–140).

If Juana Villegas had been able to demonstrate authorized presence in the United States, the arresting officer might have released her with a citation for reckless driving or driving without a license. Since she could not prove authorization, per the officer, "she goes to jail." After asking the brother-in-law whether Villegas was "here legal or illegal [sic]," the officer also said, "I don't do immigration, that's the federal government" (Armenta 2017). And yet, during this traffic stop, the officer assumed authority to interrogate both Villegas and her brother-in-law about Villegas's immigration status. That the police officer felt comfortable raising the question of Villegas's immigration status during a misdemeanor traffic stop and discussing immigration consequences suggests that law enforcement officers do not always recognize the existence of a firm boundary between the streets and the jail, despite the language of a 287(g) memorandum of agreement.

The first memorandum of agreement for 287(g) authority was signed with the state of Florida in 2002, but the 287(g) program as a whole did not gain momentum until after 2006 (Capps et al. 2011).[6] Even so, relatively few law enforcement agencies across the United States have implemented 287(g); during the Bush and Obama administrations, there were never more than seventy to eighty signed memoranda of agreement at any one time. In part, this might be because some jurisdictions have other means to engage with ICE, such as through the Criminal Alien Program, which allows ICE officers to enter jails and interrogate inmates. Other jurisdictions decline to participate because of limited local resources and the program's potentially high fiscal cost to local governments. Jurisdictions that participate in 287(g) are primarily responsible for covering expenses associated with the program, including start-up costs and the salaries and benefits of officers who receive 287(g) delegation of authority. In Prince William County, Virginia, start-up costs for the county's 287(g) program were estimated at more than $1 million, with a projected cost of $26 million to the county over the first five years of operation (Singer, Wilson, and DeRenzis 2009).

For the most part, these costs accrue to local jurisdictions, although there are variations. In North Carolina, for example, the state legislature has granted additional funding to local sheriffs interested in pursuing immigration enforcement authority. Jurisdictions also cover the majority of costs associated with detaining unauthorized immigrants. Even though these costs are partially reimbursable through the State Criminal Alien Assistance Program, the program has been consistently underfunded to the extent that its budget has been recommended for elimination at times due to its ineffectiveness.

Beyond these expenses, local jurisdictions are liable for civil rights violations related to the 287(g) program, a problem with no small cost. In 2011, a federal judge ruled that Davidson County corrections officers had demonstrated "deliberate indifference" to Juana Villegas's suffering and medical needs. The court case stemming from Villegas's treatment by the Davidson County Sheriff's Office resulted in a judgment of nearly half a million dollars in damages against the county. At the urging of the judge, Villegas eventually received a U visa, a special visa available to noncitizen victims of crime who aid the government in the investigation and prosecution of criminal activity; in Villegas's case, the perpetrator was the Davidson County Sheriff's Office.

Knox County, Tennessee: The Fall and Rise of 287(g)

The case of Knox County, Tennessee, is instructive for understanding the fall and eventual rise of 287(g) under successive federal administrations. The Knox County Sheriff's Office (KCSO) originally applied for 287(g) jail enforcement authority in 2009. At the time, the program was expanding nationally: twenty-nine jurisdictions had memoranda of agreement for delegation of authority, and the Obama administration announced its intention to authorize eleven new agreements. Yet a report by the Government Accountability Office, also released in 2009, identified significant concerns with the program. The Government Accountability Office noted that the program's stated purpose—"to enhance the safety and security of communities by addressing *serious criminal activity*" (Government Accountability Office 2009: 10; emphasis added)—did not align with how the program functioned in some 287(g) jurisdictions. To the contrary, the report found that several jurisdictions appeared to use the program to process noncitizens for removal based on minor violations, including traffic offenses. Of course, the Government Accountability Office was not taking issue with the legality of removing people on minor offenses but rather with the practicality and expense of doing so. The report suggested clarification of the program's purpose and stronger supervision over existing and future 287(g) programs.

When the Knox County Sheriff's Office applied for 287(g), it submitted a needs assessment for the program, a standardized document that outlines the jurisdiction's perceived enforcement challenges. In this assessment, the KCSO noted a "large number of illegal [*sic*] persons arrested in our jurisdiction" and a "need to investigate and process illegal [*sic*] persons on [a] daily basis."[7] The assertion that the Knox County jail processes a "large number" of unauthorized immigrants is somewhat perplexing. Certainly, Tennessee is a new destination for immigrants, but Knox County does not have a large foreign-born population, unauthorized or otherwise. In 2009, the county boasted a scant sixteen thousand foreign-born residents—3.7 percent of the county's total population—more than a third of whom were naturalized citizens (US Census Bureau 2009).[8]

At the time of the 287(g) application, the Knox County jail reportedly housed thirty thousand inmates per year, roughly 5 percent (1,575) of whom were foreign-born,[9] indicating that immigrants were overrepresented in the jail compared with their proportion of the county population. The number certainly stood out to one of Tennessee's U.S. senators, Lamar Alexander, who wrote a letter of support on behalf of the KCSO's application, noting that the jurisdiction "arrests an average of 1575 illegal [*sic*] immigrants each year" and that "approval of this application would allow Knox County to expedite the investigation and processing of illegal [*sic*] immigrants and lead to more successful deportations."[10] Senator Alexander's reference to the jail's population of unauthorized immigrants appears to be taken from the KCSO's estimate of the total number of *foreign-born* inmates per year. To be clear, an inmate's country of birth reveals nothing about his or her immigration and citizenship status; after all, temporary visa holders, lawful permanent residents, and naturalized citizens are all foreign-born. The senator's use of foreign-born as a proxy for "illegal" reveals more about his perceptions of belongingness than it does the illegality—or, more generously, the deportability—of those inmates.

Still, what to make of the fact that the foreign-born population of Knox County was overrepresented in the jail? One way of interrogating this issue is by analyzing differences in criminal charges for U.S.-born and foreign-born inmates. For the U.S.-born, the top five charges included driving on a suspended license, public intoxication, possession of drug paraphernalia, simple possession/casual exchange, and criminal trespass. In contrast, the top five charges for foreign-born inmates included three license-related charges—driving without a valid license, driving without a license in possession, and failure to provide evidence of insurance—as well as public intoxication and driving under the influence.[11] In states that deny driver's licenses to unauthorized immigrants, license charges are often de facto status offenses; thus, many of the Knox County jail's foreign-born inmates may be unauthorized. In the logic of "common sense" enforcement via police-ICE interoperability, they are also criminals and threats to public safety.

For nearly three years, 287(g)-related communications between the KCSO and ICE included little more than periodic check-ins between the two agencies. By 2012, when the KCSO's application for 287(g) came up for consideration, some jurisdictions around the nation had already begun to abandon their agreements. Davidson County—facing ongoing pressure from Nashville-based immigrant rights groups and elected officials over the program's targeting of immigrants with low-level offenses and civil rights violations, such as the abuse of Juana Villegas—decided not to renew its 287(g) program (the sheriff announced that the program was no longer necessary, since it had been so successful at removing unauthorized immigrants).

The federal government had also ended 287(g) task force programs in Maricopa County, Arizona, and Alamance, North Carolina, due to allegations of racial profiling and racially biased policing practices. Multiyear investigations of these jurisdictions found that officers disregarded constitutional policing practices by explicitly targeting Latinx communities (U.S. Department of Justice 2011, 2012b). In 2011, the Department of Homeland Security terminated Maricopa County's 287(g) agreement, citing reasonable suspicion that the Maricopa County Sheriff's Office had engaged in discriminatory policing practices against Latinx residents, including unlawful stops, detentions, and arrests, as well as differential treatment of Latinx inmates. The following year, DHS terminated a 287(g) agreement between Alamance County and ICE, citing a pattern of biased policing that included differential treatment for Latinx people during traffic stops and at checkpoints.

By 2013, 287(g) was on the decline nationwide. The Department of Homeland Security announced that it would discontinue memoranda of agreement for task force jurisdictions that were "least productive" in apprehending "criminal aliens," noting that another program—Secure Communities—had become "more consistent, efficient and cost effective" (U.S. Department of Homeland Security, 2013: 16). That same year, DHS announced that it would consider no new requests for 287(g), even when jurisdictions expressed interest in the jail model. Although 287(g) was never entirely phased out under Obama, DHS requested substantially less in budget appropriations for 287(g), signaling the administration's lack of commitment to the program.

Within this context, the federal government declined to approve Knox County's application, issuing its formal decision in 2013. State and local immigrant rights groups, which had actively opposed the program's implementation, learned of the rejection before the Knox County sheriff did. When the sheriff learned, via the media, that ICE had declined to approve Knox County's memorandum of agreement, he released the following statement on the KCSO website:

> Once again, the federal government has used sequestration as a smokescreen to shirk its responsibilities for providing safety and se-

curity to its citizens by denying Knox County the 287(g) corrections model. An inept administration is clearing the way for law breaking illegal [sic] immigrants to continue to thrive in our community and ultimately be allowed to reside in the United States. Hopefully, the denial of this program will not create an influx of illegal [sic] immigrants who think that without this program they will be able to break the law and then be less likely to be deported.

The vast majority of Knox County citizens feel just as I do when it comes to the issue of illegal [sic] immigration. I strongly support the 287(g) program and will continue to make every effort to pursue its implementation. *I will continue to enforce these federal immigration violations with or without the help of U.S. Immigration and Customs Enforcement (ICE). If need be, I will stack these violators like cordwood in the Knox County jail until the appropriate federal agency responds.* (emphasis added)

The callousness of the sheriff's comments garnered widespread attention, as the graphic visualization of bodies stacked "like cordwood" evoked histories of mass atrocities. As Lawrence Downes (2013) of the *New York Times* noted, "That's brutal imagery, befitting a violent demagogue, not a sworn peace officer." In Knox County, immigrants and allies rallied outside the sheriff's office, piling wood on the ground in protest of the sheriff's statement about human bodies. The Knox County sheriff dismissed the public outcry, noting that his comment was a common colloquialism from his childhood.

Like others, I was deeply disturbed about the sheriff's comparison of unauthorized immigrants to cordwood. I was also concerned by his declared intention to violate due process protections: in his statement, the sheriff threatened to enforce immigration laws "with or without the help of U.S. Immigration and Customs Enforcement" and to indefinitely detain people based solely on immigration status "until the appropriate agency responds." Since the Knox County jail had not received 287(g) authority, attempts by county officers to enact immigration consequences would violate federal laws and constitutional protections. It is worth noting that the sheriff easily won reelection in 2014 despite ongoing outcry from local immigrant rights groups.

By the end of the Obama administration, just thirty-two agencies were participating in the 287(g) program, down from more than seventy in 2010. All of these operated under the jail enforcement model. Shortly after taking office, however, the Trump administration immediately expanded collaborative partnerships between federal, state, and local law enforcement agencies. In January 2017, the administration noted its goal of reinvigorating the 287(g) program to "empower State and local law enforcement agencies . . . to perform the functions of an immigration officer . . . to the maximum extent permitted by law" (Executive Order 13491 2017). By May 2019, eighty agencies, nearly half in the U.S. Southeast, had 287(g) authority.[12]

It came as no surprise that Knox County was one of the first jurisdictions to apply for and receive 287(g) authority under the Trump administration. In a new application submitted before Trump's inauguration, the KCSO expressed its hope to partner with ICE through 287(g) to "combat illegal [*sic*] immigration, especially illegal aliens [*sic*] committing criminal acts with prior criminal records" and to "assist with identification and removal proceedings of those criminal aliens [*sic*] who have deportation proceedings and are arrested for local crimes."[13] Although the Knox County jail's justification for 287(g) had changed since the 2009 application—which mainly referred to the need to process a "large number of illegal [*sic*] persons"[14] rather than unauthorized immigrant residents with criminal records, it is notable that the jail's self-reported top five charges for foreign-born inmates in the Knox County jail prior to implementation of 287(g) had not changed considerably. Once again, the top five charges for foreign-born inmates included three license-related charges (driving without a valid license, driving without a license in possession, and driving on a suspended license),[15] public intoxication, and driving under the influence.[16] The number of foreign-born inmates in the jail also remained relatively static, at 1,600 per year—roughly 5.9 percent of the inmate population—presumably not all of whom were unauthorized or deportable.

Surprisingly, the KCSO signaled its expectation to use 287(g) to identify, process, and turn over to ICE approximately 150 inmates per month—a total of 1,800 per year—higher even than the total yearly average of foreign-born inmates in the jail. If the KCSO actually intends to identify 1,800 deportable noncitizens each year, it may be that the only way to reach this goal is for officers on patrol—those without 287(g) authority—to target anyone and everyone perceived to be unauthorized, opening the jurisdiction to racial profiling allegations. Another strategy to boost numbers of foreign-born inmates is to process noncitizens arrested elsewhere: in 2018, the Knox County jail contracted with ICE, through an intergovernmental services agreement with the U.S. Marshal Service, to become a hub for immigrant detainees from surrounding counties. Preliminary analyses of those with ICE holds in the Knox County jail reveal that 88 percent of those arrested on local criminal charges between January 2018—when 287(g) went into effect—and March 2019 were charged with misdemeanor offenses, including driving without a license, public intoxication, and simple possession of marijuana (Conley 2019). These findings suggest that the Trump administration's iteration of 287(g) continues to primarily impact people with low-level offenses, just as 287(g) functioned throughout the Southeast under Obama prior to the implementation of targeted enforcement practices (Kee 2012; Nguyen and Gill 2010; Shahshahani 2009, 2010).

Secure Communities: The Story of Alejandro Guizar Lozano

It is true that Alejandro Guizar Lozano had been drinking.

Just eighteen years old, Alejandro Guizar had spent the evening with friends celebrating his recent graduation from high school. His life had changed considerably in the last few years, and he had much to celebrate. Eight years earlier, Guizar had arrived in the United States speaking no English whatsoever; by graduation, he had mastered the language, developed a love for writing, and aspired to higher education. Enrollment at a four-year university was out of reach for the moment, both financially and as a result of his immigration status—undocumented students are prohibited from receiving federal financial aid, and Tennessee bars unauthorized residents from receiving state financial assistance as well as in-state tuition regardless of their length of residency in the state. Still, Guizar intended to sustain his commitment to learning by taking a few credit hours per semester at the local community college.

Barely a month after high school graduation, Alejandro Guizar found himself in an unfamiliar part of town and separated from his friends when he was stopped by a police officer. Slightly drunk, his footing uncertain in the darkness, Guizar stumbled into the street in the wee hours of the morning. Perhaps he seemed suspicious. "So I got arrested," he explained. "And this didn't . . . this didn't red flag in my head while it was happening, but looking back at it, it red flags now. While I was getting arrested, the police officers were asking me about my status. And looking back on it," he continued, "I don't know if it was because of my intoxication, or if this really happened, but I don't remember them reading my Miranda rights to me. I was talking to them, and I thought that if I answered everything that they asked me, that they would eventually just let me go. And that was not what happened. They arrested me. And I went down to the county jail."

With little ceremony, Guizar was handcuffed and ushered into a police cruiser. The officers transported him to the Knox County jail, nicknamed "Maloneyville" after its street address, where he was booked and his fingerprints were taken. Guizar noted,

It all went by very fast because I was sleeping the whole time. But once I woke up and was sobered up, I was just . . . it just hit me, and I was like, "Oh wow, I'm in here." And I don't know what was going through my head, but I honestly did not think about my status, that factor of it, until somebody told me that I was gonna get picked up by ICE . . . I don't know how I did such a great job at ignoring that part of my life, to the point where I was in jail and I didn't even think about that. And when I found out about it, it was mind-crippling.

In a matter of hours, Guizar transitioned from celebrating his graduation to painfully confronting his immigration status, something he had worried about before primarily in terms of how it would impact his ability to drive or attend college. After more than a decade of living in the United States without authorization, Guizar was illegalized when he was arrested for public intoxication and interrogated about his immigration status.

Like many undocumented immigrants, Alejandro Guizar had never heard of Secure Communities, a federal program that enables local jails to share arrest information with the Department of Homeland Security. Debuting in 2008 with just fourteen activated jurisdictions, the Secure Communities program proliferated rapidly, becoming one of the nation's preeminent tools of interior immigration enforcement. By 2013, Secure Communities functioned in more than three thousand law enforcement jurisdictions across the United States.

Secure Communities facilitates the interoperability of two national fingerprint databases, one operated by the Federal Bureau of Investigation and the other by the Department of Homeland Security. When Guizar was arrested and booked into the Maloneyville jail, his fingerprints and booking information were submitted to IAFIS—the Integrated Automated Fingerprint Identification System—a national database operated by Criminal Justice Information Services, a division of the Federal Bureau of Investigation. IAFIS is renowned as the largest biometric database in the world; it compiles criminal histories, fingerprints, mug shots, aliases, and outstanding warrants to aid criminal investigations and apprehensions. Since Guizar had no outstanding warrants—this was the first time he had gotten into trouble of this nature—ordinarily he might have sobered up in jail overnight and been released the next morning with little more than a court date and an admonition of the legal drinking age.

However, Knox County—Alejandro Guizar's home for more than a decade—had activated the Secure Communities program in the summer of 2010. By January 2011, just a few months prior to Guizar's encounter with the police, the Secure Communities program functioned in every law enforcement jurisdiction across the state of Tennessee. Accordingly, Guizar's fingerprints were automatically transmitted from IAFIS to IDENT—the Automated Biometric Identification System—an immigration database maintained by the Department of Homeland Security through the United States Visitor and Immigrant Status Indicator Technology program. Precisely as intended by Secure Communities, Guizar's fingerprints were transmitted to the Department of Homeland Security as soon as he was booked into jail. By the time Guizar was flagged as unauthorized, he had neither spoken to his family nor seen a lawyer; he had been convicted of no crime whatsoever. The entire process—from his arrest, through booking, to the revelation of his immigration status—took only a matter of hours.

The process of connecting the DHS's immigration database with the Federal Bureau of Investigation's criminal database is referred to as IDENT/IAFIS interoperability. Its purpose is to streamline how law enforcement agencies identify the immigration and criminal status of arrestees. However, the system of database interoperability enabled through Secure Communities does more than promote information sharing between federal, state, and local law enforcement agencies. In many cases—as in Guizar's—IDENT/IAFIS interoperability prompts additional involvement from immigration authorities. When the IDENT database identifies an arrestee as foreign-born—whether authorized or unauthorized—the Department of Homeland Security automatically notifies Immigration and Customs Enforcement, its interior enforcement arm. ICE then determines whether the person arrested is removable due to immigration violations, criminal charges, or criminal convictions. ICE may issue an immigration *detainer*—a request that the local jail voluntarily detain the arrestee for up to forty-eight hours, not including weekends and holidays, until ICE can assume custody.

It took far less time for ICE to determine Alejandro Guizar's fate. Guizar explained, "They called my name. And they said, 'You're leaving.' And so I thought that I was *really* leaving. Like, I thought that I was gonna get to go home. And, you know, I got my box of stuff, and I walked down the aisle all the way up to the office where they gave me my clothes back. So I was like, 'Okay, I'm going home. This is cool.'" Dressed in his regular clothes, Guizar was impatient to leave. "I'm just like, 'Okay, what's going on? I'm ready to go.' And I wait for, like, five minutes, and this guy shows up. And he's talking to a lady, and she says, 'We've only got one for you today.'" Guizar shrugged, shaking his head. "I was just . . . not knowing what was happening. And then he started talking to me, and then he put me in cuffs from hands and feet, and I was just like, wow. Because I had honestly—just five minutes ago—I honestly thought that I was going home."

To my surprise, Guizar's eyes glistened with tears as he recounted the details of his story. When we first talked about this incident, more than a year had passed since he had been arrested for public intoxication and subsequently detained by ICE, yet it was evident that the shock was still fresh in his mind. I offered Guizar a tissue, and he gently dabbed at his eyes. His voice cracked, heavy with memories, as he recalled, "He was taking me to his office [which] was very close to [my parent's house]. I didn't know what was going on." After a long pause, Guizar continued, "For some reason I kept getting hopes." He smiled ruefully, recalling his impressions at the time: "He's gonna do something, and I'm just gonna . . . I'm gonna get to walk home. 'Cause I can [walk home] from here." Guizar shook his head again, seemingly incredulous at his own naiveté as he coiled the tissue into a dense spiral. In the end, he was not released that day, and it would be weeks before he would see his family again. That day, Alejandro Guizar boarded a bus to a federal immigration detention center in Jena, Louisiana, more than six hundred miles from his home.

———

SECURE COMMUNITIES, even more so than 287(g), is described as a "simple and common sense" method of immigration enforcement in assisting state and local law enforcement agencies in removing "threats" to their communities (U.S. Immigration and Customs Enforcement 2018b). Because the system is automated at the point of booking, it requires no additional investigative work on the part of the arresting officer or local jail to determine an arrestee's immigration status. The ICE Enforcement and Removal Operations field office director who oversaw operations in several southern states, including Tennessee, explained the program's benefits: "We want to make sure that our local law enforcement partners know as much as possible about the people in their custody. . . . By using sophisticated biometrics, the Secure Communities initiative allows us to quickly and accurately identify aliens [*sic*] *who pose the greatest threat* to our communities. And the program requires no additional costs to the local law enforcement agency" (U.S. Immigration and Customs Enforcement 2010b; emphasis added).

It is hard to imagine how Alejandro Guizar's story fits this narrative. With his open demeanor and easygoing smile, Guizar seems like a far cry from the "greatest threat" to his East Tennessee community. Yet people like Guizar—nonviolent offenders who are arrested, though not necessarily convicted, for minor misdemeanors—have been persistently identified and detained because of the indiscriminate nature of the Secure Communities program. Between 2008 and 2014, the program processed more than 42 million submissions, resulting in more than 2.1 million matches in the IDENT database. Of those, more than 375,000 people were subsequently removed or returned to their countries of origin. Less than a third of the 375,000 had been convicted of "high priority" criminal offenses such as murder, kidnapping, and aggravated assault; 28 percent had been convicted of low-priority offenses, primarily misdemeanors (U.S. Immigration and Customs Enforcement 2014). Another 18 percent were immigration violations—for example, people who had overstayed a visa or entered without inspection, or who had been ordered to leave and failed to do so.

In justifying the mandatory implementation of Secure Communities, the Obama administration argued that the program was an important tool in identifying and apprehending "criminal threats" to the community. Yet the program acted less like a precision instrument and more like a vacuum, sucking up all noncitizens who came into contact with state and local law enforcement for any reason whatsoever, even as a result of minor misdemeanors (C. Thompson and Flagg 2016). In 2010, a year before Alejandro Guizar was arrested for public intoxication and flagged under Secure Com-

Alejandro Guizar poses during a public hearing in Birmingham, AL. (Author's collection)

munities, ICE developed priorities for apprehending, detaining, and removing noncitizens. The memo, written by ICE director John Morton, gave top priority to noncitizens who presented a risk to national security and public safety, including those suspected of terrorism, gang involvement, and criminal activity. Noncitizens who were "criminal offenders" were further prioritized based on the severity of the crime they had committed: high-priority "level one" offenders were those who had been convicted of an aggravated felony, and low-priority "level three" offenders were those who had been convicted of a misdemeanor. Still, ICE's application of "criminal offenders" has always deserved further scrutiny: at the time, level one offenses leading to deportation included traffic violations, disorderly conduct, obstruction of justice, possession of marijuana, and possession of liquor (Transactional Records Access Clearinghouse 2012). Apparently, ICE's priorities were not as straightforward as they appeared.

In the Southeast and across the country, immigrant rights groups mobilized to highlight Secure Communities as a funnel into the deportation pipeline. Activists started referring to the program as "Insecure Communities," suggesting that it functioned to destabilize communities rather than make them safer. In 2014, DHS announced its decision to discontinue the program, acknowledging widespread criticism: "The goal of Secure Communities was to more effectively identify and facilitate the removal of criminal aliens [*sic*] in the custody of state and local law enforcement agencies. But the reality is the program has attracted a great deal of criticism, is widely misunderstood, and is embroiled in litigation; its very name has become a symbol for general hostility toward the enforcement of our immigration laws" (U.S. Department of Homeland Security 2014b).

To be sure, the Obama administration had not backed away from the intent of Secure Communities—the identification and removal of "criminal aliens" through police-ICE interoperability. Instead, the DHS memo outlined a replacement—the Priority Enforcement Program—which would provide a "fresh start" (U.S. Department of Homeland Security 2014b) to reflect the administration's enforcement priorities as they shifted toward "criminal offenders." The program was designed to function in much the same way as Secure Communities: through the sharing of biometric data between state and local law enforcement agencies, the Federal Bureau of Investigation, and DHS. However, ICE was directed to take custody of noncitizens held in local jails only under specific circumstances. Noncitizen inmates who were suspected of terrorism; who had been apprehended while attempting to enter without authorization; or who had been convicted of felonies, gang activity, or significant misdemeanors (such as domestic violence or driving under the influence) were priorities (U.S. Department of Homeland Security 2014a). Those who had been convicted of minor offenses were not.

The deportation pipeline through state and local jails was immediately impacted by the Obama administration's termination of Secure Communities and implementation of the Priority Enforcement Program. The percentage of interior arrests leading to detention and removal, which declined during Obama's second term in office, continued to fall relative to the numbers of unauthorized entrants removed from the border (this also corresponded to increased apprehensions along the border). Moreover, the share of people removed from the interior with "serious" criminal convictions increased to 90 percent of those removed (Chishti, Pierce, and Bolter 2017).

As with 287(g), the Secure Communities program gained new life under the Trump administration. In his first days in office, Trump directed the Department of Homeland Security to abandon the Priority Enforcement Program and reinstate Secure Communities. The administration also outlined new enforcement goals, thoroughly upending Obama's priority categories. Under Trump, guidelines for enforcement included noncitizens who had been convicted of any criminal offense; had been charged but not yet convicted; had committed an offense but had not been charged; had committed fraud or misrepresented themselves to a governmental agency; had "abused" public benefits; had failed to depart after ordered removed; or who, "in the judgment of an immigration officer, otherwise pose[d] a risk to public safety or national security" (Executive Order 13768 2017).

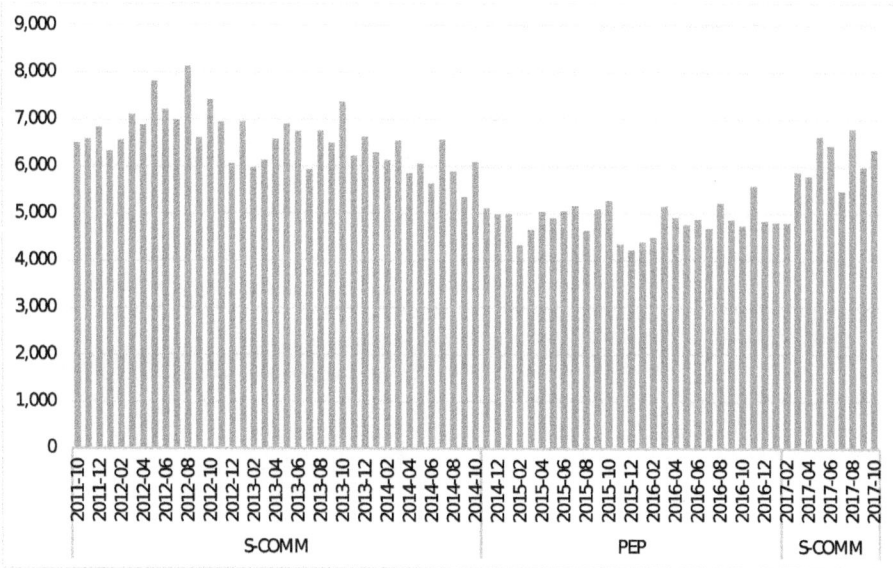

ICE removals through Secure Communities (S-COMM) and the Priority Enforcement Program (PEP), October 2011–October 2017. (Transactional Records Access Clearinghouse 2018)

Following the Trump administration's expansion of enforcement priorities and its reinstatement of police-ICE collaboration programs such as Secure Communities, interior removals increased rapidly. The increase is especially notable because a growing number of noncitizens have been removed following misdemeanor charges (Nowrasteh 2018; U.S. Immigration and Customs Enforcement 2017a). In essence, the Trump administration prioritized all removable noncitizens for enforcement. In the words of the administration's acting ICE director, Thomas Homan, "If you're in this country illegally and you committed a crime by entering this country, you should be uncomfortable. . . . You should look over your shoulder, and you need to be worried." Homan continued, "Most of the criminal aliens [sic] we find in the interior of the United States, they entered as a non-criminal. . . . If we wait for them to violate yet another law against a citizen of this country, then it's too late. We shouldn't wait for them to become a criminal" (quoted in Foley 2017).

Notes

1. Rapid expansion in border enforcement personnel comes at the expense of transparency and oversight, a point raised by Gil Kerlikowske, Obama's commissioner of U.S. Customs and Border Protection. The Border Patrol has faced allegations of systemic abuse, including persistent corruption (Homeland Security Advisory Council

2015), use of excessive force (Macaraeg 2018), sexual abuse of migrants (Graff 2014), and a "culture of cruelty" (No More Deaths 2011). The Trump administration's call for a hiring surge suggests the possibility of loosening qualification standards for applicants, deepening concerns about the agency's culture of impunity.

2. *Sign-cutting* refers to specialized tracking skills used by Border Patrol agents to track unauthorized entrants through footprints, clothing fibers, depressions in the soil, and disturbances in plants and wildlife.

3. In 2008, Texas launched the Texas Virtual Border Watch Program, a virtual surveillance plan that uses existing surveillance technology to enable volunteers to monitor the border from personal computers. Users watch streaming video of the border and report sightings of unauthorized entrants to the Texas Border Sheriff's Coalition, which refers reports to the Border Patrol (Koskela 2011).

4. Prevention through deterrence is a framing strategy that emphasizes entry prevention rather than alleviation of push factors.

5. Homan is referencing eighteen Texas jurisdictions that, in 2017, received 287(g) authority for police-ICE collaboration.

6. Salt Lake City, Utah, considered 287(g) in the late 1990s but ultimately declined due to concerns over racial profiling (Capps et al. 2011).

7. KCSO Needs Assessment, 2009. Via records request.

8. The ACS does not gather data on immigration status other than naturalization. Presumably, many of the remaining noncitizens were authorized, including lawful permanent residents.

9. KCSO Needs Assessment, 2009. Via records request.

10. Correspondence between L. Alexander and J. Napolitano, 2010. Via records request.

11. Correspondence between T. Wilshire and S. Flores, 2011. Via records request.

12. Most of the remaining memoranda of agreement were concentrated in Texas, which had twenty-five 287(g) jurisdictions, mostly signed in 2017.

13. KCSO Needs Assessment, 2016. Via records request.

14. KCSO Needs Assessment, 2009. Via records request.

15. Readers may wonder how unauthorized immigrants are charged with driving on a suspended license if they are ineligible to obtain a license in Tennessee. The Tennessee Department of Safety auto-generates license numbers to track people who lack driver's licenses when they are charged on license charges. To unsuspend a person's license and reinstate driving privileges (even though the individual may be ineligible for such privileges), the person must pay fines associated with the original charge and provide proof of car insurance. Thus, unauthorized immigrants may be charged with driving on a suspended license if they are convicted for driving without a license, fail to pay associated fees, and are stopped again on a license charge. Of course, since the Knox County jail's measure uses "foreign-born" (rather than unauthorized), this number may include naturalized citizens or authorized noncitizens whose suspended licenses are unrelated to their immigration status.

16. KCSO Needs Assessment, 2016. Via records request.

4

The Enforcement Lottery

POLICE-ICE INTEROPERABILITY has expanded the risk of enforcement for unauthorized immigrants like Juana Villegas and Alejandro Guizar. As state and local law enforcement agencies have been transformed into force multipliers for ICE through 287(g) and Secure Communities—programs that were expanded and then contracted under the Obama administration and that have been revitalized by the Trump administration—enforcement becomes ubiquitous at traffic stops, flea markets, apartment complexes and neighborhoods, homeless shelters, day laborer pickup sites, work sites, courthouses, and jails as well as near churches, schools, and health facilities (see, for example, Blitzer 2017; Castillo 2017; Coleman and Kocher 2011; Hernández, Lowery, and Hauslohner 2017; Menjívar and Abrego 2012; Poe 2017; Southern Poverty Law Center 2009; U.S. Immigration and Customs Enforcement 2018a; Weissman and Headen 2009).[1]

Police-ICE interoperability renders the threat of immigration enforcement omnipresent but never certain. As Nicholas De Genova (2002) and others have argued, any interaction between unauthorized immigrants and law enforcement officers could reasonably—though not necessarily—result in an immigrant's detention and eventual removal. In this way, police-ICE interoperability can be imagined as a lottery system, a seemingly random, neutral process with outcomes determined by the arbitrariness of chance or luck. Of course, the process is anything but random and neutral: federal, state, and local policies shape the sociopolitical status of illegality, and hence the lottery's outcomes. Those who are obligated to enter this *enforcement lottery* by virtue of their immigration status do not compete for money or prizes; rather, they risk the consequences of detection, discretion, detention, and deportation. Each of these stages creates opportunities to illegalize immigrants, thereby reproducing vulnerability in everyday life.

Detection

Unauthorized immigrants may reside in the United States for years, even a lifetime, without detection. Nearly two-thirds of the unauthorized adult population has lived in the United States for more than a decade, and 35 percent has lived in the country for more than fifteen years (Taylor et al. 2011). Their status may be known to family, friends, neighbors, teachers, and employers. As a population, however, unauthorized immigrants largely evade detection by those with power to engage in immigration enforcement. This point, of course, is used as justification for expanding police-ICE interoperability based on the idea that state and local law enforcement officers with immigration authority are uniquely positioned to help ICE identify, apprehend, and deport removable noncitizens.

Unauthorized immigrants cultivate resources and tools to function without authorization (Marquardt et al. 2013). They also develop strategies to avoid detection. Some anonymize themselves, deliberately or unconsciously taking on manners of speech, dress, and behavior to blend seamlessly into mainstream society. This is particularly true of undocumented youth who grow up in the United States and who are sometimes referred to—by both immigrants and advocates alike—as "Americans in every way except on paper," a rhetorical strategy that reinforces claims to belongingness. Immigrants who defy stereotypes of "foreignness" or unauthorized status—such as through markers of age, race, ethnicity, socioeconomic class, and language—may have less burden to defend their belongingness (Hing 2004; Molina 2014). Unauthorized immigrants may also embrace co-ethnic communities, both as a practical strategy for survival and as an effort to shield themselves from the prying eyes of outsiders.

Deliberate avoidance of law enforcement officers is another key strategy to evade detection. Many unauthorized immigrants describe a constant state of vigilance, and they are ever alert to the presence of officers (Marquardt et al. 2011). In an interview, an undocumented person in Georgia expressed to me his perpetual awareness of law enforcement as follows: "Today we [drove] to the market. We saw [an officer] and we were like, go right, go left, go left, pull in there. So it's just always constant, it's always there." The normalization of constant vigilance that results from policies and practices of illegality is itself a form of "legal violence" (Menjívar and Abrego 2012), an ever-present reminder to unauthorized immigrants that they do not belong and thus do not have the right to expect benevolence in their interactions with police officers.

Unauthorized immigrants avoid interacting with law enforcement—even as victims or witnesses of crime—out of fear that any contact could result in detection of their status and subsequent immigration enforcement consequences. In the preface, I shared the story of Jesús, whom I met in Georgia, both of us there to protest the state's restrictionist legislation. When I happened upon him in the parking lot, his car window had just been smashed and a great deal of cash—likely his entire savings—had been stolen. However, Jesús chose not to report this incident to police. He was conscious of his vulnerability and resigned to the possibility that officers might be more interested in his immigration status than the burglary.

Jesús's decision may be unsettling to people who see law enforcement as a force for protection, especially when abstracted to the 11.1 million unauthorized immigrants in the United States today and to the range of victimization they may experience. Yet Jesús's story is not uncommon, and his decision not to contact police is in no way unique to immigrants in new destinations. Empirical research and anecdotal stories indicate that the involvement of state and local law enforcement in immigration matters—or even the perception of involvement—has significant, negative effects on the willingness of both U.S.-born and foreign-born Latinx residents to report crime. Nik Theodore's (2013) research on Latinx residents of Chicago, Houston, Los Angeles, and Phoenix found that 44 percent of those surveyed reported that they were less likely to contact law enforcement if they were the victim of a crime, and 45 percent were less likely to volunteer information about a crime that they had witnessed, when they perceived that police officers were collaborating with ICE. Among those who were unauthorized, 70 percent reported that they were less likely to contact law enforcement to report a crime out of concern that officers would ask about their immigration status or the status of people they knew.

Unauthorized immigrants are often reticent to contact law enforcement regardless of the severity of infractions committed against them. In Knoxville, just two months after Donald Trump's inauguration and shortly after revelations of the Knox County sheriff's renewed application for 287(g), an entire community of undocumented families was terrorized in the middle of the night, and no one called the police. The incident was brought to my attention a few hours after it happened by Eva, a woman who lived in the neighborhood. In the early hours after midnight, a group of four men, all dressed in black, invaded a quiet mobile home community and proceeded to bang on doors, shine flashlights through windows, rifle through mailboxes, and photograph license plates. Families cowered under beds and in closets in their dark homes, fearful that an organized gang, an anti-immigrant group, or ICE had come to tear their families apart. That morning, children were afraid to go to school, worried that their mothers and fathers would not be home when they returned.

By that afternoon, a handful of advocates across the city had heard similar stories from different sources in the neighborhood. I received a call from one bewildered tutor who, upon hearing about the night terror from a young student, was unsure whether the "raid" had actually happened or was the invention of an active, anxious imagination. Calling on an informal network of local allies, I helped organize a team of investigators to interview the neighborhood's residents in hopes that we could better understand what had happened and determine how to respond in case this was to become the new normal.

Who were these men who had invaded the community, and what did they want? At the outset, a number of possibilities seemed plausible, including white nationalist vigilantes. Knoxville was not a hotbed of anti-immigrant organizing, but the campaign and election of Donald Trump had certainly inspired extremists across the nation (Levin 2016; Southern Poverty Law Center 2016a) who saw in this candidate a platform for their white racial grievances. After consulting with an immigration attorney who has extensive experience with ICE enforcement actions in the state, we ruled out ICE, to Eva's relief; ICE raids are more likely to happen at dawn as people leave for work or in the late afternoon or evening as families commune over dinner.

Should they call the police if the men came back? Eva wondered. That depends, I responded. Did the men have guns? And was the community inside the Knoxville city limits, where the police chief had recently affirmed that immigration enforcement was a federal matter, or was it in Knox County, where the sheriff's "stack them like cordwood" comment still lingered nearly four years later and was freshly ominous from the county's renewed application for 287(g)? In effect, I was advising Eva to process a risk analysis of her situation, to weigh the relative costs and benefits of enduring another such event, should it happen again.

Of course, the community would have good reason to be wary of city police, too; even though the city of Knoxville claimed to be uninterested in federal immigration enforcement, city police would still act to maintain "public order" (Armenta 2015), and any arrest would result in transfer to the Knox County jail, which was operated by the sheriff. How likely might it be, then, that one of the neighborhood's mobile homes or cars had a delinquent registration, a fact of life for low-income communities? How likely might it be that a simple conversation over a delinquent registration would escalate into an interrogation? It is impossible to know for sure, of course; for vulnerable communities, doubt over the trustworthiness of law enforcement officers expresses as avoidance.

Had this incident happened to me, to my community, I might not have hesitated to call the police—a problematic reaction, perhaps, and one that reveals layers of structural privileges that I benefit from and that have been systematically denied to Eva and her neighbors. The truth is that the community did not call for help from law enforcement because the residents believed that police or ICE might have been responsible for the terror campaign inflicted overnight on the neighborhood. And even if the invaders had not been agents of law enforcement, the residents believed that an official investigation would be more likely to jeopardize their security than protect them from future threats.

The fear that any encounter with law enforcement, no matter how trivial, could result in immigration consequences is not unfounded. The American Immigration Lawyers Association, a group of more than fifteen thousand attorneys and law professors who practice and teach immigration law, once reported that "any contact with the police, no matter how innocent or trivial, can result in immigration enforcement and removal" (Alonso et al. 2011: 3). Advocacy groups have detailed myriad encounters between unauthorized immigrants and law enforcement officers that resulted in removal proceedings under the Obama administration's peak interior enforcement years, from calling the police to report intimate partner violence to being approached by an officer while changing a flat tire on the side of the road (Alonso et al. 2011; National Community Advisory Commission 2011; Weissman and Headen 2009).

The threat posed by interaction with law enforcement is particularly pervasive in the absence of reasonable guidelines for prosecutorial restraint. Following the Trump administration's elimination of enforcement priorities and reinvigoration of collaborative police-ICE partnerships, the law enforcement agencies of several major cities documented an aggregate decrease in crime reports by Latinx residents. Houston's police chief noted that Latinx residents reported 42.8 percent fewer sexual assaults and 13 percent fewer other violent crimes than the same period in the previous year, even though non-Latinx residents reported these crimes at a higher rate (B. Lewis 2017). The Los Angeles police chief similarly noted that reports of sexual assaults committed against Latinx residents had dropped 25 percent compared to the same period in the previous year, attributing the cause to immigrants' fears of immigration enforcement (Queally 2017). An analysis of crime reporting in three other cities—Dallas, Denver, and Philadelphia—found that Latinx residents had reported fewer crimes since the beginning of the Trump administration, even as crime reports from non-Latinx residents remained steady (Arthur 2017).

It is no coincidence, then, that some state and local law enforcement officials are less than enthusiastic about aspects of police-ICE interoperability. Programs such as 287(g) and Secure Communities undermine the contemporary community policing model, which seeks to build relationships of trust between residents and officers to deter and resolve crime. Officials worry that these programs jeopardize the willingness of marginalized and vulnerable people and communities to report their own victimization or crimes that they have witnessed.

Several law enforcement officials spoke against the expansion of police-ICE interoperability programs under the Bush and Obama administrations. Both the International Association of Chiefs of Police (2007) and the Police Foundation (Khashu 2009) expressed concerns about their involvement in immigration enforcement and its impact on the communities they police, specifically in terms of diverting officers and resources from pressing public safety issues. Similarly, the former district attorney of New York County (Manhattan) condemned police-ICE collaboration, arguing, "When immigrants perceive the local police force as merely an arm of the federal immigration authority, they become reluctant to report criminal activity for fear of being turned over to federal officials" (National Community Advisory Commission 2011: 9).

The reinvigoration of police-ICE interoperability under Trump as well as the administration's threats to target cities that refuse to fully cooperate with ICE have renewed outcry among law enforcement. In 2017, the police chief of Tucson, Arizona noted a "growing sense of fear and distrust" among Latinx residents corresponding to the "[Trump] administration's crackdown on immigrants" (Magnus 2017), and he urged the administration to encourage community confidence in law enforcement by expanding reforms initiated under Obama. The next year, the Law Enforcement Immigration Task Force—a group of sixty-three police chiefs and sheriffs that formed in 2015—sent a letter to Congress stating that state and local law enforcement agencies would "best serve our communities by leaving the enforcement of immigration laws to the federal government" (Law Enforcement Immigration Task Force 2018a). In a separate letter to members of the House Judiciary Subcommittee on Immigration and Border Security, the task force wrote, "When state and local law enforcement agencies are required to enforce federal immigration laws, undocumented residents may become fearful that they or people they know will be exposed to immigration officials and are less likely to cooperate" (Law Enforcement Immigration Task Force 2018b).

To be sure, law enforcement officers and agencies that oppose some aspects of police-ICE interoperability do not, as a rule, oppose immigration enforcement in general; the Law Enforcement Immigration Task Force itself reinforces the importance of immigration enforcement as a federal matter. For the most part, agencies that are generally unenthusiastic about police-ICE collaboration are willing to collaborate with ICE on requests to detain noncitizens with significant criminal histories and when ICE provides a court order for an arrest. These jurisdictions argue that immigration enforcement should be managed by federal agents with minimal involvement from state and local law enforcement agencies. Essentially, this is a strategy for maintaining a division of labor, not for dismantling the immigration enforcement system.

In any event, we should not assume that the preservation of a strict boundary between state and local law enforcement officials and federal immigration authorities will automatically encourage communities to trust police. In the *Nuevo* South, where belongingness is racialized and Latinx residents are persistently seen as other, many unauthorized immigrants easily perceive that everyday interactions are fraught with risk (Bustamante and Gamino 2018), and these fears cannot be extricated from the broader context of differential enforcement of criminal laws against communities of color.

Still, community advocates broadly agree that disentangling the police-ICE regime is the bare minimum required to ease immigrants' fears of detection and their willingness to fully engage in their communities. The extent to which such entanglement occurs appears to vary by region. States and communities in the Southeast are at the forefront of collaborative immigration enforcement: jails in this region operate nearly half of all 287(g) agreements, and some of the nation's harshest anti-immigrant legislation has been proposed and enacted in these states. In Georgia, a state that has actively pursued 287(g) and antisanctuary legislation, one community advocate voiced the perception that it was "open season on immigrants, anybody who looks foreign or is brown, or [is] a person of color." Certainly, this sense is heightened in jurisdictions that rebuff attempts at community oversight and accountability of law enforcement, that pursue arrests for racialized public order crimes, that lack robust policies against racial profiling, and that actively pursue and engage in police-ICE interoperability programs.

Azadeh Shahshahani, legal and advocacy director for Project South, notes that police-ICE collaboration programs have led to "an atmosphere of terror for [immigrant] communities, who are reluctant to contact the police for any reason, because they are afraid of ending up in deportation." This is true not only of undocumented people who refuse to report nonviolent crimes but also for those who decide not to come forward in much more severe situations. Isabel Rubio, the executive director of the Hispanic Interest Coalition of Alabama (¡HICA!), related one such example: "We have had several cases of young women—and I say young women like teenagers—who have been raped. And in one case, the mom just refused to make a police report because of her fear that the police would be more interested in their immigration status than in the crime that had been committed."

As immigration enforcement becomes ubiquitous, the pervasive threat of detection and its consequences may be perceived as too detrimental to risk interaction with the police. This means that both violent offenses and nonviolent crimes—including assault, harassment, workplace exploitation, and burglary—may be largely unreported by unauthorized immigrants who experience or witness these transgressions. In the words of one Sunday school teacher who testified to the community impact of police-ICE collaboration in Alabama, "The people . . . are afraid to come forward, afraid to report abuse, because . . . to complain is to admit you are undocumented."

Discretion

Unauthorized immigrants are not always able to avoid detection. Since unauthorized status is a sociopolitical identity marked by policy decisions around commonplace tangible matters such as access to identification and employment authorization, engagement with society creates risk for revelations of status and enforcement consequences. Once detected, unauthorized immigrants may be subject to a variety of discretionary—and sometimes internally contradictory—enforcement policies, which further determine whether they will be exposed to a series of enforcement consequences.

Discretion is pervasive throughout the immigration system. At the federal level, discretion involves systemic choices surrounding the articulation of priorities for the apprehension, detention, and removal of noncitizens (Motomura 2011). The Obama administration prioritized "criminal offenders" as a matter of discretionary enforcement—a misleading term, to be sure, especially since the label was generously applied to those with minor offenses and those whose offenses involved criminalized violations of civil immigration laws, such as illegal reentry. Over time, the Obama administration developed a more targeted approach to enforcement of unauthorized residents, even as it expanded criminalization of unauthorized entrants apprehended along the U.S.-Mexico border.

The Obama administration also developed policies surrounding prosecutorial discretion—or the ability to enforce immigration policies in accordance with the administration's shifting enforcement priorities applied to individuals on a case-by-case basis. In 2011, ICE was directed to exercise discretion in cases where removable noncitizens, including unauthorized immigrants, had—in ICE's terminology—certain *equities*, or factors meriting special consideration. These included cases in which the noncitizens were minor children or elderly people, those who served the United States in the armed forces, those who had been present in the United States since childhood, those with mental or physical disabilities or serious health conditions, and those who were victims of crime.

The favorable exercise of prosecutorial discretion does not generally confer authorization on unauthorized immigrants or automatically provide access to work permits, driver's licenses, or other benefits. Those who benefit from discretion in one situation are not automatically considered nonremovable in future or different circumstances; ICE simply declines to pursue removal for a given individual in a particular situation. The application of discretion occurs on an individual level, and unauthorized immigrants—

even those who meet most of the equities outlined in the memo—are in no way entitled to the "favorable exercise of discretion" (Morton 2011: 6). In this way, the collective hardships induced by the policies and practices of illegality are treated on a case-by-case basis.

Notably, the Trump administration has sought to limit favorable exercise of enforcement discretion at the federal level, pushing a universal approach to immigration enforcement. The administration's elimination of enforcement priorities in particular exempts no "classes" or "categories" of removable noncitizens from enforcement consequences (Executive Order 13768 2017). This means that ICE's ability to exercise discretion for noncitizens with equities, such as those who have lived in the United States since childhood, is severely restricted.

This does not mean that discretion is no longer an important aspect of the enforcement lottery. To the contrary, federal constraints on ICE's discretionary authority have elevated the importance of state and local policy decisions, especially with regard to cooperation with federal immigration authorities. This plays out in geographically specific ways as much of the Southeast actively pursues police-ICE collaboration. As a result, noncitizens who are arrested on relatively minor criminal charges in jurisdictions that collaborate with ICE, such as Knox County, may be more likely to end up in ICE custody than noncitizens who are arrested on more severe charges in places that do not collaborate.

Federal policy directives on immigration enforcement have individual impacts on an immigrant's progression through the enforcement lottery. However, policies are also enforced—or not—by officials at the state and local level, and discretion is as pervasive in the criminal justice system as it is in the immigration system. The enforcement decisions of state and local law enforcement agencies and officers in particular may advance the enforcement lottery or temporarily suspend its progression for individual noncitizens. Law enforcement agencies make decisions about how to allocate agency resources, such as which communities to patrol heavily and where and when to establish routine traffic checkpoints. The results of these choices are highly consistent in the communities and populations they target for policing, a fact that influences the demographic characteristics of those most likely to be monitored, stopped, and arrested (Pierson et al. 2017; Russell-Brown 1998; Varano et al. 2009). Notably, such choices produce disparate impacts for specific sociodemographic groups, a pattern that has been well documented for low-income and black and brown communities (Ghandnoosh 2015; Pierson et al. 2017; Warren et al. 2006).

It is precisely the standard use of discretion by state and local law enforcement agencies that has substantiated allegations of racial profiling in the local enforcement of immigration law, resulting in the disproportionate arrest of U.S.-born Latinx people and foreign-born Latinx people of varying immigration statuses. In this way, the racialized policing and mass incarceration system intersects with a racialized immigration system to primarily impact immigrants of color. Black and brown immigrants are disproportionately likely to be apprehended, a fact that reflects the criminalization and overpolicing of low-income communities of color. These immigrants are also disproportionately likely to be detained and removed (Aranda and Vaquera 2015; Golash-Boza 2015a). Black immigrants, in particular, are disproportionately likely to be removed on criminal charges. Although they make up just 5.4 percent of the unauthorized population, black immigrants comprise 10 percent of those in removal proceedings and 20 percent of those in removal proceedings based on a criminal charge (Morgan-Trostle, Zheng, and Lipscombe 2016); this disproportionality is largely due to shifts in immigration policy that mandate removal for certain criminal convictions, such as drug offenses.

Latinx communities are likewise disproportionately policed, and the effects of this are especially stark in jurisdictions that maintain police-ICE interoperability programs. In North Carolina, Matthew Coleman and Austin Kocher (2011) found that law enforcement agencies with 287(g) agreements were more likely to establish traffic checkpoints in neighborhoods with higher concentrations of Latinx residents, resulting in a disproportionate number of traffic stops and arrests of Latinx people. Civil liberties and advocacy groups have documented similar findings for communities in Georgia (Shahshahani 2009, 2010), Tennessee (Kee 2012), and other jurisdictions with police-ICE collaboration programs. Importantly, these findings hold true even for jurisdictions with 287(g) jail enforcement models.

Local law enforcement officers exercise a great deal of decision-making authority, often referred to as officer discretion, in the course of their regular duties. Key to this stage of the enforcement lottery is the fact that officers do not fully enforce every criminal and civil statute; instead, officers make determinations about whom to arrest and whom to release. Although states may implement mandatory arrest policies for some violations, such as domestic violence offenses, officers generally have broad discretionary powers in their arrest authority. An officer's decision whether to make an arrest may be shaped by factors such as the situational context, officer biases, sociodemographic characteristics of the arrestee, and departmental resources. These determinations are also situated in broader policy responses to crime more generally: the broken windows theory of policing, for example, encourages arrests as a method of maintaining "public order," even in response to relatively minor criminal charges or civil offenses (Beckett 2016).

An officer's determination may result in immigration consequences for noncitizens, including detention and removal, even when the initial charge is unrelated to an immigration violation. As a reminder, this is the premise of police-ICE collaboration; ICE asserts, for example, that local law enforce-

ment officers will "encounter foreign-born criminals and immigration violators who pose a threat to national security or public safety" (U.S. Immigration
and Customs Enforcement 2010a). Accordingly, Juana Villegas was detained
by ICE after she was stopped for rolling through a stop sign and arrested for
driving without a license, and Alejandro Guizar was placed in removal proceedings after he was arrested for public intoxication. Under Tennessee code,
neither of these offenses requires arrest. For unauthorized immigrants, arrests for minor charges will have outsize impacts, especially in the context
of broader discretionary choices surrounding immigration enforcement priorities at the federal level and state and local collaboration with enforcement
policies and practices.

In truth, the vast majority of interactions between unauthorized immigrants and local officers likely result in outcomes other than arrest. An officer's arrest authority and its disproportionate impact on unauthorized
immigrants as a result of police-ICE collaboration are particularly salient in
the case of César Bautista Sánchez, an undocumented immigrant from Mexico. Bautista Sánchez told me, "The police officers that I have dealt with have
actually been, like, just nice to me as they can possibly be. Only one asked
me why don't I have a license. And I told him why, and he just gave me a
ticket and let me go. And he said specifically, 'I'm gonna go this way.' And he
said, 'Don't tell me where you're gonna go, just go. Just take care of the ticket and you'll be fine.' And that's what I've done. And I've been pretty lucky,
I guess, that I have met cops like that."

When I first met César Bautista Sánchez, he was a young activist working with the Tennessee Immigrant and Refugee Rights Coalition (TIRRC).
On a warm, sunny day, when he was in Knoxville working to organize undocumented youth, I invited him for coffee at a nearby café. Born in Mexico
City, Bautista Sánchez lived most of his childhood in Nashville. He had recently graduated high school and completed a nine-month medical assistant
degree, even though his status made it impossible to work in his chosen
profession. "I still wanted to go ahead and improve myself," he said, explaining why he pursued the credential. "I knew there was probably no chance [of
working as a medical assistant], but I still wanted to go ahead and take the
risk. Go ahead and study, do something with my life. Even if it meant that I
probably would not work."

Over time, Bautista Sánchez became increasingly outspoken about his
status. Frustration at his inability to work in his chosen profession combined
with a desire to "make a difference, whether it's for me or other people," fueled his entrance into immigrant rights activism. Unlike many of his friends
and family, Bautista Sánchez was relatively unconcerned by the threat of
interaction with police, a sentiment he attributed to knowing his rights,
being involved in a community of activists, and participating in campaigns
to stop others' deportations. His parents, on the other hand, were more fear-

ful—reflecting a generational divide in wariness of law enforcement (Abrego 2011) as well as discretionary practices that often looked favorably on undocumented youth. Echoing a sentiment familiar to many unauthorized immigrant youth, Bautista Sánchez explained, "Parents—they fear for their children to be okay, that they're always safe, that, you know, drive carefully." Undocumented parents have additional fears, however. Bautista Sánchez explained, "For an undocumented parent, they worry even more, because if your kid gets deported, what are they going to do? They're over here, they already have a life over here, and they will have to pretty much give up everything just to go save them. So they tend to watch them more, tell them, 'Be careful. Don't do this, don't do that.' You know, 'Drive carefully.' Maybe, you know, 'Don't hang around with the wrong crowd, that will get you in trouble, get us in trouble.'" Bautista Sánchez recognized that one small incident could lead to a chain reaction of consequences. "One thing could lead to another thing," he noted, "and maybe a whole family could get in trouble, and the whole family could get deported. And, so, that's why my mom, my parents, they worry."

Heeding the pleas of his parents, Bautista Sánchez had organized much of his life to avoid activities that might cause him to be noticed. Another undocumented youth expressed the impact of immigration status similarly: "Being undocumented, it's a tremendously stressful situation, you're not allowed to be yourself." In fact, being yourself or hanging with the "wrong crowd" might invite unwanted attention and the potential for detection, which might invite the discretionary power of police to advance the enforcement lottery.

Nevertheless, Bautista Sánchez has had occasional interactions with police, each time as the result of a minor traffic infraction. In each of these interactions, César Bautista Sánchez saw himself as lucky—and he was. After all, he was not labeled a "criminal offender" when he was stopped for speeding and ticketed for driving without a license. Thus far, he has never been arrested or detained as a result of his interactions with law enforcement, even though an officer could have decided to make an arrest, arguing that a citation could not be issued without verification of identity and place of residence. In this situation, though, the officer's assessment of the situation and subsequent use of discretion benefited Bautista Sánchez.

However, it is precisely Bautista Sánchez's luck—and that of many other unauthorized immigrants—that structures his illegality within the enforcement lottery; the possible unfavorable application of discretion reinforces the pervasive threat of immigration-related consequences, including deportation. The persistent threat posed to Bautista Sánchez, and all unauthorized immigrants, would mean very little if it were not actualized in some circumstances. Thus, not all unauthorized immigrants are as lucky in their interactions with local law enforcement, and not all officers are willing to use their discretionary authority to overlook criminalized activities—even relatively minor misdemeanors, such as driving without a license, that result from broader sociopolitical decisions about immigration.

As an active member of Jóvenes Unidos por un Mejor Presente (Youth United for a Better Present)—a group of undocumented youth who organize for tuition equity and other pro-immigrant polices under TIRRC's sponsorship—Bautista Sánchez was very familiar with the story of Mercedes, another undocumented youth from Mexico who grew up in Nashville. Likewise a member of Jóvenes Unidos por un Mejor Presente, Mercedes was also stopped for speeding; however, as Bautista Sánchez described, Mercedes received very different treatment:

> [Mercedes] got pulled over for going seven miles over the speed limit. No license, no ID. And the cops arrest her. They didn't give her a phone call to call her parents or somebody. She didn't sign [any] documentation to be deported,[2] so she was let go within three days.[3] The cops told her, "You're going to get deported." She was only one week away from graduating high school. But she got out [of jail]. [The police] didn't offer her a ride home. She actually had to walk home. She was in deportation status. It was just a speeding ticket, with no license.

The frustratingly unpredictable nature of the enforcement lottery becomes apparent through the disparate interactions that unauthorized immigrants have with law enforcement based on discretionary determinations of law enforcement officers. Whereas César Bautista Sánchez's progression through the enforcement lottery was suspended when the officer used discretionary authority to issue a citation, Mercedes advanced through the lottery when she was arrested. When I asked Bautista Sánchez to consider the disparity in outcomes between his situation and that of Mercedes, he remarked that he had never thought about it before. He paused for a moment and then conjectured, "I've been, just, I really say lucky. I don't believe in luck, but I think . . . *blessed.* Because if it wouldn't come out that way, maybe I would've gotten deported or something. I wouldn't help Mercedes, I wouldn't be helping other students." Bautista Sánchez elaborated:

> I think that God had a plan for me, and that's for me to help out more people, so that's why he's keeping me here. Same thing with Mercedes. Maybe that happened to her so that people can open their eyes to a student that was pulled over just for a ticket, and a big mess was made out of this. Now everybody in the country—or maybe just in Tennessee—knows about this. She even got to meet President Obama face-to-face, and she gave him her cap and gown after her graduation

from high school. And she [asked] him, is he going to do something about it. He said that they are still working on it, but you know how that goes.

After some consideration, Bautista Sánchez continued, "I think that the difference between me and [Mercedes] is because we just have different purposes in life. Mine was probably just to keep it easy, so that I can do something big, the stuff I'm doing right now. And for her it was probably to start rough and get out of there and make herself somebody great so everybody can be, like, 'Well, she went through this, I don't want to go through it.' Maybe other people can learn from that. So," he concluded, "I think this is God working on behalf of us, really."

In Bautista Sánchez's conjecture, the difference between his and Mercedes's experiences can be explained as part of a divine plan intended to bolster the capacity for unauthorized immigrants to support one another and prepare themselves for enforcement consequences. Certainly, every interaction with law enforcement adds more information to those struggling to identify patterns in enforcement behaviors. However, the seemingly random and arbitrary exercise of discretion—which, again, may be highly patterned for officers and agencies around perceptions of belongingness, including sociodemographic markers—is also an important means of structuring illegality, constraining the lives of undocumented immigrants by sustaining the pervasive threat of immigration enforcement. Even when individual officers and agencies are patterned in their behaviors, unauthorized immigrants can never be sure whether any interaction with any particular police officer will result in benevolence, indifference, or enforcement. Despite Bautista Sánchez's hope that immigrants can learn something from Mercedes's experience, there may be very little they can do, practically speaking, to influence the outcome of this stage of the lottery. Any contact whatsoever with law enforcement is deemed suspect and undesirable—hence, the effort to remain undetected. Unauthorized immigrants are impacted by the enforcement lottery not only during their real interactions with police but also through the very possibility of interaction, which is perceived as deeply threatening.

The relationship between the discretionary choices of local officers and the procedures of the enforcement lottery, and thus the structuring of illegality, applies even for officers who are not authorized to enforce immigration laws. Programs that enable cooperative partnerships between local law enforcement and ICE allow local officers to use their discretionary arrest authority to activate immigration enforcement mechanisms, even when the arresting officer cannot directly bring about immigration consequences. Although the officers who arrested Juana Villegas and Alejandro Guizar were not deputized to enforce immigration law, their willingness to inquire about and act upon suspicions of unauthorized status advanced the enforcement lottery for these immigrants by pushing them further into the deportation machine. The officers' choices, combined with broad federal enforcement priorities and established collaborative partnerships in these jurisdictions— the 287(g) jail model in Villegas's case and the Secure Communities program in Guizar's case—enabled the officers to instigate enforcement consequences indirectly through arrest. Conversely, officers may decide not to make an arrest, thereby enabling unauthorized immigrants to circumvent—at least temporarily—potential immigration consequences. In the case of misdemeanor traffic violations, such as driving without a license or speeding, an officer's decision to issue a citation (as in César Bautista Sánchez's case) or make an arrest (as in Mercedes's case) will significantly impact outcomes at this stage of the enforcement lottery.

Detention

The power of discretion intersects closely with the third stage of the enforcement lottery: detention. An officer's arrest of a noncitizen instigates a series of interrelated consequences that impact the immigrant's progression through the enforcement lottery. These consequences depend on various programs and policies at different levels of government that either mandate, enable, or restrict cooperation between state and local agencies and federal authorities.

Following arrest, the federal, nationwide Secure Communities program automatically reports noncitizens to ICE as soon as they are booked into state and local jails.[4] Once an incarcerated noncitizen is reported to federal immigration authorities, ICE may issue a formal request called a detainer (sometimes referred to as an ICE hold), asking the jail to detain the immigrant for up to forty-eight hours, not including weekends and holidays, so that ICE may take custody. The detainer takes effect once the inmate is set for release on the criminal charge or conviction, such as when they attempt to bond out of jail, when the charge is dropped, when the inmate completes the sentence, or when they otherwise satisfy the terms of the sentence. This is precisely what happened in Alejandro Guizar's case. Once Guizar was booked into the Knox County jail for public intoxication, his fingerprints were automatically transmitted to ICE through Secure Communities. ICE then issued a detainer requesting that the jail hold him past release on his criminal charge until it could assume custody.

Ostensibly, ICE detainer requests occur in the context of enforcement priorities. The Obama administration prioritized immigration enforcement consequences against "criminal offenders," an expansive term that encompassed low-level offenses and immigration violations (Thompson and Flagg 2016). Thus, even though Guizar's violation was relatively minor, the fact that ICE sought to detain him is not especially surprising. The Transactional Records Access Clearinghouse (2012) found that more than two-thirds of ICE detainer requests issued between 2008 and 2012 were for noncitizens who had no criminal record whatsoever. Of the 22 percent of those detained who were convicted of a crime, only 8.6 percent had been convicted of priority ("level one") offenses—a category that, at the time, included minor traffic violations. Given the flawed and inconsistent nature of ICE's "criminal offender" label, the Transactional Records Access Clearinghouse (2013) has suggested that "far fewer than even this small proportion . . . actually would meet the more objective standards of having been convicted of crimes that pose a serious threat to national security or public safety."

In 2012, ICE revised its policies on discretion in immigration detainers, dictating that ICE should issue detainers only under certain conditions, such as when a person had three or more misdemeanor convictions, a "serious" misdemeanor conviction (such as driving under the influence), or a felony charge or conviction. As the Obama administration shifted to prioritize "serious" criminal offenses and retired Secure Communities in favor of the Priority Enforcement Program, the number of immigration detainers declined sharply. The smaller number of noncitizens who were detained for ICE custody were more likely to have serious charges. Notably, the Trump administration's elimination of enforcement priorities and reinvigoration of Secure Communities corresponds to an increase in ICE detainers, from 85,000 in 2016 to 142,000 in 2017 (U.S. Immigration and Customs Enforcement 2017a). In 2017, the category with the highest growth in detainers was noncitizens with low-level offenses and those without criminal convictions (Transactional Records Access Clearinghouse 2018).

Once ICE issues a detainer request, state and local jails play a crucial role in advancing or halting the enforcement lottery's progression. In Guizar's case, the Knox County jail complied with ICE's request, a decision that enabled ICE to take custody of Guizar and transfer him to an immigrant detention facility for further processing. However, detainers are not legally binding under federal law, and state and local jails are not generally obligated to detain noncitizens for ICE. Thus, even as the mandatory Secure Communities program gives jails little discretion over reporting noncitizens to ICE, many jurisdictions may still exert discretion in deciding whether to honor ICE detainers.

Some state and local governments have sought to limit the discretionary authority of jails in ways that are favorable to immigrants by legislating noncompliance with ICE detainers. Under mounting concerns over ICE's targeting of low-level offenders and the impact this has had on the willingness of immigrants to interact with police, some jurisdictions have pursued "sanctuary" policies during both the Obama and Trump administrations. Although the term lacks a consistent legal definition, *sanctuary* is broadly used

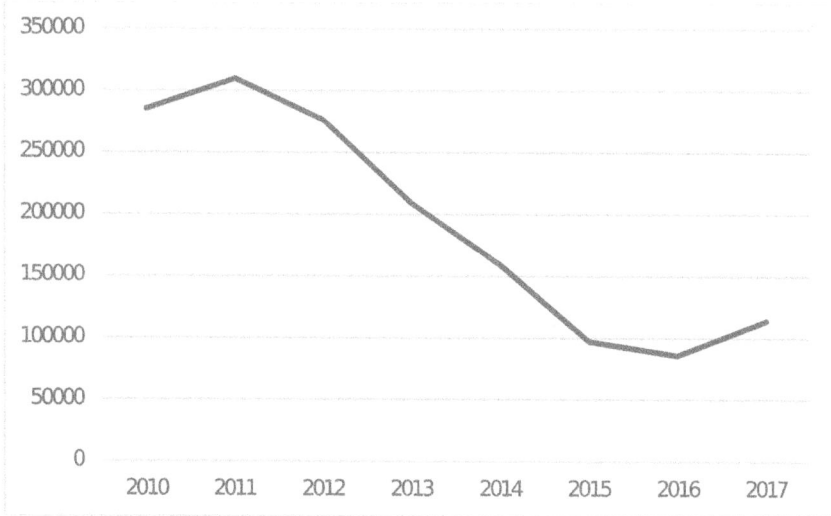

ICE detainers issued for all U.S. jails, 2010–2017. (Transactional Records Access Clearinghouse 2019)

to describe states and cities with policies that prohibit degrees of police-ICE collaboration, particularly with regard to detainers. California occupies one end of the sanctuary spectrum. The California Trust Act, which took effect in 2014, restricted law enforcement jurisdictions across the state from cooperating with ICE detainer requests except under limited circumstances, such as when an inmate had a violent criminal history or felony convictions. The California Values Act, a more expansive sanctuary policy that became law in 2018, entirely prohibits state and local law enforcement agencies from detaining noncitizens for ICE and even restricts jails from informing ICE about an inmate's release date, except under certain circumstances, such as when ICE has a judicial warrant. The Values Act also prohibits state and local police officers in California from inquiring about immigration status and prohibits jurisdictions from entering into police-ICE interoperability programs such as 287(g).

Many jurisdictions have policies that limit police-ICE cooperation, though not to the extent of California. Jurisdictions such as Washington, DC, and Ithaca, New York, refuse to honor ICE detainers for noncitizens booked on minor charges. Several county jails refuse to detain inmates for ICE regardless of the criminal charge unless presented with a warrant. Potentially significant constitutional issues are at play. In 2017, the Massachusetts Supreme Court ruled in *Commonwealth v. Lunn* that ICE detainers were unconstitutional violations of Fourth Amendment rights to due process, since detainers are based on civil immigration violations rather than criminal offenses, and state and local jails without 287(g) have no authority to enforce federal immigration laws. In 2018, a federal district court in California issued a similar ruling, stating that officers "have no authority to arrest individuals for civil immigration offenses, and thus, detaining individuals beyond their date for release violate[s] the individuals' Fourth Amendment rights" (*Duncan Roy et al v. County of Los Angeles* 2018: 21).

It is significant that the majority of sanctuary jurisdictions are in places with large and well-established immigrant populations and/or progressive political agendas, such as cities in the Northeast and Northwest. States in the *Nuevo* South, in contrast, have pushed for policies to limit the discretionary authority of jails, but in the opposite direction. Several states in the Southeast have pursued antisanctuary legislation to require jails to honor all detainer requests from ICE regardless of constitutional concerns or the jurisdiction's own discretionary policies. In 2018, for example, the Tennessee legislature passed H.B. 2315, which prohibits state and local governments and officials from adopting sanctuary policies, including policies that limit cooperation between local law enforcement and ICE and those that prevent officers from asking about immigration status and detaining people for ICE. H.B. 2315 also encourages state and local law enforcement agencies to enter into 287(g) agreements. As jurisdictions in California, New York, and elsewhere restrict and refuse police-ICE collaboration, the detention stage of the enforcement lottery plays out most critically in states such as Tennessee, where even minor offenses have significant immigration consequences.

Once detained by ICE, noncitizens may be remanded to short- or long-term custodial supervision in one of the nation's more than 250 public and privately contracted federal, state, and local immigration detention facilities while they await an administrative decision on their immigration case. Since unauthorized presence is a civil violation rather than a criminal infraction, detention is often part of a broader administrative process to determine whether a noncitizen will be permitted to remain in the United States—if the person has certain equities that render them a potential candidate for asylum, adjustment of status, cancellation of removal, or other discretionary relief—or whether they will be removed. This is true not only of unauthorized immigrants but also of authorized immigrants whose criminal charges or convictions make them removable.

The number of detention facilities nationwide has proliferated in the post-9/11 rise of the homeland security state (Mittelstadt et al. 2011). In addition to federal and private, for-profit detention facilities, state and local jails have contracted with ICE through intergovernmental service agreements, which enable them to hold noncitizens in custody beyond the forty-eight-hour detainer. As capacity to detain immigrants has increased, so, too, has the number of immigrants in detention; this fact is reflected in a legislative "bed mandate"—a statutory quota on the number of detainees that ICE is required to maintain on any given day. In 2012, more than thirty thousand unauthorized immigrants were detained per day in immigration detention facilities across the nation (Siskin 2012); this jumped to more than forty thousand in 2016, corresponding to an increase in unauthorized entrants fleeing violence and environmental degradation in Central America. An average of more than 395,000 unauthorized immigrants have been detained every year since 2010, with a high of 464,000 in 2012 (Baker 2017). Although the number of detainees decreased to 307,000 in 2015 following implementation of Obama-era priorities, the Trump administration has sought to expand detention for broad categories of immigrants, including unaccompanied minors and those seeking asylum. The Trump administration has also announced plans to increase detention capacity through the construction of new detention facilities, the expansion of intergovernmental service agreements, and the use of military bases for temporary camps and shelters.

Immigration detention is a civil matter; hypothetically, detention is not meant to be punitive. Yet detention centers resemble penal carceral institutions in their appearance and daily operations (Schriro 2009)—so much so that civil liberties and advocacy organizations have referred to facilities in the South as "shadow prisons" (Southern Poverty Law Center, National Lawyers Guild, and Adelante Alabama Worker Center 2016b).[5] These detention centers are typically located in remote areas and have hardened boundaries accomplished through the use of guards, gates, bars, and barbed-wire fences. Those who are incarcerated involuntarily in such facilities are surveilled and supervised, their routines are strictly managed, and they have little autonomy.

Alejandro Guizar recalled his first experiences with detention: "I knew we were going to some kind of detention center where I was going to be with a bunch of people. I didn't know what to expect, if it was going to be a cell. It just looked like a big building with barbed-wire fences. We all got out. The first person that talked to us was a nurse, trying to figure out if we have any medical conditions." Guizar remembered waiting for what seemed like an interminable amount of time at each stage of the journey. "What was the worst was the constant lingering," he recalled. "It took forever to get booked at every place we stopped at, and every holding cell was just terribly cold, so it was, like, hours and hours of trying to sleep in this cold room." As he waited to be processed, night turned into morning.

> We got there at eleven [P.M.], something like that, and it turned into daytime before we got our inmate clothes and shoes and we finally got booked. And afterwards we get put where we're going to be at, and it's just a pod with a hundred bunk beds in it. And that was where I lived for two weeks. And then, after that, I got moved to this federal place, where it was, like, two people to a cell. In the first place, you stayed in that room all day, and you never go outside. [In the

second place,] you went outside all day. So, like, when it was time to go back to your room, you didn't want to do anything. You just wanted to go to bed. Days went fast like that.

César Cuauhtémoc García Hernández (2015) argues that immigration detention must be understood in terms of the harm that it causes and that this must be considered independently of any harms associated with deportation. Much of this harm is due to the fact that detention extracts people from their families and communities, often for lengthy periods—and this occurs even in the absence of a criminal conviction (Koulish 2016). In fact, immigrants may languish in detention facilities for weeks, months, or even years (American Civil Liberties Union 2009). Since immigrant detention facilities are often far removed from people's communities, family members—even those who are U.S. citizens—may not be able to visit. Detention facilities have also been implicated in guards' systematic abuse and punishment of immigrant detainees, including forced labor, assaults, sexual assaults, denial of adequate and timely access to medical services, and deaths of detainees (García Hernández 2014; Greenwald 2017; Kalhan 2010; Schriro 2010; Speri 2018). The Office of Inspector General of the Department of Homeland Security (2017) has documented that detainees are kept in prolonged solitary confinement, often for minor infractions.

Detention has often been the rule rather than the exception (García Hernández 2015), and this is despite the fact that ICE has generally had discretion in terms of whether to house noncitizens in detention facilities. It is true that 1996 laws—the Illegal Immigration Reform and Immigrant Responsibility Act and the Antiterrorism and Effective Death Penalty Act—expanded mandatory detention for certain criminal offenses and immigration violations (Hincapié 2009).[6] Still, many immigrants in detention are potentially eligible for release, but they may not have access to legal representation to explain the administrative process and advocate for their release; in fact, only 35 percent of detained immigrants are represented by counsel (Stave et al. 2017). Others may not be able to afford their immigration bond, which may exceed thousands of dollars.

Still other detainees may be eligible for release on immigration bond or on their own recognizance instead of being processed for ICE detention, but there is little consistency and transparency in this process—a situation that is intensified by lack of access to legal counsel for civil immigration violations. During the Obama administration, ICE regularly detained so-called low-risk and nonviolent immigration offenders who would be prime candidates for alternative supervision programs (Finnie, Guzik, and Pinales 2013), particularly prior to the administration's full implementation of prosecutorial discretion and the Priority Enforcement Program. In fact, 58 percent of detainees held in custody in January 2009 did not have a criminal record and were not subject to mandatory detention; of those with criminal records, nearly 20 percent were held on traffic violations or civil immigration violations (Kerwin and Lin 2009), neither of which constitutes a serious criminal infraction. Under the Trump administration, ICE has increasingly denied bond to immigrants with low-level criminal offenses and immigration violations, such that noncitizens are now more likely to be detained without bond once they are apprehended and turned over to ICE through police-ICE collaboration (Oberhaus 2018; Rosenberg and Levinson 2018). The Trump administration has also terminated programs that offer alternatives to detention, including one program for asylees that had a near universal rate of compliance for immigrants reporting to their court dates (Fernández Campbell 2018).

Alejandro Guizar, who spent much of his childhood in the United States, was just one of many low-risk and nonviolent "offenders" transferred to immigration detention after being flagged as unauthorized through police-ICE interoperability. Luckily, Guizar eventually qualified for release, and his parents were able to scrounge together $2,500 to pay his immigration bond— one of the lowest possible bonds granted to detainees—which enabled him to leave the detention facility.

The trip home was its own labyrinthine struggle. "When you're released you have to have enough money to prove that you can pay a taxi driver, because Jena and La Salle are in the middle of nowhere, Louisiana," Guizar recalled. "You have to prove that you can pay a taxi driver to drive you from the detention center to this random gas station where the Greyhound picks people up. The cab ride was, like, a hundred-something dollars. So you not only have to pay the bond; you have to show [that you have] all these other funds to get a cab ride and pay for a bus back home." Here, too, people wait. "When the bus came, in our case, the bus was full. I was just lucky enough that I was one of the people that got on the bus. A bunch of other people didn't get on because the bus was full, and they had to wait at that gas station for another bus to come."

In all, five weeks had passed between Guizar's arrest for public intoxication and the moment he finally walked through the door of his parent's home. "I tried to act like nothing happened," he said, brushing it all aside. "I tried to think that I never really left home."

Deportation

Unauthorized immigrants have few choices in the enforcement lottery, and the choices they do have are heavily influenced by the sociopolitical construction of illegality, which is expressed through the decisions of policy makers and those who enforce immigration and criminal laws. Thus, unauthorized immigrants may attempt to avoid detection (the first stage) by avoiding interactions with immigration officials, law enforcement, and other authorities perceived to participate in enforcement activities. Once detected, however, the choices of unauthorized immigrants are, to a great extent, dependent on the discretionary choices of law enforcement officials (the second stage), jailers, and immigration authorities (the third stage).

The final stage in the enforcement lottery is deportation, formally referred to by the Department of Homeland Security as removal. It is during this fourth and final stage of the enforcement lottery that some unauthorized immigrants may shape the lottery's outcomes, though the extent to which they are able to do so is often dependent on factors entirely beyond their control.[7] In this stage, unauthorized immigrants who are charged with civil immigration violations—alone or in addition to misdemeanor criminal violations—may be allowed to choose between leaving the United States (by agreeing to a stipulated order of removal or a voluntary departure) or fighting their deportation.

One of the swiftest ways to end involuntary confinement to an immigration detention center is to agree to a stipulated order of removal, which is a petition for "voluntary" removal (not to be confused with voluntary departure). In this procedure, a noncitizen waives the right to a removal hearing by an immigration judge on their civil immigration case; as a result, the removal may be processed much more quickly than otherwise. A stipulated removal is, in effect, the same as an involuntary removal in that it carries the same legal penalties and future prohibitions associated with a removal ordered by an immigration judge. Unauthorized immigrants who receive orders of removal are prohibited from petitioning to reenter the United States for a period of three to ten years (depending on the duration of unauthorized residency), a policy established under the 1996 Illegal Immigration Reform and Immigrant Responsibility Act and often referred to as the "three- and ten-year bar." Under certain circumstances, depending on conditions of the removal and whether the person has been removed in the past, bars on admissibility may be longer or permanent. Unauthorized immigrants who, once removed, reenter the United States without legal authorization—regardless of whether the removal was voluntarily stipulated by the unauthorized immigrant or ordered by an immigration judge—face additional civil and criminal penalties for reentry if they are later apprehended.

In contrast, a voluntary departure, sometimes referred to more generally as a return, is a form of discretionary relief granted by an immigration judge that may not negatively mark a noncitizen's record.[8] Unauthorized immigrants who qualify for and agree to voluntary departure may not be restricted in future visa applications.[9] Moreover, those who return to their countries of origin through voluntary departure are not subjected to heightened criminal penalties on future unauthorized entry, as in the case of removal (Koh, Srikantiah, and Tumlin 2011).[10] This makes voluntary departure attractive to many unauthorized migrants, particularly Mexican nationals, who may attempt to immediately reenter the United States to reunite with their families.

Generally, the length of time it takes to receive voluntary departure depends on when an unauthorized immigrant initiates the request. Unauthorized immigrants can request voluntary departure at two different stages of the administrative process: during initial court proceedings or at the conclusion of court proceedings. In either case, the decision is entirely at the discretion of an immigration judge. Those who are granted voluntary departure at the conclusion of their case must often submit to additional penalties (for example, bond payments) or fulfill additional requirements (for example, a record of "good moral character") as determined by an immigration judge. Post-conclusion recipients of voluntary departure are given less time to arrange their affairs and depart the country than if they had requested voluntary departure during initial proceedings (Johnson et al. 2015).

Despite the relative attractiveness of return compared with removal, the average yearly number of returns has declined while removals have increased. In the 1990s, more than one million people per year were granted return, a number that dropped to just over 100,000 by 2016. In the same period, the number of removals—including stipulated orders of removal—increased exponentially, from thirty thousand in 1990 to more than 340,000 in 2016, with a record high of more than 433,000 in 2013 (U.S. Department of Homeland Security 2017).

The increase in removals (and decrease in returns) can be attributed to several policy changes in immigration law surrounding border and interior enforcement. Most prominently, the Illegal Immigration Reform and Immigrant Responsibility Act expanded the ability of immigration officers to expedite the removal of unauthorized entrants, streamlining the process by blocking access to judicial review (Rosenblum et al. 2014). Although unauthorized entry has declined, unauthorized entrants who are apprehended along the border are now less likely to be returned and more likely to be summarily removed or transferred to ICE for detention and removal, often with criminal penalties attached to their immigration violations (Lopez, Gonzalez-Barrera, and Motel 2011; Rosenblum and McCabe 2014).

The Trump administration's zero-tolerance policy for unauthorized entrants has increased criminal prosecution of migrants apprehended along the border, the vast majority of whom are charged with misdemeanor unauthorized entry. In 2018, over a matter of weeks, this policy led to the forcible separation of hundreds of families: parents were criminally prosecuted for unauthorized entry and placed in detention awaiting their deportation, while their children, who are required by law (under *Flores v. Reno*) to be housed in the "least restrictive conditions" possible and quickly released to nongovernmental custodians in the United States, were housed in separate facilities. After international outcry, DHS ended the family separation policy. The Trump administration's proposed solution is to expand family detention facilities so that entire families may be detained together—possibly indefinitely if the *Flores* agreement is overruled by the courts.

Immigrants who are detained may be pressured into signing stipulated orders of removal, which count toward overall ICE removal statistics. This pressure is intensified for parents who crossed the border with children during the Trump administration's separation policy and who were subsequently told that they would be reunited with their children only after they agreed to removal. Even though many of these immigrants may have been eligible for asylum, voluntary departure, or some other form of discretionary relief, research indicates that immigration officials do not explain the differences or consequences associated with these choices (Koh, Srikantiah, and Tumlin 2011). Those who must navigate removal proceedings without competent counsel may not even be aware of such forms of relief.

Changes in interior enforcement, too, have affected rates of removal. Interior enforcement expanded during the George W. Bush administration and into Obama's first term in office, marshalling police-ICE interoperability as a force multiplier to escalate removals of unauthorized residents, including those who lived for years in the United States. In the interior, DHS has relied on enforcement procedures that are difficult to square with its own discretionary goals, including mining records from the Department of Motor Vehicles for information about foreign-born applicants, sending ICE agents to traffic checkpoints, and pursuing unauthorized immigrants booked into jails on low-level offenses (Heath 2013). Despite the Obama administration's discretionary enforcement policies, the staggering number of removals during his terms in office—approximately three million in eight years—earned President Obama the nickname "deporter in chief." Interior removals peaked during Obama's first term, when they outpaced removals from the border (Chishti, Pierce, and Bolter 2017). Although interior removals declined during Obama's second term, they have increased under the Trump administration (Nowrasteh 2018) as a result of the elimination of enforcement priorities, the reinvigoration of police-ICE collaboration, and the expansion of ICE raids on businesses that employ unauthorized immigrant workers.

Overall, stipulated orders of removal and voluntary departure are attractive to eligible noncitizens for their ability to provide a degree of certainty in a time that is otherwise fraught with ambiguity. The entire enforcement lottery, no less the final stage of deportation, is shaped by this uncertainty, because enforcement is always possible but never guaranteed. For the detained immigrant who is a primary wage earner or caregiver, a lengthy stay in detention while fighting removal or awaiting an immigration hearing is untenable. A stipulated removal or voluntary departure signifies less overall time incarcerated in immigration detention, meaning less time separated from loved ones and more time to provide for one's family.

Even so, not all detainees agree to be removed or returned to their country of origin. Some, like Alejandro Guizar, opt to fight their deportation. As Guizar recalls, "[The ICE officer] said, 'You don't have to answer this right now, but you will have to eventually. You have to make a decision if you want to sign this voluntary deportation, or if you want to fight your case.'" To Guizar, there was no question: "Immediately I was like, 'I want to fight my case.'"

Those who attempt to fight removal must await a judicial decision, which may or may not result in some form of discretionary relief. Just so, Alejandro Guizar spent nearly two years on bond awaiting his immigration hearing and a final decision on his possible removal. At the time of his release, Guizar had no idea what it meant to fight his deportation; he only knew that he did not want to leave his family or the home he had known for more than a decade. Other detainees advised him to move constantly after he was released, operating under the mistaken belief that each change of address would require the court to postpone his court date. Guizar had considered, and rejected, this option: "In the back of my head I thought that maybe I could buy some more time until something happens, you know? But, of course, that wasn't any solid strategy."

It did not seem that Guizar had much chance to avoid removal. Nevertheless, he had hope, if for no other reason than the fact that he had stared into the abyss of his fear from inside the detention center and had not been summarily deported. "It felt like I had a shot, I guess. It wasn't a *good* shot," he emphasized, "and I always knew that. But coming face-to-face with my deportation, I felt like I could do something." And so, as he awaited the hearing that would decide his fate, Guizar became involved with state and local immigrant rights groups—TIRRC, AKIN, and the Comité Popular de Knoxville (Knoxville People's Committee)—and cultivated a community of advocates and defenders. In collaboration with these organizations, he collected letters of support from teachers and friends and spoke to congregations and community gatherings, hoping to accumulate enough support to somehow convince an immigration judge to allow him to stay.

Then, in June 2012, as Guizar waited for a date on his immigration hearing, President Obama directed DHS to deprioritize the removal of unauthorized immigrants who came to the United States as children. This new policy—Deferred Action for Childhood Arrivals (DACA), a specific application of prosecutorial discretion—affirmed that certain young people who had come to the United States at a young age and who had not committed serious crimes were low priorities for deportation. Perhaps more importantly, DACA provided qualifying young people with the opportunity to receive temporary relief from the threat of deportation proceedings as well as temporary work authorization.[11]

An estimated 800,000 young people benefited from the program. It could not have come at a more opportune moment for Alejandro Guizar. His lawyer was able to argue that he should not be deported since the crime for which Guizar had been arrested—public intoxication—was a minor misdemeanor, and Guizar met every requirement for discretion through the DACA memo. The Department of Homeland Security agreed. Guizar applied for DACA in 2013, and shortly thereafter his case was administratively closed—a discretionary form of relief that acknowledged the deprioritization of his removal.

————

ALEJANDRO GUIZAR'S ability to remain in the United States was based on a confluence of policy changes, discretion, access to counsel, community support, and luck. Now, more than seven years after his arrest for public intoxication, Guizar remains in the United States, but he is once again undocumented. Although he was eligible to renew his DACA status in 2016, he declined to do so out of fear that the Trump administration would direct ICE to use DACA applications to track and deport recipients. He explained, "I went out of my way to make sure the government didn't have my address. I was working hard to stay off their radar. I just knew that there wasn't going to be another Democratic president, and I didn't want to risk it." He paused, reflecting silently as the weight of his choice hung heavily in the air. Then he continued, "When I was inside [the detention center,] I met lots of people that were green card holders, so there's no real protection out there. I knew that Trump was going to be ramping up to get people out of here. And even though I'm not going to crawl under a rock, I felt more comfortable with the government not knowing where I live."

In Guizar's assessment, the potential risks associated with reapplying to DACA—namely, the government having his current address—outweighed the benefits of the program. He explained, "DACA to me felt like it was never going to be anything more than just DACA; [it's not] a pathway to become a citizen, and that's the only way to avoid deportation." He continued, "I got what I needed out of DACA, which was having my name with a photo. And I was able to get some jobs and get some good experience, so I got what I needed."

Alejandro Guizar's status renders him vulnerable to enforcement, but who can say definitively whether he made the right choice when he declined to renew his DACA? On one hand, it is an empirical fact that ICE has not begun rounding up and deporting DACA recipients en masse. It is also true that "deporter in chief" is a dubious honor that has yet to be bestowed on Trump, as rates of deportation under his administration have not approached the height of removals under Obama. At the same time, it is also a fact that the Trump administration has gone to great lengths to terminate DACA—an effort that has only been temporarily halted by the courts—and that his administration has vowed to exempt no classes or categories of "removable aliens" from deportation. More broadly, the Trump administration has tried—thus far unsuccessfully—to rewrite the entirety of modern immigration policy to reduce pathways for authorized residency and citizenship.

A greater truth lies beyond these facts. Fundamentally, illegality is a sociopolitical condition created around boundaries of belongingness and expressed through laws and policies that illegalize. Just as unauthorized immigrants are illegalized by macro- and micro-level policy decisions and implementation, immigrants with marginal status—such as DACA recipients or those with temporary protected status—as well as authorized immigrants—such as green card holders—can also be rendered "illegal" (Golash-Boza 2015b; Kanstroom 2007). We may disagree with Guizar's assessment that "there's no real protection out there," even for immigrants with green cards, but our difference of opinion should only be a matter of degrees. After all, Guizar's vulnerability to the enforcement lottery is not based on whether he has DACA or even on whether he has a green card; rather, it is based on boundaries of belongingness that structure illegality.

Guizar's story also illustrates the cyclical nature of the enforcement lottery. Although unauthorized immigrants may be granted some form of discretionary relief from immediate deportation—such as through temporary deferred action, stay of removal, or cancellation of removal—the cycle may begin anew because these actions offer only limited relief; in general, they do not confer authorization.[12] Authorized immigrants, too, are vulnerable to the lottery, because authorization can be revoked based on expiration or termination of a visa[13] or through increasingly expansive definitions of criminality. Although deportation may be the final stage of the enforcement lottery, an unauthorized immigrant will reengage this cycle by reentering the United States without authorization after a removal or return. Finally, even though individual noncitizens may avoid particular stages of the enforcement lottery, the overall structure and consequences of the system remain activated.

It is exactly this degree of unpredictability that leads De Genova (2002) to speak of "deportability" rather than actual deportation as the fundamental threat structuring the illegality of unauthorized immigrants. Certainly, the abstract possibility of deportation is both constant and eminent, and this is true regardless of whether a noncitizen is placed in removal proceedings or deported. The threat of enforcement, however, is much broader than the potential for removal as the entirety of the enforcement lottery—through detection, discretion, detention, and finally deportation—contributes to an immigrant's experiences of the vulnerabilities of illegality. As a whole, the enforcement lottery is a system of control (Hay 1975) that perpetuates the vulnerability of noncitizens. It forces unauthorized immigrants in particular to doubt their security at each stage of the process, and it requires them to make constant adjustments to their lives in search of some measure of stability.

Notes

1. ICE discourages and/or severely limits enforcement activity in "sensitive loca-tions"—schools, hospitals, institutions of worship, and public demonstrations (U.S. Immigration and Customs Enforcement 2011). Reports of enforcement activity near these locations suggest that ICE may not be following the spirit of the policy under the Trump administration.

2. Bautista Sánchez likely refers to the stipulated removal, in which detainees agree to deportation. Some accounts suggest that detainees are pressured to sign these orders.

3. Mercedes was released from the jail within three days due to regulations on immigration detainers. In some jurisdictions, jails may voluntarily detain noncitizens for a set time (up to forty-eight hours, not including weekends and holidays) until ICE assumes custody. ICE may also request to be notified when a jail releases noncitizens.

4. The pervasiveness of Secure Communities reflects shifts in enforcement strategy. DHS initially portrayed the initiative as voluntary; in 2011, however, DHS announced that Secure Communities was mandatory. This claim was hotly contested—to no avail— by state and local jurisdictions. By 2013, Secure Communities was activated in every jurisdiction across the nation. Although the program was phased out in 2014, the Trump administration revitalized Secure Communities in 2017. Like the Obama administra-tion, the Trump administration has made participation mandatory.

5. Until 2009, half of noncitizens in civil immigration custody were held in state and local facilities designed for penal detention (Schriro 2009). In 2009, under scru-tiny for its detention practices, ICE proposed guidelines for greater accountability and transparency in the detention system. Since then, ICE has centralized detention contracts under ICE supervision and has constructed several federal civil detention facilities. Still, many continue to be housed in penal carceral institutions.

6. ICE rationalizes mandatory detention as protecting the public from the threat of immigration violators who commit criminal offenses. However, noncitizens subject to mandatory detention are not particularly dangerous to public safety (Koulish 2016).

7. Some noncitizens may be forced into expedited removal, which allows immigra-tion officials to summarily deport without judicial review (Johnson et al. 2015).

8. DHS uses the term *return* to refer to the departure of inadmissible or deport-able noncitizens not based on a removal order. Returns can include noncitizens who receive discretionary relief through voluntary departure as well as those who receive voluntary return, an informal process that does not involve court proceedings (Johnson et al. 2015).

9. Unauthorized immigrants who have lived in the United States for more than 180 days but less than one year and who receive voluntary departure are not affected by the three-year bar if: (1) they receive "advanced consent" from DHS; (2) departure is granted by an immigration judge; and/or (3) they qualify for a hardship waiver.

10. Unauthorized immigrants who return without authorization after a volun-tary departure may face civil penalties (including a temporary bar on future entry), but criminal penalties are not heightened as they are with those who return without authorization after removal.

11. DACA recipients must conform to certain qualifications, including restrictions on age, length of residency, age at entry, year of entry, physical presence, and education or military service. Additionally, DACA recipients must not have a significant criminal record, including a felony conviction, a significant misdemeanor (for example, domes-tic violence, driving under the influence), or more than three misdemeanors of any

kind, and they must not pose a threat to national security or public safety. Applicants were required to pay a $500 processing fee, which funded the program. DACA was renewable every two years, at which point applicants could reapply for consideration. The DACA memo was rescinded by Donald Trump in 2017; however, courts have temporarily halted its termination.

12. In limited circumstances, an immigration judge may determine that a noncitizen is eligible for more permanent relief from deportation, such as an adjustment of status through asylum or a U visa.

13. The Trump administration, for example, attempted to terminate temporary protected status for citizens of El Salvador, Haiti, Honduras, and others.

5

Welcome to Alabama

LUÍS ESCOTO was crossing the border into Alabama.

"I got chills," he later recalled over dinner at a Laotian restaurant in Nashville, Tennessee. "I felt like there was a noose around my neck, in a sense. I was very . . . not wanting to show my face out of the window. So I was, like, slightly down."

Escoto hunched over in his chair, his thin frame almost disappearing behind a large bowl of curry as he demonstrated how he crouched in the backseat of the car as it barreled down the interstate. At twenty, Luís Escoto was crossing a border that, to him, seemed every bit as significant as the border he had crossed seventeen years earlier, when his uncle carried him atop his shoulders across the Río Bravo del Norte (known in the United States as the Río Grande). In fact, he had every reason to seize up with terror as the car zipped past the sign marking the Alabama border. Born in Mexico and raised in Nashville, Escoto was one of an estimated 2.9 million undocumented young people living in the United States (Hoefer, Rytina, and Baker 2012). On that day, counting the minutes in miles, he was traveling deeper and deeper into a state that had just passed the most punitive immigration law in the country.

"It's a very intense feeling," Escoto continued, straightening in his chair. "I wouldn't want someone to ever have to feel that feeling . . . to go to a place where they're . . . not wanted. It's one thing to have a group of people tell you that you're not wanted, and it's a whole different thing where it's a law that says that you're not wanted. It's . . . a bit more serious, and it just goes straight to home."

"Welcome to Alabama the Beautiful." (Author's collection)

———

WHEN CROSSING THE BORDER INTO ALABAMA, the first thing you see is a giant sign that towers over the interstate. "Welcome to Alabama the Beautiful," it reads, the letters rounded and graceful. Undeniably, the view from Interstate 59 traveling southbound into Alabama is stunning. Northern Alabama boasts the southern reaches of the Appalachian Mountains, and there are few signs or buildings to distract from the evergreens that frame the mountain range's blue ridges. Against this backdrop, the welcome sign seems indisputable.

Beneath the inviting script of Alabama's border sign appears the name of the governor, at the time Robert Bentley—the man responsible for signing into law the now infamous Beason-Hammon Alabama Taxpayer and Citizen Protection Act, known simply as H.B. 56. Enacted in the summer of 2011, H.B. 56 was the harshest and most comprehensive state immigration law that the United States had ever seen. Although much of this law has been significantly amended or permanently dismantled, H.B. 56 intended to expand the roles and responsibilities of state and local law enforcement agencies as well as public- and private-sector actors in determining the immigration and documentation status of Alabama residents. In this way, H.B. 56 sought to structure the illegality of unauthorized residents not only through mechanisms of police-ICE collaboration but through bureaucratic enforcement practices that criminalize the commonplace activities of daily life.

Arizona S.B. 1070 and the Origins of State Crimmigration Policies

Alabama was not the first state to pass wide-ranging restrictionist legislation. The state followed a nationwide trend that was consciously oriented at comprehensive strategies to regulate interactions between unauthorized residents and state and private entities. In 2006, for example, the Georgia legislature passed S.B. 529, the Georgia Security and Immigration Compliance Act. Georgia state senator Chip Rogers, a sponsor of the legislation, noted that the bill's purpose was to "tak[e] what we thought was [sic] the best, workable ideas and put them into a comprehensive bill as opposed to doing this piecemeal and bill by bill by bill" (quoted in Bohon 2006: 99). In the words of one *New York Times* editorialist, S.B. 529 was a strategy of "deterrence by bureaucracy" (Downes 2006). In subsequent years, other states passed or attempted to pass similarly comprehensive measures as legislatures targeted unauthorized residents through bureaucratic provisions related to driver's licenses, employment verification, and public benefits.

Alabama was also not the first state to enact comprehensive legislation to criminalize unauthorized residents. Arizona, most notably, garnered national attention in 2010 when the state's legislature passed S.B. 1070, the Support Our Law Enforcement and Safe Neighborhoods Act. With the passage of the law, unauthorized immigrants and immigrant rights advocates across the nation shuddered in horror at this new iteration of Sensenbrenner, the 2005 federal legislation that had tried—and failed—to criminalize unauthorized residents and those who aid the unauthorized.[1]

The central feature of Arizona's law, known as the "show me your papers" provision, required police officers to make a "reasonable attempt" to determine a person's citizenship or immigration status during the course of regular patrolling duties—such as during traffic stops or arrests—whenever officers had a "reasonable suspicion" that the individual was unlawfully present in the United States. The law also enabled officers to make warrantless arrests of unauthorized immigrants and required officers to ascertain the immigration status of anyone who was booked into custody, jailed, or convicted of a crime, regardless of the severity of the crime for which the person was arrested or convicted.

Beyond outlining new responsibilities for state and local law enforcement officials in identifying and apprehending unauthorized residents, S.B. 1070 criminalized a multitude of activities related to violations of civil immigration law. The legislation criminalized those who hired unauthorized immigrants as day laborers as well as those who "harbored" or transported unauthorized immigrants. S.B. 1070 also criminalized immigrants who failed to carry their immigration documents and unauthorized immigrants who solicited or performed work in the state.

Although Arizona claimed that its policies simply mirrored federal statutes, S.B. 1070 pushed the boundaries of state regulation and criminalization of unauthorized immigrants (Fan 2012). In modern times, the authority to enact and enforce immigration law, including the right to grant permission to enter the country and determine who is unauthorized, has fallen to the federal government. Programs such as 287(g) and Secure Communities—which encourage specific methods of police-ICE collaboration—are designed to allow states to assist federal agents in the enforcement of federal law; however, these programs are managed by the federal government and require federal oversight. In contrast, S.B. 1070's provisions were enacted by the state of Arizona and were intended to be managed by the state. Arizona's law also went much further than laws in other states in criminalizing unauthorized residents. When Colorado passed S.B. 90 in 2006, requiring state and local law enforcement to notify federal immigration officials of individuals suspected of being unauthorized, it did not give agencies the authority to determine an individual's documentation status or authorize them to enforce immigration consequences. In contrast, S.B. 1070 initiated a state-sponsored expansion of the role of state and local law enforcement agencies in matters of criminal immigration enforcement.

Response to the Arizona law was mixed. In this border state, where roughly 5 percent of the total population was estimated to be unauthorized when the legislation passed (Passel and Cohn 2016), an *Arizona Republic* (2010) poll found that 55 percent of Arizona residents favored the law. The same poll found that 62 percent of Arizona residents approved of allowing unauthorized immigrants to remain in the country as long as they were employed and had no criminal record—reflecting, perhaps, a broader ambivalence toward unauthorized residents who are deemed respectable as well as the political saliency of rhetoric that frames the unauthorized as an economic burden or criminal threat (Conley 2015). A national study by the Pew Research Center for the People and the Press (2010) found that approximately 59 percent of those polled approved of S.B. 1070. Disaggregated by political affiliation, the same poll found that 82 percent of Republicans and 64 percent of Independents approved of S.B. 1070, while just 45 percent of Democrats approved of the law. Other national polls reflected similar findings: respective of one's political ideology, S.B. 1070 was considered to be either a rational and justified response to the failure of the federal government to secure the nation's borders or an egregious violation of the civil and human rights of Arizona residents, particularly immigrants and people of color, who would be presumed foreign-born.

The Obama administration objected to Arizona's immigration law. Days after S.B. 1070 was signed into law, during remarks to a naturalization ceremony for active-duty service members, Obama suggested that the legislation was "misguided" and "threatened to undermine basic notions of fairness . . .

as well as the trust between police and their communities that is so crucial to keeping us safe" (White House Office of the Press Secretary 2010). Shortly thereafter, the federal government filed suit against Arizona, charging that the law could not be enforced because its provisions were preempted by federal law and conflicted with existing federal statutes. The district and federal appeals courts agreed, respectively issuing and upholding injunctions against S.B. 1070. In response, Arizona appealed to the Supreme Court, which agreed to review the state's petition in December 2011, more than a year and a half after the law passed. In 2012, the Supreme Court ruled in *Arizona v. United States* that much of S.B. 1070 was, in fact, preempted by federal law, including provisions that allowed Arizona officers to make warrantless arrests and criminalize immigrants who failed to carry their documents. However, the Court allowed the law's centerpiece—the "show me your papers" provision—to stand (see also Campbell 2011; Menjívar and Enchautegui 2015).

The intervening uncertainty about the legitimacy of Arizona's law did not prevent other states from introducing and enacting similar legislation prior to the Supreme Court's ruling. To the contrary, representatives in more than half of the nation's state legislatures introduced similar bills in 2010 and 2011. The Tennessee House of Representatives (2010) passed a joint resolution commending the Arizona law, stating that the House "salutes the initiative and the courage of the Arizona State Legislature and Governor Jan Brewer in their actions to protect their citizens and the borders of our great nation." In spring 2011, Utah, Indiana, and Georgia passed comparable legislation with provisions similar to S.B. 1070; South Carolina and Alabama passed copycat bills that same year in the early summer.

H.B. 56: The Alabama Twist

On June 9, 2011, Governor Robert Bentley signed into law H.B. 56, Alabama's version of the Arizona legislation, even as many of the provisions of the Arizona law and copycats in other states were enjoined or facing impending injunctions. Despite its newcomer status, the Alabama law was swiftly acknowledged as unparalleled by previous state-level immigration laws. Enacted barely a month after a series of tornadoes had devastated much of the Southeast—killing more than fifty people in the state of Alabama alone and leaving many communities struggling to rebuild—Representative Micky Hammon, cosponsor of H.B. 56, claimed that the legislation was "an Arizona bill with an Alabama twist" (quoted in *USA Today* 2011).

Alabama's immigration law contained many of the same provisions as Arizona's law, such as Arizona's emphasis on empowering state and local law enforcement to engage in immigration enforcement duties. H.B. 56 boasted the "show me your papers" provision, which enabled state and local law enforcement officers to check an individual's immigration status during the course of a lawful stop or arrest and required that officers check the immigration status of individuals who were booked, jailed, or convicted of a crime. Unlike S.B. 1070, however, Alabama legislators did not include a provision for warrantless arrest of unauthorized immigrants, perhaps recognizing that this portion would not withstand a Fourth Amendment challenge. H.B. 56 preserved the Arizona law's provisions to criminalize those who harbored or transported unauthorized immigrants, immigrants who failed to carry their immigration documents, and unauthorized immigrants who solicited or performed work. Finally, the Alabama law mandated that employers use the federal E-Verify program, an electronic employment eligibility verification system intended to determine the legal status of newly hired employees.[2]

However, H.B. 56 went much further than legislation enacted in Arizona and other copycat states, and it extended far beyond outlining responsibilities for law enforcement. The "Alabama twist," as it was referred to by Representative Hammon, revolved around comprehensive bureaucratic enforcement measures that went above and beyond those specified by federal immigration law, essentially structuring and enforcing the illegality of unauthorized immigrants through bureaucratic processes.

Years earlier, other states and localities had passed or attempted to pass bureaucratic enforcement measures intended to curb settlement of unauthorized immigrants by denying public services, limiting language access programs, and restricting access to housing and employment. One well-known example is California's Proposition 187, which in 1994 attempted to deny access to public K–12 education for unauthorized immigrants (Jacobson 2008). In 2006, the city of Hazleton, Pennsylvania, passed the Illegal [sic] Immigration Relief Act Ordinance, which declared that the city was "empowered and mandated . . . to abate the nuisance of illegal [sic] immigration by diligently prohibiting the acts and policies that facilitate illegal [sic] immigration and punishing the people and businesses that aid and abet illegal aliens [sic]."[3] Hazleton's ordinance threatened to fine property owners who rented to unauthorized residents and to penalize employers who hired unauthorized immigrants (McKanders 2007). Similar ordinances passed elsewhere, including in Riverside, New Jersey, and Farmer's Branch, Texas. None of these policies was as extensive or elaborate as that implemented in Alabama, and all were ultimately rescinded by local governments or litigated and ruled unconstitutional.

In crafting H.B. 56, Alabama's legislators sought to target routine aspects of living and working in Alabama, or what Donald Kerwin (2014: 327) suggests amounts to "criminaliz[ing] the exercise of fundamental rights." The Alabama law required people to provide proof of citizenship or lawful immigration status prior to entering into business transactions with the state, and it rendered unenforceable any existing or future public- and private-sector contracts with unauthorized immigrants. H.B. 56 also mandated that school administrators determine the citizenship or immigration status of newly enrolling students. Taken together—and taken to the extreme—these provisions, on top of newly expanded roles for police, intended to make everyday life in Alabama even more arduous for unauthorized immigrants.

Those who try to understand the origins of H.B. 56 puzzle over the fact that the nation's most draconian immigration law was enacted in a state that is not known for having a large population of immigrants, unauthorized or otherwise. Certainly, when compared to Arizona and several other states that passed copycat legislation—as well as a multitude of states that either rejected or failed to pass similar legislation—Alabama has a relatively small population of unauthorized immigrants. Estimated at barely 1.8 percent of the state's population in 2010, approximately ninety thousand people—the majority of whom were Latinx people of Mexican origin (Passel and Cohn 2016)—Alabama had fewer unauthorized immigrants per capita than half the states in the nation, and its share at the time was more than a percentage point below the national average (Passel and Cohn 2011). At the same time, Alabama's estimated population of unauthorized immigrant residents had also increased considerably over the previous two decades, by more than 1,700 percent since 1990 (Passel and Cohn 2016), reflecting a similar pattern of immigrant settlement throughout the Southeastern United States.

Perhaps it was the dramatic and visible increase of Latinx newcomers who were presumed to be unauthorized—rather than their actual status or numbers in the population—that led Alabama lawmakers to target unauthorized immigrants during the 2011 legislative session. Since there is no way to identify an unauthorized immigrant by sight alone, members of communities—legislators, police officers, doctors, teachers, neighbors—make assumptions about a person's status based on biases of what it means to be or look "American," and these boundaries are often drawn in racially specific ways. Mae Ngai (2004: 58) elaborates, "Europeans and Canadians tended to be disassociated from the real and imagined category of illegal alien, which facilitated their national and racial assimilation as white American citizens. In contrast, Mexicans emerged as iconic illegal aliens. Illegal status became constitutive of a racialized Mexican identity and of Mexicans' exclusion from the national community and polity." In this way, people of Latin American ancestry or origin are often unambiguously portrayed and understood as "alien." Unauthorized immigrants are racialized as nonwhite—and, more specifically, as Latinx or Mexican. These biases, in turn, impact political and social landscapes at the local, state, regional, and national level.

Certainly, immigrant rights advocates in Alabama and other Southeastern states detect a generalized, widespread hostility toward those perceived as different and "foreign." Many argue that the region's changing demographic profile, combined with a history of racialized oppression and systemic economic inequalities, provides ample opportunity for legislative scapegoating. Many simply shrug off the question of why policy makers across the Southeast openly embrace harsh immigration enforcement policies. In an interview, one advocate noted his state's "sordid history of dealing with racial problems and racial challenges," suggesting that "unreconciled racial problems from the past [have been] directed towards a new community." Another long-time community organizer declared simply, "You just need to review the history of the state and you'll find your answer."

The United States in general and the Southeast in particular have a long and complex history of racial hierarchies and racialized caste systems intended to exclude racial minorities from full participation in everyday life (Alexander 2012; McConnell 2011). This hierarchy has been further complicated by the in-migration of Latinx people into the Southeast region (Jones and Brown 2017; Marrow 2009). Jerry Gonzalez, founder and executive director of the Georgia Association of Latino Elected Officials—a nonprofit organization dedicated to civic engagement and leadership development—suggested: "There is hostility in politics against immigration, against Latinos. And [Arizona-style legislation] is a cheap political trick for politicians to take advantage of that." In fact, some research indicates that anti-immigrant legislation is more closely tied to partisanship than demographic change, as Republican-controlled jurisdictions are more likely to advance restrictionist policies regardless of demographic composition (Ramakrishnan and Wong 2010).

Like Alabama, the state of Georgia also passed Arizona copycat legislation after recent decades of settlement by Latinx immigrants and other immigrants of color had substantially altered the state's demographic characteristics. Reflecting on this, Gonzalez noted, "Georgia is a hostile state to foreign-born people and to anyone that looks foreign-born. It's not a friendly state. There's a lot of open hostility. There's open discrimination. It is not a welcoming state." Asked to elaborate, he enumerated several examples: "[There are] people talking to their children in the grocery store in Spanish—U.S. citizens—and then others coming up to them and saying, 'This is America. Speak English.' Children playing in the playground, Latino children, Puerto Rican children, playing in the playground, being approached by other teenagers, being slapped and told they should 'Speak English because this is America.' And at a Starbucks, Korean Americans were—instead of their name being written on their cups, [the staff] drew what's called 'chink eyes' instead, to determine who the coffee belonged to." Gonzalez continued, "Puerto Ricans are being asked for immigration documentation at DMV [Department of Motor Vehicles] offices across the state, and their citizenship is being questioned. They [DMV personnel] are asking for their visas to be in this country. Things like that are very prevalent across the state." Finally, he cautioned, "I'll mention that these are just the things that we know about. So there's many, many more examples that we have heard of, and again, these are just the things that we have heard of."

Receiving populations in new destinations are often ambivalent about demographic changes (Fennelly 2006; Marrow 2011b; Naples 2007; Shutika 2008). However, antagonisms and microaggressions similar to those described by Gonzalez are well documented, particularly in places that have experienced steady growth in the Latinx and immigrant population (Gouveia 2006; Lippard and Gallagher 2011; Mohl 2003; Naples 2007; Neal and Bohon 2003). Without discounting people's experiences of discrimination by individual antagonists, it is important to acknowledge that individual acts of discrimination are often impelled by, and rooted to, institutional policies. In their research on the role of social services administrators in policing the boundaries of deservingness around immigration status, Natalia Deeb-Sossa and Jennifer Bickham Mendez (2008) found that decisions to provide care were shaped by barriers created through institutional markers of belongingness, such as social security numbers. They argue, "The institutional positions of gatekeepers in social services and clinics placed these workers . . . in the role of border enforcers" (627)—regardless of whether administrators wanted to serve in this role and regardless of whether individual workers explicitly intended or desired to prohibit immigrants from accessing services.

In Georgia, Arizona copycat legislation had similar effects. One key example, described by Gonzalez, revolved around private businesses' refusal to accept the Matrícula Consular, an identification card issued by Mexico to Mexican nationals who reside outside the country. Gonzalez explained, "Just yesterday, a staff person [at the Georgia Association of Latino Elected Officials] came up to me and said that one of her close relatives was trying to get pain medication at a local drugstore, and the local drugstore was telling them they couldn't use their Matrícula Consular ID card to get their medication because it was outlawed with the H.B. 87 that was recently passed. So there is a hostile climate in Georgia against foreign-born immigrants. If they look different and sound different, they will be treated harshly."

Unauthorized immigrants of Mexican nationality often use the Matrícula because they are prevented from obtaining U.S.-issued state identification by federal and state policies that limit access to these documents. The Matrícula is generally accepted as legal identification, even in interactions with law enforcement and private businesses, but it does not provide proof—or absence—of authorized residency. The Georgia law, through the Secure and Verifiable Documents Act, explicitly prohibited use of the Matrícula Consular for identity verification, noting that "secure" and "verifiable" documents were only those issued by "a state or federal jurisdiction or recognized by the United States government and that is verifiable by federal or state law enforcement, intelligence, or homeland security agencies." This specifically excluded the Matrícula Consular and similar identification cards issued by other nations (Georgia House of Representatives 2011). Importantly, this portion of the law applied only to transactions with state agencies, such as applications for public benefits; it did not prohibit private businesses from accepting the Matrícula as valid identification. Yet, in Gonzalez's story, the drugstore clerk cited the law as reason to refuse service to a customer who presented the Matrícula as proof of identification. Whether the store clerk actively intended to discriminate matters less than the fact that the law, in targeting the Matrícula, created the conditions for discrimination and bureaucratization of immigration enforcement.

Hostility toward immigrants of color also manifests at the legislative level, as policy makers promulgate supposedly race-neutral mythologies of immigrants as scapegoats, especially in relation to economic woes (Jones and Brown 2017). Concerns over Alabama's economy occupied a substantial part of state legislators' professed support for the bill. Senator Scott Beason, the bill's cosponsor, argued, "[H.B. 56] is a jobs bill. We have a problem with an illegal [sic] workforce that displaces Alabama workers. We need to put those people back to work. That's the number one priority" (quoted in White 2011). Certainly, the Alabama economy, like much of the nation, had been in a deep recession for some time. When H.B. 56 was approved by the state legislature and signed into law by Governor Bentley, the state's unemployment rate stood at 9.9 percent, slightly higher than the national unemployment average of 9.1 percent. But it would be a mistake to center the state's appetite for restrictionist legislation solely on the economic woes of its residents. In fact, at the time of the bill's passage, unauthorized immigrants—who, again, comprised roughly 1.8 percent of the state population—were a fraction of the state's labor force.

How is it, then, that such a small population warranted such a strong reaction? Isabel Rubio, executive director of ¡HICA!—a nonprofit organization devoted to social, civic, and economic integration of Latinx families in Alabama—offered one possible explanation. Noting the large number of white Alabamans living below the poverty line, Rubio indicated that some politicians cultivated racial animosities around perceptions of economic threat. She explained, "Politicians were running on this platform [of anti-immigrant sentiment]. There was a lot of embedded racism here. Often times these poor white people end up voting against their own self-interest in lots of things. So I think that what really happened is that the politicians who were running for election used fear as a tactic." Acknowledging the state's economic downturn, she continued, "Of course, the economy has been bad, but the reality is that immigrants aren't taking jobs away from Alabama citizens who want them. The population in Alabama of immigrants, generally speaking, is very small. Very small."

When H.B. 56 was introduced in 2011, Alabama was among the poorest states in the nation, and this continues to be true. Although Alabama's residents of color—especially black and Latinx people—are disproportionately likely to live in poverty, nearly half of Alabama's poor, in absolute numbers, are white. Some politicians exploited fears of white economic decline through stories of white demographic decline, such as by conflating unauthorized immigrants with people of Latin American ancestry and origin. For example, Representative Micky Hammon repeatedly cited the numbers of Latinx people in Alabama as a measure of the state's unauthorized population in order to articulate the necessity of H.B. 56. (Notably, one judge who blocked portions of H.B. 56 pointed to Hammon's statements as evidence of racial animosity).

But what of Rubio's other suggestion—the idea that economically disadvantaged white people vote for politicians who champion restrictionist legislation regardless of whether these same politicians reflect the class interests of poor white people? Certainly, economic interests are assumed to be an important motivating force in white support for immigration restrictionism, and anti-immigrant sentiment in the United States often fluctuates around periods of economic recession and recovery. Immigrants—of all statuses and throughout the nation's history—have been described as union busters who undercut the employment of U.S. citizens and authorized residents by accepting low-wage work. Alternatively, immigrants are portrayed as willingly engaged in dirty, dangerous, and demeaning jobs that U.S.-born citizens refuse to do. Both narratives are troublesome in their framing of labor relationships as individual choices rather than rooted in structural conditions of vulnerability and exploitation.

Aside from this, the preservation of specifically white economic, demographic, and political supremacy is, in itself, a manifestation of group interests. Thus, white people who vote for immigration restrictionism are not voting against their class interests so much as they are voting for the preservation of white racial hierarchy, the benefits that accrue to the "public and psychological wage" of whiteness (DuBois 1935). As Rubio suggested in her comment about embedded racism, the fears of economically disadvantaged white people may be expressed through an economics of scarcity, but they are premised on the racial scapegoating of immigrants of color.

It is undeniable that politicians used fear as a tactic in their advocacy for H.B. 56. However, this fear was also felt by Latinx immigrants, and with good reason. Representative Mo Brooks, a staunch ally of the bill, claimed, "As your congressman on the House floor, I will do anything short of shooting them. . . . Anything that is lawful, it needs to be done because illegal aliens [sic] need to quit taking jobs from American citizens" (quoted in Camia 2011). Senator Beason seemed to take this advocacy a step further when he called on other Republicans in the state legislature to "empty the clip, and do what has to be done" (quoted in Rolley 2011).

As time passed, the state's unemployment rate dropped, leading Beason to claim that the law had succeeded. Beason (2012) noted, "Since the anti-illegal [*sic*] immigration law went into effect, Alabama has seen a tremendous drop in unemployment. A drop that far outpaces the other states in the region. . . . I promised that the anti-illegal [*sic*] immigration law would open up thousands of jobs for Alabamians, and it has done that. People are going back to work. . . . The critics may whine, but many of our neighbors have jobs again. I know those folks are thankful for the opportunity to work and support their families, and that opportunity was opened up by H.B. 56."

It is true that the state's unemployment rate dropped slightly after the implementation of H.B. 56. However, despite Beason's assertion, little evidence links the declining unemployment rate to the new law. To some extent, the state's official unemployment rate dropped alongside a sizable contraction in the formally recognized labor force, as Alabama residents who were not actively seeking employment were no longer counted in official unemployment statistics. In the year following passage of H.B. 56, the officially acknowledged labor force decreased by more than fifty thousand people, while the total number of employed Alabamans fluctuated marginally but remained relatively static over time, thereby accounting for an overall decrease in the unemployment rate. Further, data from the U.S. Department of Labor's Bureau of Labor Statistics indicate that employment rates in Alabama actually fell in the areas of agriculture, construction, hospitality, and food preparation (Alabama Department of Labor 2013), four sectors that traditionally employ a larger-than-average percentage of unauthorized immigrant workers (Passel and Cohn 2009).

At the same time, employers in some traditionally immigrant-heavy sectors reported a shortage of workers who were willing and able to fulfill tasks associated with these jobs. This should have come as no surprise to Alabama, since the neighboring state of Georgia experienced immediate labor shortages in similar sectors following passage of H.B. 87, Georgia's own copycat version of S.B. 1070. In Georgia, farmers reported record losses as crops were left to rot when immigrant workers—including those with work authorization—largely abandoned the fields after passage of H.B. 87, fearing direct or indirect consequences of increased enforcement. Georgia farmers claimed that they could not employ enough U.S.-born residents to fill these vacancies, resulting in an overall loss of agricultural goods. Research conducted in collaboration with the Georgia Department of Agriculture, the Georgia Fruit and Vegetable Growers Association, the Georgia Farm Bureau, and the Georgia Agribusiness Council (McKissick and Kane 2011) confirms that these anecdotal reports were part of a broader pattern of labor shortages across the agricultural sector in Georgia. This contradicts the Georgia governor's insistence that formerly incarcerated people could be required to work the fields if they were unemployed. A similar strategy was advocated by John McMillan, commissioner of the Alabama Department of Agriculture and Industries, who offered that Alabama farmers should use people incarcerated in the state's correctional facilities to remedy Alabama's labor shortage.

When similar labor shortages emerged in Alabama after the passage of H.B. 56, farmers recruited Haitian and Eritrean refugees from other states to fill the vacancies of jobs formerly occupied by unauthorized immigrants, who supposedly had taken those same jobs from native Alabamans. In learning this, the reaction among unauthorized immigrants was unequivocal. "It's nonsense," exclaimed one undocumented woman who I heard testify before a delegation of Washington officials on the impact of the Alabama law. She continued:

> Hundreds and hundreds of people were laid off . . . that had been working there for twenty years. They were laid off who have, like, U.S. citizens [children]. They were laid off. And, for a while, they bring people from Thailand, taking poor people from Thailand to take the place of the undocumented people who have U.S. citizen children, who need the job. And I don't know what the point of—you don't want—you import people, and you take away the jobs of the people that [are] already here, and have attachments, and . . . have U.S. citizen children, and take away their job. Doesn't make any sense.

If jobs such as these were being abandoned by unauthorized immigrant workers as a result of H.B. 56—as the anecdotal evidence suggests—the recent vacancies had not been filled by eager U.S.-born workers (Addy 2012). Perhaps this is in no small part related to the fact that such jobs are quite physically demanding yet offer comparably little in terms of compensation and respect.

H.B. 56 in Practice: Expanding State Involvement in Bureaucratic Enforcement

On November 21, 2011, I stood among hundreds crowded into the Council Chambers of Birmingham's City Hall. The simple room, with its long wooden benches and dim lighting, looked as though it might ordinarily be quite spacious; on that day, however, it was overflowing with media, grassroots leaders, advocates, civil rights activists, and eleven Democratic members of the U.S. Congress. This ad hoc congressional delegation, led by U.S. Representative Luis Gutiérrez of Illinois, had traveled to Birmingham to hear testimony on the impact of H.B. 56 in the lives of Alabamans.

The legislation—in the words of Alabama State Representative Micky Hammon, a cosponsor of H.B. 56—had been designed to "attack every aspect of an illegal alien's [sic] life" (quoted in Chandler 2011). But how successful had the law been in accomplishing its task? Mary Bauer, legal director of the Southern Poverty Law Center, an Alabama-based civil rights and legal advocacy organization, noted that the law had been quite efficacious. In testimony before the congressional delegation, Bauer explained, "H.B. 56 has devastated the immigrant community in Alabama. It would be hard for me to overstate the human tragedy that has been unleashed upon Alabama by H.B. 56." She continued, "Under the provisions of this law that are currently in effect, undocumented persons are unable to interact with the government—in any way and for any purpose. It has turned a significant class of people, effectively, into legal non-persons, subjecting them to a kind of legal exile. It has destroyed lives, ripped apart families, devastated communities, and left our economy in shatters" (Conley 2015: 154–155).

Once H.B. 56 was approved in the Alabama legislature, the Southern Poverty Law Center joined other legal advocacy organizations, including the National Immigrant Law Center, the American Civil Liberties Union, and the Asian Law Caucus, in filing a lawsuit against Alabama seeking an injunction against the law's implementation. Although parts of the law were blocked a few weeks after H.B. 56 went into effect, most of the law's major provisions were allowed to stand, at least temporarily. Advocates insisted that the provisions left intact would wreak havoc in people's lives.

Bauer's assertion—that unauthorized residents of Alabama were unable to "interact with the government in any way and for any purpose" in the wake of H.B. 56—was hardly an exaggeration. H.B. 56, whose wording claimed that "illegal [sic] immigration is encouraged when public agencies within this state provide public benefits without verifying immigration status" (Alabama House of Representatives 2011), compelled state and local governmental employees to ascertain the immigration and documentation status of anyone who applied for state services and, in some cases, to make decisions about how or whether services were rendered based on an applicant's status. Correspondingly, this provision in the law prohibited Alabama's state and local governments from entering into "business transactions" with unauthorized immigrants. However, the law did not initially specify the scope of this provision.

In practice, this meant that some employees of state services, including utility companies, public libraries, and even the Department of Human Services, required clients and patrons to provide proof of citizenship even when proof was not technically required by law. In the days and months immediately following the bill's implementation, as institutions scrambled to interpret the law's ambiguity, employees often erred on the side of caution by denying routine services. Accordingly, in Blount County, Alabama, an area with a larger-than-average population of both Latinx and foreign-born residents compared with the rest of the state, the Allgood Alabama Water Works Company displayed the following notice: "Attention **ALL** water customers: to be compliant with new laws concerning immigration you must have an Alabama driver's license or an Alabama picture ID card on file at this office . . . or you may lose water service" (emphasis in original).

From countless stories told in organizing and advocacy workshops that I attended, and as chronicled by several media outlets, Alabama residents were denied access to utilities (including water and electricity), child welfare assistance (even for U.S.-born children), library cards, public school–sponsored after-school programs, and business licenses (Fleischauer 2011; Kennedy 2011; Pilkington 2011; Southern Poverty Law Center 2012). Immediately following passage of the law, unauthorized immigrants worried about whether they would be able to pay property taxes and the required fees to register their automobiles and mobile homes, since these constituted business transactions with the state.

H.B. 56 also prohibited Alabama's courts from enforcing existing contracts between unauthorized immigrants and private entities, causing lawyers and immigrant advocates to question whether child support payments, work contracts, and rental agreements for cars, trailers, and houses would be legally binding and enforceable under the new law. To be sure, unauthorized immigrants are entitled to workplace protections and compensation for work performed, even if they are not authorized to enter into formal employment relationships. However, many advocates worried that unscrupulous employers would invoke this section of the law to prey upon already vulnerable workers, refusing to pay for services rendered by day laborers and other contract employees, and threatening to call police or immigration authorities if unauthorized workers asserted their rights to compensation or safe working conditions. Private business owners took advantage of H.B. 56. In one such case, detailed by the Southern Poverty Law Center (2012), a used-car dealership in northern Alabama repossessed a family's vehicle—even though the owners were current on their loan and had made more than $3,000 in payments; the manager of the dealership explained simply that he "could no longer sell to 'illegals' [sic] because he might lose his business license" (27–28).

Finally, H.B. 56 required public elementary and secondary schools to collect data on the immigration and documentation status of newly enrolling children.[4] This provision in particular was disturbing to community members, who worried that school officials with access to this information would report children or their families to immigration agents. Teachers and school administrators worried that the fear or perception of this happening would keep children away from school. This was a subject of intense discussion during an Alabama field hearing held by the United States Commission on Civil Rights (USCCR), a bipartisan federal agency that investigates civil rights issues. During the hearing, one resident testified about the days immediately following implementation of this portion of the law. She explained, "The [school] bus was empty, none of the kids want to go to school, because they were scared that their parents won't—when they come back, their parents won't be there." Her voice pained, the woman continued:

> I saw this, like, twelve-year-old running to the bus because she got a test that day. And the mother went running after her, crying, saying, "You cannot go to school." She was scared. And I was at the window looking at this—this scene. And I couldn't—They start crying. [The girl] said, "I want to go to school, Mom," and [the mom] said, "No, you can't. . . . They can take you." And they start crying, and I start crying too. And at that point I was like, this cannot be happening. People with good hearts, with sense of justice could see that this is not right. (Conley 2015: 156)

Contrary to the mother's fears, H.B. 56 did not actually empower public school employees to directly enforce immigration law or report unauthorized immigrant children and their parents to ICE. Rather, it mandated that school administrative officials—not teachers—collect information on the immigration and documentation status of newly enrolling students. The law further required that schools submit this information to the state board of education, which, in turn, was mandated to compile data on the fiscal costs to the state of providing educational instruction, supplies, and extracurricular activities to students who were unauthorized immigrants. Finally, under this provision, the Alabama Board of Education was required to submit an annual report detailing these outcomes to the state legislature. In doing so, the law cautiously tiptoed around *Plyler v. Doe*, the 1982 Supreme Court ruling that prohibits states from denying access to primary and secondary public education for unauthorized immigrant children. By law, Alabama must provide public primary and secondary education for all residents of the state regardless of immigration status or the status of their parents; thus, H.B. 56 did not explicitly deny access to education to unauthorized student residents.

Nevertheless, the wording of the law differed markedly from the practice of the law, a contention leveled by the U.S. Department of Justice (2012a) among others. Some school personnel across the state blatantly misunderstood the law, such as when a teacher asked a previously enrolled fourth-grader about her immigration status and that of her parents (Lyman 2011). Mary Bauer of the Southern Poverty Law Center noted in her 2011 testimony to the congressional ad hoc delegation that a mother was refused entry to a book fair at her daughter's school when she could not prove that she was an authorized resident. Although this provision of the law was temporarily

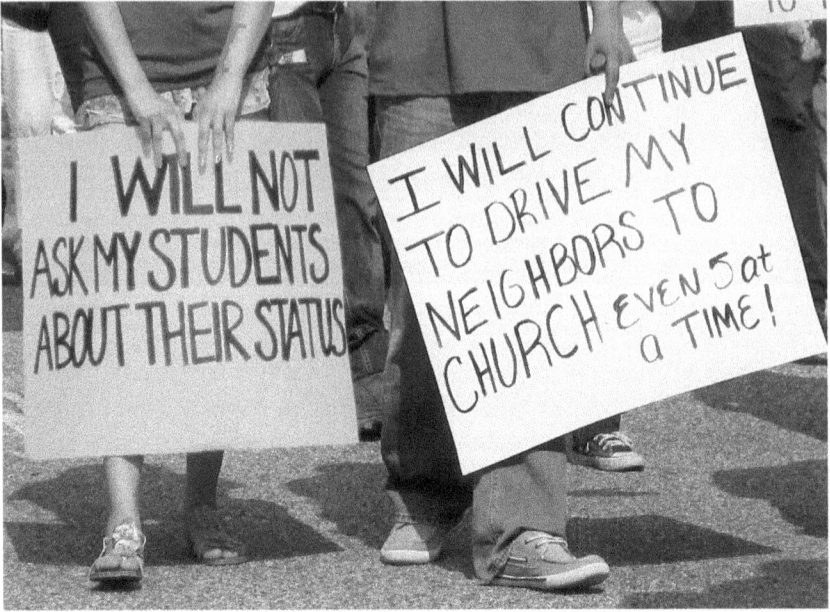

Demonstrators protest H.B. 56 in Montgomery, AL. (Author's collection)

blocked pending further review just two weeks after taking effect, reports of discrimination and abuse in schools continued to emerge. Isabel Rubio of ¡HICA! noted one incident at a school in northern Alabama where the principal had separated schoolchildren based on perceived citizenship and immigration status. At another school, Latinx children, including those born in the United States, were harassed by school officials and students alike and told to "go back to Mexico."

Despite the fact that Alabama is legally required to provide access to education, the implementation of this provision undermined parents' confidence that schools were safe and off-limits to immigration enforcement, a fact made abundantly clear during the USCCR field hearing. After the hearing, Martin R. Castro, chair of the USCCR, told me that he believed the law to be "the most draconian of all of the anti-immigrant laws that have been passed in the last couple of years." After emphasizing that he was speaking only for himself and not on behalf of the commission, which had yet to issue an official report, he elaborated, "These immigration laws—particularly the Alabama law, but each of them encompasses a number of civil rights issues: racial profiling, discrimination, bullying, violations and denial of educational benefits, and violation of *Brown versus Board of Education*." In his view, the Alabama law "sought to deny children an educational benefit that is their right regardless of immigration status at the primary and secondary school level." Chairman Castro said, "While [Alabama officials] claim that that's not the intent, certainly the information that I was able to glean from the [testimony] presented to us at the briefing said that there were children that did not register for school this year, but had registered for school last year, that were undocumented. They were clearly fearful of this law, and so, to me, that is a clear example of a situation where this law has a chilling effect on the rights of children to an education." He continued, "I personally believe education is an important civil rights issue because education is the basis by which every person in this country can move forward to achieve the American dream, and enforce their rights, and have economic and electoral opportunity. And when we deny access to education, we're denying access to all the civil rights that flow from that."

Given the potentially serious consequences of the enforcement lottery, made eminently more tangible through Alabama's law, many parents were deeply fearful and kept their children home from school. Craig Witherspoon, the Birmingham superintendent of schools at the time, testified to the congressional ad hoc delegation that the city's schools experienced a higher-than-usual rate of student absences immediately after H.B. 56 was implemented, and newspaper articles from that time indicated that an estimated two thousand Latinx children across the state of Alabama stayed home from school in the days following implementation of the law (Gomez 2011; Robertson 2011). School officials, including superintendents and principals, responded by reaching out to local communities to assure parents that schools would not report children or their relatives to immigration officials. Nevertheless, officials across Alabama believed that some parents continued to keep their children home out of fear, even after this provision of the law was enjoined.

When reporters asked Alabama representative Mo Brooks directly about the "unintended side effects" of Alabama's law, such as these impacts on schoolchildren, he responded contrarily, "Those are the *intended* consequences of Alabama's legislation with respect to illegal aliens [sic]. We don't have the money in America to keep paying for the education of everybody else's children from around the world. We simply don't have the financial resources to do that. Second, with respect to illegal aliens [sic] who are now leaving jobs in Alabama, that's exactly what we want. . . . These aren't unintended consequences. We want illegal aliens [sic] out of the state of Alabama" (quoted in Trowbridge and Weinger 2011; emphasis added).

Attrition through Enforcement: "Self-Deportation" by Any Means Necessary

Like Luís Escoto, I, too, traveled to Alabama shortly after H.B. 56 was enacted into law. Like Escoto, I noticed the border sign welcoming me to "Ala-

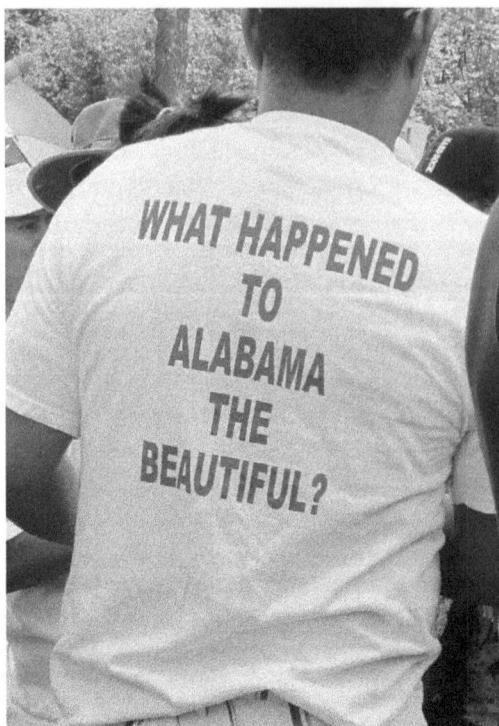

"What Happened to
Alabama the Beautiful?"
(Author's collection)

bama the Beautiful" perched neatly amid a backdrop of greenery and the blue ridges of the Appalachian Mountains. However, unlike Escoto, and perhaps many undocumented people before him, I did not experience a rush of fear at the sight of this sign. Nor did I immediately contemplate the contradiction inherent in the juxtaposition of its phrasing. After all, "Alabama the Beautiful" is not just a phrase on an interstate welcome sign; it is also the state slogan. Evelyn Servín, a grassroots organizer in Russellville, Alabama, later laughed with me at the irony. She explained, "It's beautiful, what is outside, the things you can see, the trees, the landscape. It's beautiful, right? But the society attacks. The society is what makes it—it doesn't allow [Alabama] to be, you know, all that it can be. Right?" She snickered, then, betraying her incredulity. "Yeah. That's what I always say."

In fact, the state slogan became a flashpoint for those who opposed the law. One group designed shirts with the phrase "What happened to Alabama the Beautiful?" inscribed across the back, which they wore to protests at the state capitol. Servín paused and then sighed, now serious. "Unfortunately, everything that you have here can be beautiful, 'Alabama the Beautiful,' your family, the roots you've planted here." She continued:

But the values that they preach on in the South—it's not the same thing that the people practice. They are so religious that you can find a church on every corner. But it doesn't have the same welcome, and all that, right? And, well, it makes me laugh to say that sarcastically, "the beauty" of Alabama, because it's not. For all of the problems that we have, all of the problems of racism that still exist, with the poverty that exists, with the attacks on the same people, the poor, African Americans, and especially Latinos . . . well, it's not so beautiful.

Undeniably, Alabama had become quite ugly—and quite unwelcoming—for many who had made the state their home. The fear in immigrant communities across the state was palpable, and as Representative Brooks articulated, that was not unintentional. H.B. 56 and other state-level immigration laws are part of a self-declared, extremist strategy of "self-deportation," a term that gained widespread notoriety—and derision—during Mitt Romney's 2012 presidential bid. Such policies are intended, in the words of Alabama representative Micky Hammon, "to make it difficult for [unauthorized immigrants] to live here so they will deport themselves" (quoted in Chandler 2011).

The term *self-deportation* was originally coined in 1994 by Mexican American comedian and political satirist Lalo Alcaraz amid the racial hostility of California's Proposition 187. Using the pseudonym Daniel D. Portado,[5] Alcaraz issued satirical press releases and political ads from a fictitious organization, Hispanics Against Liberal Takeover (HALTO), calling on Mexicans to "self-deport." Joking aside, the philosophy behind the strategy of self-deportation is quite stark. According to such reasoning, unauthorized immigrants will pack their belongings and return voluntarily to their countries of origin once the perceived costs of living in the United States outweigh the perceived benefits. Alternatively, from the perspectives of states like Alabama, unauthorized residents could be strong-armed into relocating from high-enforcement states to those with laxer policies (Bohon 2006). In a simple cost-benefit analysis, unauthorized immigrants are rational choice actors who weigh the expected future costs of enforcement—perhaps including lengthy detention stays and eventual removal—against the likelihood of any benefits they may derive—such as wages—if they are not detained and deported. The possibility of future benefits, it may be noted, is intended to decrease significantly thanks to the devolution of immigration enforcement powers to state and local law enforcement and to the bureaucratic enforcement provisions of laws such as H.B. 56.

Immigration restrictionists claim that this strategy of "attrition though enforcement" has the added benefit of being cost-effective for the United States. If unauthorized immigrants deport themselves, restrictionists reason, the federal government will save on the costs of service provision and enforcement measures, including costs incurred for lengthy detention stays for detained immigrants awaiting their immigration hearings.[6] Of course, this belief invariably overlooks the well-documented, long-term economic benefits that accrue to federal and state tax systems as a result of the labor and purchasing power of unauthorized immigrants (Bohon and Conley 2015; Congressional Budget Office 2007; Goss et al. 2013), not to mention benefits that accrue to U.S. employers and consumers through commodities and services extracted from often-exploited unauthorized immigrant bodies (Conley 2012b).

Initially, it seemed that H.B. 56 had succeeded in its strategy of self-deportation. Anecdotes from teachers, clergy, employers, and community members suggested that many unauthorized immigrants—their students, congregants, employees, and neighbors—had abandoned the state, fleeing the law and its punitive effects. One teacher in the town of Russellville, Alabama, attested, "When H.B. 56 came into effect, my classrooms became empty." She continued, "The students were crying. My nieces received goodbye letters from their friends saying they had to leave" (Conley 2015: 158). Similarly, Isabel Rubio confirmed that she, too, had noticed a pervasive sense of dread among Latinx immigrants in ¡HICA!'s outreach efforts. Rubio explained, "There's really been this huge terror in the Latino community, people who have been afraid to go to school, go to church, go to work, just because they're afraid that they'll get stopped for 'driving while Latino.' It's created a large amount of fear." Then, quietly, she added, "And some people have left."

For some time, organizers and advocates whispered about these outcomes, fearing that we would somehow speak them into existence or acknowledge their legitimacy simply by expressing them aloud. Others were more outspoken, hoping that the cumulative effect of often-nightmarish accounts of outrageous abuses would shame the state legislature into backing down. Alabama's newspapers were full of such stories. Nonetheless, many Alabama politicians loudly proclaimed their apparent victory over the state's unauthorized population.

I witnessed the devastating impact of H.B. 56 on one community when I was invited to Alabama to help organize and mobilize against the law, and against the criminalization of immigrants across the Southeast more broadly. Community members and organizers from across Alabama and the Southeast converged in Albertville, a rural town in the northeastern part of the state with a relatively sizable Latinx immigrant population. We were there to support the work of Alabama organizers in cultivating local leadership against the law, to participate in a door-knocking campaign to raise awareness about the law, and to encourage residents to turn out for a community meeting to discuss how communities could protect and defend themselves.

A quiet place, far removed from the hustle of the state's major cities, Albertville was placed in the state spotlight when Senator Beason cited the town as an example of the extent to which unauthorized immigrants brought harm to the state. He argued, "The reality is that if you allow illegal [sic] immigration to continue in your area you will destroy yourself eventually. . . . If you don't believe illegal [sic] immigration will destroy a community go and check out parts of Alabama around [the towns of] Arab and Albertville" (quoted in Rolley 2011). At the time, Albertville's population was 24.1 percent Latinx, nearly 42 percent of whom were either U.S.-born or naturalized citizens. Arab's population was approximately 1.1 percent Latinx, and nearly 85 percent of these were U.S.-born (US Census Bureau 2011).

Albertville mayor Lindsey Lyons gently disputed Beason's claims of the city's destruction, noting that his comments were "a little overboard" (quoted in Rolley 2011). A more forceful challenge could be made, however, as the settlement of immigrants into small towns across the nation is often credited with revitalizing communities—demographically and economically—that have otherwise experienced stagnant population growth or massive out-migration of residents (Vitiello and Segrue 2017; J. Wilson and Singer 2011). Even Lyons later acknowledged that "our industries would shut down" if immigrants left the area entirely (quoted in Constable 2012). Still, Representative Kerry Rich of Albertville, a staunch supporter of H.B. 56, agreed with Senator Beason, arguing that the district had been overwhelmed for some time by unauthorized immigrants. In an interview with the *Birmingham News*, Representative Rich argued, "The illegals [sic] in this country are ripping us off. . . . If we wait for the federal government to put this fire out, our house is going to burn down" (quoted in Chandler 2011).

We who converged in Albertville saw the fire very differently. In teams of twos and threes, we dispersed into Albertville's Latinx neighborhoods, many of which were mobile home communities that had seen better years. Equipped with a rudimentary map of the neighborhood and flyers advertising our meeting, my door-knocking partner and I walked together through our designated area. At first glance, the community seemed like any other. As we made our way past parked cars and stepped around haphazardly strewn children's toys and bicycles, we carefully inspected each home for signs of life. Door after door, though, we knocked with no response. At a few homes, young children peered at us from closed windows and then quickly disappeared behind tightly drawn curtains. In the early twilight of the crisp Alabama fall, we wondered whether the neighborhood's residents were too afraid to answer their doors.

I would not have been surprised. In my travels across the state, I had heard stories of immigrants who refused to answer the door to strangers for fear that they were opening the door to *polimigra*—the merger of police officers (*la policía*), or local law enforcement officers more generally, and immigration agents (*la migra*) that serves as a force multiplier for immigration enforcement. In Clanton, a rural Alabama town similar to Albertville, an undocumented man named Héctor told me that officers often knocked on doors in his neighborhood looking for unauthorized immigrants with outstanding warrants. If someone who was not under investigation happened to answer the door, the officer would nonetheless interrogate or arrest that unlucky person on suspicion of his or her own immigration status, a practice known as collateral arrest. Sometimes, Héctor claimed, an officer would wait outside in an unmarked car for those who refused to answer the door. Once someone—anyone—emerged from the house and headed to work or to the grocery store, the officer would follow, stop the car, and arrest the individual for driving without a license. Mission accomplished.

For unauthorized immigrants who lived in mobile home communities— who were many, since mobile homes are often more accessible to the unauthorized than apartments and houses—their homes would have been easy to identify. The Alabama law prevented unauthorized immigrants from entering into business transactions with the state; as a consequence, those who lived in mobile homes could not pay the annual fee required to renew their home's registration. They could not update the decals on their homes, and this was visible to any passersby.[7] Many unauthorized immigrants who lived in mobile homes thus felt that they were easy targets; better to not answer at all than to risk opening the door to an official intent on inquiring about a delinquent trailer decal.

After we knocked at several homes that appeared inhabited, with not a single person answering the door, my door-knocking partner and I had nearly given up hope. It seemed that no one wanted to talk with us, and I wondered if our appearance was the cause. My colleague was a large Latino man, friendly looking but possibly intimidating to those peering at us from behind curtains and peepholes; in contrast, my stature is quite small, but my appearance—marked by red hair and pale, freckled skin—is unmistakably other. Still, we smiled and knocked, knocked and smiled. No answer.

Finally, we came to an older mobile home in the middle of the neighborhood; it was just one of many in a long line of such homes, virtually indistinguishable from the others. The paint was worn, but the home was otherwise well maintained. I climbed the rickety wooden steps to the front door, knocked, and then quickly retreated to the packed dirt ground; the door could not have budged otherwise, because the stairs were so narrow. To our surprise, the door opened a crack and then wider as a middle-aged man cautiously poked his head through the narrow opening. We smiled. "*Hola, buenas tardes,*" we called, and rushed to explain why we had disturbed his privacy. The man waved as if to signal that he understood why we were there and he was glad we had come. He invited us inside, and his wife emerged from the kitchen—differentiated from the cramped living room by an oven and a few narrow cabinets—and urged us to sit at the small dining table. The man brought an extra chair, and the woman returned to the stove to hover over her *pozole* as we talked.

The *pareja* was familiar with the law; so, too, were their neighbors. Most of the community had long since gone, the man explained, abandoning their homes shortly after the law was enacted. Many had left homes filled with belongings—furniture, toys, clothing—taking only their most prized possessions. Many left in the middle of the night without warning; there was no time to pack, no time to sell property, no time to find homes for pets, some of whom now wandered the dusty gravel roads in the community of vacant trailers looking for scraps of food. The houses that we thought inhabited were occupied not by people, then, but by the possessions and memories of those who had left. According to media reports, the same had happened across the entire state of Alabama. One day people were there; the next day they were just gone.

As the months wore on, however, it became apparent that unauthorized immigrants had not packed up and left, abandoning Alabama en masse, at least not for an extended period of time. In my travels across the state, not once did I meet a single person who knew of anyone who had "self-deported" to Mexico or any other country. Perhaps some had left Alabama and settled elsewhere in the United States, out of reach of the Southeast's transition toward punitive state crimmigration measures. Indeed, analysis from the Pew Research Center indicates that Alabama is one of a handful of states that saw a decline in unauthorized residents, even as the unauthorized population in the United States overall has remained steady (Passel and Cohn 2016). The exact causes of this decline are unclear and could be attributed to a number of factors—adjustment of status, removal, death. It is also possible that some people relocated. Héctor, the man from Clanton, expressed frustration at those who left voluntarily: *After the law is passed, they leave the state; they go somewhere else, to another state. But I always tell them the law will just follow you until it exists everywhere in the United States. They say if that happens, they will just go to Mexico. But I say you should stay here and fight.*

Still, many who initially left Alabama eventually returned, drawn back to their neighborhoods despite the state's pursuit of harsh policies. Although Representative Hammon argued, "We really want to prevent illegal [*sic*] immigrants from coming to Alabama and to prevent those who are here from putting down roots" (quoted in Preston 2011), he overlooked the fact that many unauthorized immigrant residents were already tied to the state and had been for some time—by jobs, children, homes, communities, and the memories of years or even decades lived in Alabama. In fact, among those settled in the Southeast, half of all unauthorized residents have lived in the United States for more than ten years (Passel and Cohn 2016), which is certainly enough time to plant oneself and begin to bloom. And so the vast majority of unauthorized immigrants and their families continued living in Alabama despite the state's draconian law. As Evelyn Servín, the grassroots organizer in Russellville, reflected, "This won't force us out. You can't [just leave]. So many roots, from so many, many years, you can't leave it without a fight. You have to. This is your home, and you'd have to leave that too." Soberly, she continued, "Maybe we're not welcome here, but you have to fight for the place where you live."

Notes

1. In 2012, the Supreme Court affirmed in *Arizona v. United States* that "it is not a crime for a removable alien [*sic*] to remain in the United States." However, legislation has successfully criminalized activities associated with unauthorized presence, including immigration-related employment fraud and identity theft.

2. E-Verify was not included in S.B. 1070. Arizona previously mandated the employment verification system under the 2007 Legal Arizona Workers Act, which also penalized businesses that hired unauthorized workers (Sáenz, Menjívar, and García 2013).

3. Hazleton, Pa., Ordinance 2006-10, §2(b).

4. This provision was permanently enjoined on August 20, 2012, in *United States v. State of Alabama.*

5. D. Portado is a sly nod to *deportado*, the Spanish word for "deported."

6. Several immigration restrictionist organizations have advocated for self-deportation. See, for example, Jessica Vaughn's 2006 report, *Attrition through Enforcement: A Cost-effective Strategy to Shrink the Illegal Population,* and Mark Krikorian's 2005 report, *Downsizing Illegal Immigration: A Strategy of Attrition through Enforcement,* both published by the Center for Immigration Studies, and the 2008 report, "Attrition of Illegal Immigrants through Enforcement," published by the Federation for American Immigration Reform.

7. This provision was permanently enjoined on August 20, 2012, in *United States v. State of Alabama.*

6

Building Structure, Building Power

I N THE END, legislators were only partially justified in believing that state crimmigration laws would leave unauthorized residents with little choice but to admit defeat and return to their countries of origin. It is true that H.B. 56 and police-ICE collaboration programs made life untenable for unauthorized immigrants in Alabama and that unauthorized residents of other Southeastern states were nervously pondering their own fates in the enforcement lottery. However, legislators erred in assuming that the little choice left to unauthorized immigrants would inevitably result in their preferred outcome of self-deportation.

In fact, undocumented people had at least one other option. Faced with the threat of illegalization in their everyday lives—driving children to school, going to work, paying property taxes, and reporting crimes—it had become clear that they could be affected by the enforcement lottery at any moment. As one organizer explained, "Seeing something like [H.B. 56] . . . if we've been fortunate enough to not fall within the net of 287(g) or Secure Communities, well, this is really going to catch us. We have to do something." Rather than inspiring unauthorized residents to "self-deport," the extreme nature of H.B. 56 and other restrictionist policies and practices galvanized many in the unauthorized community. Isabel Rubio of ¡HICA! observed, "The weird twist is that we have really gotten people engaged, just realizing that [they] might be undocumented, but [their] kids were born here, and so they have a right to be here, and [they] have a stake in this fight, so [they] have to stay and fight. People have stepped up." People "stepped up," so to speak, because they realized they would lose the lives they had built for themselves and their families if they did not. And so, worried for their children, their partners, and themselves, unauthorized residents and their allies chose an option that legislators had not expected: they fought for the right to remain.

A month after H.B. 56 went into effect, nearly forty people gathered in an unfinished, unheated church in rural Alabama. Days earlier, spread out in communities across the Southeast, we had been invited by the Southeast Immigrant Rights Network (SEIRN), the Alabama Coalition for Immigrant Justice, and the National Day Laborer Organizing Network for a four-day emergency workshop on H.B. 56. We were a diverse group for the town of Albertville, including black, white, and Latinx people of all ages, from various walks of life, some born in the United States and some abroad. Most of those present were Latinx residents of cities and towns across Alabama. We huddled together in heavy sweaters and jackets as we strategized to build grassroots resistance to the policies and practices structuring illegality in the Southeast. We had gathered to fight for the communities we called home.

Much of the workshop was dominated by discussions of strategy and structure—how to build a movement in resistance to H.B. 56 as well as against the region-wide push toward criminalization. How could we, as a region confronting some of the nation's harshest immigration policies and practices, work together against the concerted efforts of legislators and law enforcement officials who wanted to expand bureaucratic enforcement and police-ICE interoperability? How would we build sustained resistance across the Southeast—not just in central cities such as Atlanta and Raleigh but also in smaller places like Knoxville and Birmingham and even rural towns like Clanton and Albertville? And how could we do this in the context of a region with a relatively recent history of immigration, a comparatively small population of immigrants, an enduring legacy of racial stratification, and a history of being consistently under-resourced, both economically and in terms of social movement infrastructure?

It is not that the Southeast had never before mobilized around immigrant rights. Plenty of marches and rallies had taken place in the region over the years. During the 2006 marches against the Sensenbrenner Bill, anger at the congressional push for criminalization brought immigrants and allies into the streets across the Southeast, just as it did in Chicago, Los Angeles, and New York—places with longer histories of immigration and significantly larger immigrant populations. At the time, however, the Southeast was not prepared to harness the collective power of these grievances. Only a handful of immigrant-oriented organizations had emerged in the region since the early 2000s in response to budding growth of immigrant communities. However, these groups were mainly dedicated to service provision, integration, civic education, and legislative advocacy. With few exceptions—such as the Georgia Latino Alliance for Human Rights (GLAHR) and TIRRC—most were not oriented toward community base building and grassroots leadership development in service to collective action. National immigrant rights organizations were largely focused inside the Washington, DC, beltway, where they lobbied for broad legislative reforms, often without input from a broad spectrum of directly affected people. To some grassroots organizers, it seemed that many national groups were not invested in strengthening the capacity of local organizing or building the movement from the ground up, especially in new immigrant destinations.

SEIRN is one organization dedicated to organizing immigrant communities and allies across the Southeast in ways that reflect the specific opportunities and challenges of the region. With the conviction that the Southeast is both intensely vulnerable to immigrant criminalization and capable of powerful resistance—especially given the region's deep history of racism and sustained racial justice activism—SEIRN organizes to create space for immigrants and allies across the region to meet with one another, share stories, and develop strategies for defending immigrant communities. Its organizing principle is to elevate the voices and leadership of immigrants in the Southeast to transform the region into one that affirms the rights and dignity of immigrants and other marginalized communities. Originally under the sponsorship of the Tennessee Immigrant and Refugee Rights Coalition, SEIRN now functions independently, and it has member groups in every state in the region.

SEIRN's founder and codirector, Mónica Hernández, has been involved in immigrant rights work for more than twenty years, including more than a decade in the Southeast. Recalling the mobilizations of 2006, Hernández believes that "organizing suffered a huge setback" during that time. She elaborated, "That was a critical event that inspired people to take action. But those of us that were around doing this work, we weren't prepared to deal with an event of that magnitude. And for real change to happen it's going to take more than these massive mobilizations, as important as they are." Hernández continued, "We weren't prepared to help people build organizations that could sustain that level of pressure. We weren't prepared to do the kind of *political education* that's necessary for people to understand that when you stand up for your rights they're going to come back at you and try to squash you. And [to understand] that it's not defeat, that it's part of this process of change. We weren't prepared."

Indeed, there was a backlash in response to the mobilizations of 2006. As Ted Wang and Robert Winn (2011: 52) note, "Anti-immigrant forces used the images of the marches to galvanize their base and to advocate for more enforcement measures targeting unauthorized immigrants," including escalation of police-ICE interoperability programs and state and local crimmigration policies. This was especially true in new destinations throughout the Southeast, which had less political will and infrastructure to respond to attacks on immigrant communities. Hernández sighed as she recollected the aftermath. "Community members would say, 'We marched, and instead of things getting better, they got worse.'" She continued, "When you're trying to work with a community that's already so repressed, you can't afford to have that kind of setback. I won't say it fully stopped people from organizing. But in many places it did. It was just too much, and people lost hope."

After the 2006 mobilizations, SEIRN and other groups continued cultivating grassroots leadership, planting seeds that they hoped would one day blossom into a strong immigrant-led voice from the Southeast. To Hernández, much of the crucial work was in "helping people build their own power by building their own organizations and having their own leadership." The Southeast needed strong organizing infrastructure to create and support decentralized, immigrant-led groups across the region, fertile ground that people could root themselves to and draw strength from as the criminalization of immigrant communities intensified. In many ways, then, even though the Alabama workshop was organized in response to H.B. 56, it was also one more step in a process that had started years before.

Much of the workshop's discussions over those four days focused on organizing immigrant communities and strategizing resistance to police-ICE collaboration programs and state-level crimmigration policies. Francisco Pacheco, an organizer with the National Day Laborer Organizing Network, described in detail the *comités de defensa del barrio* (CDBs), or neighborhood defense committees, that had arisen in Arizona in the weeks and months surrounding the passage of S.B. 1070. Modeled after the *comunidades eclesiales de base* (Christian base communities) and other grassroots communities of resistance developed in El Salvador, Guatemala, and elsewhere in Latin America (Shefner 2008; Walker and Armony 2000), these groups are often composed of families, neighbors, and friends who work together to support and defend one another in times of threat and crisis. CDBs intend to provide the foundations of resistance to the onslaught of crimmigration laws and the vulnerabilities of unauthorized immigrants by empowering directly affected community members with tools to challenge these practices.

In principle, a *comité de defensa del barrio* is organized into seven *equipos*, or teams: *equipo de vigilancia y respuesta rápida* (vigilance and rapid response team); *equipo de actividades cívicas* (civic activities team); *equipo de asuntos legales* (legal issues team); *equipo de arte y cultura* (art and culture team); *equipo de organización y movilización* (organization and mobilization team); *equipo de recaudación de fondos* (fund-raising team); and *equipo de la*

Francisco Pacheco describes organizational structure at a *comité* workshop in Clanton, AL. (Author's collection)

escuela de la libertad (freedom school team). Though each team of the CDB operates independently, all the teams are managed collectively by a coordinating council of representatives from each team.

Each team of each CDB fulfills an important role in challenging crimmigration policies and practices and empowering and protecting community members. The organization and mobilization team, for example, might organize civil disobedience actions or turnout for demonstrations, while the civic activities team might coordinate voter registration drives. Meanwhile, the freedom school team might create accessible educational materials to teach community members about police-ICE collaboration, and the art and culture team might host cultural events to celebrate immigrant histories and experiences. The vigilance and rapid response team might organize civilian patrols to monitor and document police checkpoints and develop warning systems about ICE raids for community members. The legal issues team might educate community members on their civil rights or host power of attorney workshops to help families make custodial arrangements for children and property in the event of a parent's deportation.

Comités in the Southeast often tackle some or all of the tasks of these *equipos* as a group, possibly due to the fact that the unauthorized population in this region is smaller and more dispersed than it is in Arizona and other

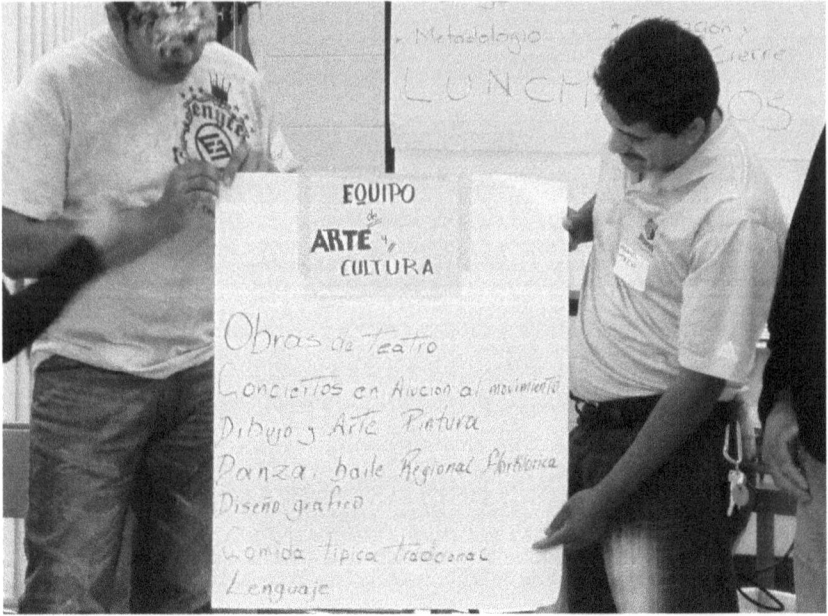

Presentation of art and culture team at a *comité* workshop in Knoxville, TN. (Author's collection)

places in the Southwest. The idea of *comités* is not entirely new to the Southeast; GLAHR, TIRRC, and SEIRN have been working to foster grassroots immigrant rights groups for some time. Dozens of active groups across the Southeast, called *comités populares*—popular (or people's) committees—or simply *comités*, have been organized with the support and guidance of state and regional organizations. Over the years, *comités* in Alabama, Georgia, North Carolina, Tennessee, and elsewhere in the Southeast have been critical in developing the organizing voices and capacities of immigrant communities and in bringing these communities into dialogue with policy makers, law enforcement, statewide advocacy groups, and the broader immigrant rights movement. In Tennessee, for example, the Comité de Mujeres Migrantes de Nashville (Nashville Migrant Women's Committee) formed around the case of Juana Villegas, and the Comité Popular de Knoxville formed around a campaign against Knox County's pursuit of 287(g). Nonetheless, the region as a whole is still in the early stages of developing independent, community-led responses to enforcement and other abuses against immigrants. Adelina Nicholls, executive director of GLAHR, noted that the *comité* structure has certainly helped articulate and advance the development of *comités* in Georgia but that the true strength of any *comité* comes in having "something to belong to that they have built, that they have grown," and that gives them "their own voice, their own power."

The Boundaries of the Problem

Organizational structure is essential to building visible, tangible resistance to illegality. Still, there is more to movement building in the Southeast than the infrastructure of *comités*. Perhaps even more critical to the struggle has been political education—in the words of Adelina Nicholls, the expansion of "voice" and "power" that stems not just from how a group is structured but from the principles by which it is organized. Political education is not merely civic education; that is, its central purpose is not to help people understand the legislative process or partisan policy debates, although this may certainly be one component. More fundamentally, political education is about cultivating political consciousness to understand relationships of power.

In the Southeast, political education of movement actors has explored illegality and the creation of alternative narratives—accounts that seek to reinterpret the "problem" of unauthorized immigration and reframe the discourse in ways that deepen community power and resistance. This became clear to me in a roundabout way during a workshop with immigrant and ally leaders from across the Southeast through an activity that—on the surface—had nothing whatsoever to do with narratives or framing. The meeting's facilitator, a spry, older woman, stood before us explaining the next *dinámica*—a type of game used in participatory education settings. We had spent the last few hours muddling through the complexities of federal immigration policy, and the *dinámica* presented a welcome break.

I want you to think of a profession—any profession at all, the facilitator said. *Something that you would have been or that you would like to be if you could have the choice. Now, imagine that—with your new identities—you are on a boat with the other people in your group. And your boat is sinking. You can only save one person on that boat. Which person would be most important to save, and why? Work in your groups to decide. You have fifteen minutes.*

Dinámicas emerge from the Freirean tradition of education for critical consciousness, in which the processes of education are participatory and its outcomes are liberatory (Freire 2013). In the popular education model, participants share production of knowledge through storytelling. Problem solving centers participants' articulation of the material conditions of their lives and livelihoods. Commonalities that emerge in dialogue of individualized experiences reveal collective social and historical context. This model of education relies on participatory techniques—methodological tools such as dialogue, role-playing, and puppetry—to engage the mind and body to disrupt the Western, linear, textual approach to knowledge production. But we should not confuse the methodology of popular education with its techniques. After all, as Pancho Argüelles once teased me, participatory games are used in corporate retreats, too.

Argüelles, a popular educator and community organizer with deep roots in the U.S. and global South, explained, "Popular education is not so much a recipe as it is a methodology of how you understand learning, how you understand teaching, and especially how you understand conscious and collective action." He elaborated, "You cannot say you practice popular education [if] you are not engaged in collective action for changing your situation, for liberation, for justice, or for survival. [Popular education] has to be directly connected to action, and that action has to be connected to a new understanding of yourself, your community, your context of history, [and] where you want to go." As a methodology, then, popular education seeks to develop strategies for real social change. Participatory techniques are manifestations of popular education only when they articulate and challenge structural causes of oppression.

In preparation for the boat *dinámica*, the workshop participants had already broken into smaller groups. Our group formed a small circle at the front of the church. One person assumed the role of facilitator: *Let's just start by saying what our professions would be—I guess you could say your dream job.*

We went around the circle clockwise, taking turns to share our dream jobs. Someone said musician, another said teacher. One wanted to be an artist. Another hoped to be an organizer. I was a doctoral student at the time, still struggling to understand my positionality in social movement work, and I offered *socióloga*—sociologist—when it was my turn. The group members' ambitions were vast, and many had been stifled in the pursuit of their dreams by their immigration status. We stared at one another as the minutes counted down. *What now?* we wondered.

Someone asked, *Is one of these jobs more valuable than the others?* Someone else responded, *They are all important.* Around the circle, others nodded: all of these were valuable jobs, we agreed, no more and no less important than the others.

Adán, an energetic man with flecks of gray streaking his dark hair, offered, *We're all organizers, right? Who here is an organizer? Everyone raise your hands. You wouldn't be here if you weren't an organizer. So we could say that we're going to save the organizer. And there: we're all saved!*

Was it a trick question after all?

Then someone else offered a simple insight: *Why should we choose who survives based on their job? There are lots of other ways we could choose.*

And thus appeared the first crack in the game's facade. The facilitator's directions implied a certain strategy to resolve the game's dilemma—selecting a survivor based on the person's chosen profession—but there was no imperative to comply with her framing of the solution.

One person proposed that we each share why we deserved to be the remaining person on the boat, a competition to determine who was best able to argue for their own survival.

Another suggested that we pick a parent, a caregiver. *Soy madre*, volunteered one woman. *I'm a mother. Tengo dos hijos. Young.* As a mother of two young children, she reasoned, she was needed to care for others. She would raise the next generation of organizers. But really, all of us had others whom we were responsible for, cared for, and inspired.

An older person said, *We should pick the youngest; the person with the most life ahead of them.* We looked at Lili, a slip of a woman, barely twenty years old and newly engaged to be married. She smiled shyly, concentrating intently on her boots, and shrugged.

Other ideas were proposed: Why not choose the wisest member of our group? The person who had the most experiences? Perhaps the person with the best chance of survival?

Adán, who had spent considerable time organizing in Arizona after the passage of S.B. 1070, suggested that we select the survivor at random by drawing straws: *It really doesn't matter who is left on the boat. We are all organizers, so we are all capable.*

Discomfited by the game's dilemma, I had been quiet for most of the conversation. Now I wondered aloud: *I really don't understand. Why do we have to pick? Why can we only choose one person?*

Yes, I was wondering that as well, murmured a woman standing next to me.

From across the circle, Adán's eyes lit up. *Tengo una pregunta (I have a question)*, he said as he beckoned to the facilitator. *What's wrong with the boat?*

The facilitator stared back, dark eyes revealing nothing. *I can't tell you what's wrong with it*, she said dismissively. *It doesn't matter. But you need to make a decision. You have to agree as a group who gets to survive. And you've only got five minutes left, so you better hurry.* Then again, louder, to the entire room, *¡Tienen cinco minutos más!*

Pressed for time, we started throwing suggestions into the circle, rapid-fire:

Maybe we can fix the boat?
But maybe it's not big enough to hold all of us.
Could we take turns, some of us in the boat, some in the water?
Can we call for help somehow?
How close are we to land? Can we swim?

Despite the facilitator's disdain for our question, our solutions to the game's problem had suddenly changed. And then, just as our solutions transformed, so, too, did our understanding of the problem:

Why is the boat sinking?
Why can we only save one person?
What are we doing on this boat?

As we asked ourselves these questions, considerations substantially broader than the facilitator's initial framing of the *dinámica*, our perspective on the game had changed. From across the room: *¡Treinta segundos! (thirty seconds!).*

How can we possibly choose just one person?
Bueno, said Adán. *So we've made our decision? Let's put it to a vote.*

———————

TOGETHER AGAIN AS A LARGE ASSEMBLY, group after group presented their solutions. Each member of each group identified their desired profession; the group spokesperson then revealed the group's decision—who was chosen to survive—and the rationale. There were several teachers and artists, a doctor, a photographer. There was even a sexologist, an announcement that drew laughter from workshop participants. The sexologist was chosen as his group's survivor—Who better to encourage the procreation of future organizers?—to enthusiastic applause from the assembly. The facilitator nodded and smiled approvingly as each group presented.

Then it was our turn. We stood in the center of the large circle, linked arm in arm, and shared our dream jobs. Adán, the spokesperson for our group, then stated our decision and explained how we had arrived at our choice: *At first, we shared our jobs, just like everyone else. But we realized that we are all organizers—and we each have strengths and ideas to contribute. And we decided that we couldn't make a decision based on our job. So we thought about other ways that we could decide—like if someone was a parent or something like that. But we didn't agree with that either. And we thought that maybe we could fix the boat if we could just understand what the problem was. We think that we can figure it out and fix it together. So we choose not to choose. We sink or swim together.*

And does everyone in the group agree with this decision? asked the facilitator, one eyebrow arched in skepticism.

Yes! We agree. It was unanimous, we chimed.

The facilitator turned to the larger group, her back to us. *This happens sometimes,* she sighed, crossing her arms. *You have a group that refuses to make a decision. They refuse to compromise. And when you don't reach a decision as a group, someone else will decide for you. So they have failed. None of them survived. They all drowned.* Turning back to us, she said, *You can sit down now.*

Chastened, deflated, we went back to our seats. *I thought it was an interesting decision*, whispered a woman sitting next to me, whose group had selected a more traditional answer. *It was different.*

THE *DINÁMICA* ENDED in a public rebuke at our group's failure to play by the rules. The game was about learning how to make concessions, we were told, and our unwillingness to compromise had resulted in the total loss of everyone involved. Ostensibly, the *dinámica* was intended to prepare us for a discussion of comprehensive immigration reform—a somewhat antiseptic term given to legislative proposals that involve, at a minimum, provisions for both amnesty and enforcement.[1] In discussions of comprehensive immigration reform, immigrant rights actors are often told (even by those within our own movement) that we must be reasonable, that we must negotiate, that we cannot expect to achieve some of our demands without conceding others. These axioms often seem to be built on the fiction—albeit well intentioned—that all parties are negotiating in good faith and that all parties have equal power.

The boundaries of the *dinámica* conceal an even deeper truth. The game's outcome—a reprimand for our group's inability to follow the rules of a supposedly simply game—illustrates far more than our unwillingness to compromise on immigration reform. In reality, the game is never as simple as it appears, even when most of the players, even the facilitator, believe that its purpose is merely to engage us in resolving a straightforward dilemma. Still, the game is presented as such, and the rules are always carefully defined. Participants who fail to play by the rules may be ignored, ridiculed, rebuked—or worse.

Of course, the stakes are much higher once we move beyond the make-believe sinking boat in the *dinámica* to the question of unauthorized immigration. Here, too, framing matters: just as the problem of the sinking boat was manufactured to be resolved in a particular way, so, too, is unauthorized immigration structured as a specific problem with specific solutions. Politicians, the media, and civic and religious institutions tell us that unauthorized immigration is a problem and that we must reach consensus on a solution to this problem. Proposed solutions vary widely—ranging from violent confrontation or "extermination"[2] to "welcoming the newcomer"[3] and everything in between—and the variations are not meaningless. However, such solutions share one important commonality: inevitably, the answers are always concealed within the boundaries of the problem that has been articulated.

"And if you choose what the conversation is about, you've already won," explained Pancho Argüelles, as we later discussed popular education as a tool of social change. Argüelles had not been present for the boat *dinámica*, but his words perfectly expressed my unease with how the game had unfolded. In straightforward terms, Argüelles encapsulates Steven Lukes's (2005) three-dimensional view of power: the ability to shape not only observable behaviors and demands of individuals and groups but also their very consciousness. In other words, power is the ability to influence one's understanding of the world (or of the conversation), thereby securing compliance with taken-for-granted assumptions about the world. As Lukes articulates: "The supreme and most insidious exercise of power [is] to prevent people, to whatever degree, from having grievances by shaping their perceptions, cognitions and preferences in such a way that they accept their role in the existing order of things, either because they can see or imagine no alternative to it, or because they see it as natural and unchangeable, or because they value it as divinely ordained and beneficial" (28).

This understanding of power is rooted in ideology, a term that has been used to describe competing and conflicting meanings. Coined by Antoine Destutt de Tracy in his call for a new branch of positivist scientific investigation, ideology was articulated as the study of ideas (Freeden 2003). Successive and postpositivist iterations brought the study of ideology into philosophy and sociology, embedding ideas within society as constructs produced and shaped by specific sociohistorical conditions. Karl Marx, for example, understood ideology as a "false idea" or "inverted world consciousness," a camera obscura that produces an inverted image of society. As with Plato's analogy of shadows on a cave wall misinterpreted for the being that causes the shadow, Marx's understanding of ideology posits that this reproduction is not reality, but a distortion of reality:

> Men [*sic*] are the producers of their conceptions, ideas . . . as they are conditioned by a definite development of their productive forces and of the intercourse corresponding to these, up to its furthest forms. Consciousness can never be anything else than conscious existence, and the existence of men is their actual life-process. If in all ideology men [*sic*] and their circumstances appear upside-down as in a *camera obscura*, this phenomenon arises just as it must from their historical life-processes as the inversion of objects on the retina does from their physical life-process. (Tucker 1978: 154)

To Marx, humans create the social relations of society; nevertheless, we perceive our material conditions as though they are natural and inevitable. Ideology decontextualizes and dehistoricizes society and its material conditions (Abercrombie, Hill, and Turner 1980; Eagleton 1991; Larrain 1983. Now perceived as natural, socially constructed outcomes seem to occupy a life of their own; we accept that conditions manifest in particular ways because, we assume, they have always existed in this way and they always will. Moreover, we perceive that this is the natural order.

John Thompson (1984: 5–6) challenged the idea of the camera obscura by noting that "ideology is not a pale image of the social world but is part of that world, a creative and constitutive element of our social lives." In other words, ideology is not a false image of reality but rather is deeply embedded within reality: it is a profound aspect of what is real about the world, even though its manifestations are created to advance particular interests. Trevor Purvis and Alan Hunt (1993: 492) elaborate, "Of course earthquakes occur, and their occurrence is independent of consciousness; but it is their construction . . . that determines whether they are 'movements of tectonic plates' or manifestations of the 'wrath of gods.'" Just so, human migration occurs, but the construction of national boundaries around borders and belongingness, narratives of illegality, and consequences for vulnerability determine how we understand and resolve the "problem" of unauthorized immigration.

Antonio Gramsci (1971) explored the role of ideology in manufacturing consent through hegemony. In the Gramscian view, ideological frameworks legitimize authority such that people do not recognize the imposition of boundaries on our thought processes. For example, white U.S.-born citizens often contend that their ancestors migrated "the right way" and that present-day would-be immigrants to the United States should "wait in line" for their turn, but they do not acknowledge historical policies that allowed open borders and U.S. citizenship for white immigrants from Northern and Western European nations or recognize constraints on contemporary authorized migration, especially for people from high-sending countries. Ideological foundations structure our social world, defining what is possible—and what is not.

Just as our group was instructed in the *dinámica* to resolve the problem as defined—by collaboratively identifying a survivor rather than trying to identify what was causing the boat to sink or, more broadly, why we were on the boat to begin with—so, too, are we coerced into addressing unauthorized immigration from within a framework that characterizes unauthorized immigrants or unauthorized immigration as a/the problem. In both circumstances, the problems—as they are understood—are manufactured, and the decision-making process that has led to this understanding has been neatly obscured—for the facilitator in the case of the *dinámica*, and for society in the case of unauthorized immigration and illegality.

Of course, we cannot deny that there are problems associated with unauthorized immigration as it is currently constructed—that is, through the lens of illegality. As a sociopolitical condition, illegality is produced through the act of unauthorized immigration only inasmuch as its idea is constructed through national borders and boundaries of belongingness as well as policies and practices that enforce these borders. The condition of illegality reproduces the eminent vulnerability of an entire class of people—and that *is* problematic. To say that unauthorized immigration exists as a problem unto itself, however, is to ignore the systematic creation of illegality and its consequences as well as the conditions that gave rise to this social relation to the state. As such, this framework takes for granted the assumption that unauthorized immigration is, in itself, problematic and naturalizes illegality as a social fact unconnected to its sociopolitical origins.

Alejandro Portes (1978) charts the transition of unauthorized migration from "pattern" to "problem," articulating a redefinition in the framing of unauthorized migration that corresponds to the needs of dominant classes. According to David Snow and Robert Benford (1998: 198), social movements use frames to "assign meaning to and interpret . . . relevant events and conditions in ways that are intended to mobilize potential adherents and constituents, to garner bystander support, and to demobilize antagonists." Frames, both embedded in and extending from ideology, guide beliefs and actions—including proposed solutions—by guiding our understanding. Thus, George Lakoff and Sam Ferguson (2006: 1) write,

> Framing is at the center of the recent immigration debate. Simply framing it as about "immigration" has shaped its politics, defining what count as "problems" and constraining the debate to a narrow set of issues. The language is telling. The linguistic framing is remarkable: frames for illegal immigrant, illegal alien, illegals, undocumented workers, undocumented immigrants, guest workers, temporary workers, amnesty, and border security. These linguistic expressions are anything but neutral. Each framing defines the problem in its own way, and hence constrains the solutions needed to address that problem.

Expressed in this way, the framing of unauthorized immigrants and unauthorized immigration as a/the problem reinforces narratives that hold immigrants accountable for their status. If the problem of unauthorized immigration is further specified as the problem of poor choices of individual unauthorized immigrants, then the solution (and the blame) must necessarily focus on rectifying the individual wrongs of individual immigrants. One solution to the problem of unauthorized immigration—criminalization of unauthorized immigrants and increased enforcement through police-ICE collaboration—derives from the narrative that unauthorized immigrants are criminals and/or terrorists who disregard the nation's borders and threaten national security (Flores 2003; Kilty and Haymes 2000; Mariscal 2005). In this framing, unauthorized immigrants are dangerous, destructive elements that bring violence and drugs to the United States and threaten the nation's sovereignty and security.

A second solution to the "problem" of unauthorized immigration—bureaucratic enforcement of illegality through state crimmigration policies—derives from narratives of unauthorized immigrants as an economic drain on citizens, authorized workers, and taxpayers (Hondagneu-Sotelo 1995; Huang 2008; Newton 2008). Here, unauthorized immigrants become a burden on society, depriving authorized residents of jobs, wages, and resources. In both solutions, individual unauthorized immigrants are held accountable for their offenses through the omnipresence of illegality and criminalization of routine aspects of everyday life.

Proposals to resolve the illegality of unauthorized immigrants sometimes manifest in alternatives that extend beyond the individual. In some instances, the problem of unauthorized immigration is articulated as a class of unscrupulous employers who preferentially hire unauthorized workers for their cheap and exploitable labor. But note here the troublesome corollary of a class of unauthorized workers who are willing to work under such conditions as though they are united with employers in bilking citizens and authorized workers out of decent jobs and pay. The solution to unauthorized immigration, then, becomes about constraining the autonomy of employers and unauthorized workers through workplace raids, employment eligibility verification systems, fines for those who hire unauthorized labor, and charges of identity theft for those employed with false documents. An administrative frame views the problem of unauthorized immigration through the backlog of visa applications or the lack of diverse, efficient, and accessible pathways to legal residency and citizenship; given this articulation, the answer to unauthorized immigration is to modernize the immigration bureaucracy and liberalize immigration policy by expanding access to visas.

Though each of these proposed solutions differs in its approach (reflecting, perhaps, ongoing disagreement over how unauthorized immigration is framed as problematic), they all begin with the premise that unauthorized immigration is the basic problem that must be resolved. This is not a false understanding of reality but constitutive of reality: conceptualizing unauthorized immigration and unauthorized immigrants as a/the problem actively creates the reality we inhabit. The framing obscures and naturalizes the conditions of unauthorized immigration, including policies and practices that contribute to the international migration of people, and the creation of borders and laws that contribute to their status as unauthorized, thereby obscuring the sociopolitical origins of illegality (De Genova 2002). Rarely is unauthorized immigration described as a symptom of a broader problem—the necessity of exploitable bodies under a system of global capitalism; the impact of neoliberalism on nations left vulnerable from histories of colonization and resource extraction; and the creation of immigration policies resulting from the violent imposition of sovereign borders—that maintains and endlessly re-creates vulnerability and illegality. And so, to paraphrase Argüelles, once you have articulated the problem, you have already won.

———————

IT WAS CLEAR FROM OUR CONVERSATIONS that Argüelles was familiar with, and had been influenced by, an understanding of ideology. Concepts of power and hegemony have informed his work as a popular educator, including his coauthorship of the BRIDGE (Building a Race and Immigration Dialogue in the Global Economy) curriculum, a collection of resources and *dinámicas* that recontextualize and rehistoricize stories of international migration. One such exercise presents a pictorial history of U.S. immigration policy, including images of slave ships, the Trail of Tears, the U.S. Border Patrol, and sky-high border fences crowned with barbed-wire spirals. There are representations of the Underground Railroad, the Chinese Exclusion Act, the Bracero Program, and the North American Free Trade Agreement. The images are accompanied by brief explanations in English and Spanish.

I first experienced this immigration history *dinámica* at a leadership summit sponsored by the Southeast Immigrant Rights Network in 2010. Those who participate in the exercise are invited to tour the time line, add their own or their ancestors' migration histories, and consider the significance of immigration policies in their own lives. Like other participants, I spent much of the activity in quiet contemplation of my migration history, reflecting on the impact of sociohistorical context on my ancestors' ability to migrate. The *dinámica* encourages participants to theorize how individual and collective histories have been shaped by the forced migration and enslavement of Africans and by the genocide and removal of Native Americans and appropriation of their ancestral lands. We contemplate how our nation's demographic profile has been shaped by the Naturalization Act of 1790, which dictated that only "free white persons" could become citizens of the United States. We reflect on how we, as individuals and as a society, have been affected by prohibitions on immigration visas for sexual minorities—only lifted in 1990—or by the Defense of Marriage Act, which until 2013 prohibited same-sex couples from petitioning citizenship through the traditional path of spousal reunification. And we reflect on what these policies tell us about the nature of our immigration system and the foundations of the nation.

The intention of the time line exercise is to contextualize contemporary expressions of immigration law (and, by extension, illegality) within sociohistorical conditions. In doing so, we reframe unauthorized immigration as broader than the simple act of a solitary individual who violates the sovereign borders of the United States. In this light, the "problem" of unauthorized immigration becomes a different problem altogether. Argüelles explained, "The main goal . . . is to define the conversation. This conversation is not just about me and you and the group of people who cross the border without papers. The conversation is not about how they are 'job-takers.'" He continued, "The conversation also has to be about how they have to cross the border . . . before it was there. Who put it there, and then who made it illegal to cross it without papers? Because that wasn't [always] true. And so you are starting to add history as the product of human interaction, not as a natural given thing. This situation is the product of human decisions and political will."

It this way, political education provides the context—or the conscious-ness—to resist illegality. As one undocumented person who had participated in an activity similar to the immigration history time line told me, "It's very important to know where you come from, and it's something that's giving me hope. It's like civil disobedience in its own right." Indeed, raising one's critical consciousness is a form of civil disobedience, and this has been a crucial component of grassroots immigrant rights organizing. In rejecting taken-for-granted assumptions about the framing of illegality through com-prehensive exploration of the nation's immigration history, we are better equipped to question—and perhaps defy—prescribed solutions. The terms of the conversation dictate the outcomes of the conversation, just as the problem's solutions are delineated by our understanding of the problem and by those who have power to define—or frame—the problem.

As it was presented in the workshop, the boat *dinámica* was about work-ing together to achieve consensus, building compromise within our move-ments, and reflecting on the difficulty of decision making under time limitations and other constraints. But our group refused to accept the terms of the game, and so we refused to commit to the game's prescribed solutions. We redefined the problem, and so the spectrum of possible solutions also changed. In much the same way, many unauthorized immigrants and allies across the Southeast grapple with redefining the "problem" of unauthorized immigration—a struggle I turn to in the next chapter.

Notes

1. Since IRCA, various proposals for comprehensive immigration reform have all ultimately failed. Under the Trump administration, comprehensive reform has come to mean provisions for amnesty and enforcement as well as curtailing authorized immi-gration by ending the Diversity Visa Lottery and restricting family-based migration.

2. In 2010, Tennessee representative Curry Todd equated immigrant women to rats who "multiply" uncontrollably. In 2011, Kansas representative Virgil Peck argued, "If shooting these immigrating feral hogs works, maybe we have found a [solution] to our illegal [sic] immigration problem" (Fertig 2011). Donald Trump consistently uses dehumanizing language to refer to immigrants of color and their countries of origin, including stating that unauthorized immigrants "infest" the nation and referring to African nations as "shithole countries."

3. The "welcoming the newcomer" frame, alternatively expressed as "welcoming the stranger," is popular with Christian and Christian-descendent associations, including the Catholic Church and U.S. Conference of Catholic Bishops, the Presbyterian Church, the National Association of Evangelicals, and the Unitarian Universalist Association. This narrative can be problematic because it frames even long-term immigrant residents as "newcomers" and "strangers."

7

Storytelling Resistance

THE "COMMON SENSE" framing of unauthorized immigration and unauthorized immigrants as a/the problem propagates narratives that legitimize the vulnerability of undocumented people. Stories that characterize unauthorized immigrants as criminals, burdens on society, and job takers justify intensification of the immigration enforcement regime through police-ICE interoperability programs and state bureaucratic crimmigration policies. These narratives and practices, in turn, structure the experiences of unauthorized immigrants, forcing them to confront illegality in even the most mundane aspects of daily life.

Immigrant rights actors challenge narratives and practices of illegality through counternarratives that resist classification of unauthorized immigration and unauthorized immigrants as problematic. Three overarching narratives of resistance—existence, deservingness, and (il)legitimacy—express alternative accounts of threat and opportunity to compete with the dominant framing of the problem. The first two narratives—existence and deservingness—challenge illegality through accounts that focus primarily on individuals. The (il)legitimacy narrative challenges illegality through accounts that focus on institutions and structures. Importantly, even as these counternarratives challenge illegality, they also limit resistance—their efficaciousness at resisting dominant stories is tempered by subtle affirmations of illegality built into the narratives themselves.

Narratives of Existence

Yovany Diaz Tolentino was born in a small village in Mexico, just outside of San Luís Potosí. "Actually," he laughed ruefully, "I was going to be born in the United States. My brother had already been born [in California], so I have a mixed status [family]."[1] Diaz Tolentino's family had been living in California for years, but after his mother became pregnant with him, they returned to Mexico because of a family emergency. "So we went back, and that's where I ended up being born." A few years later, his mother returned to the United States for work. "I was three or so," he recalled. "I milked the cows, cut the yard with machetes. We missed her a lot. I was really hurt. I felt like I had nobody." Diaz Tolentino and his older brother lived with their maternal grandparents on their small *rancho* until his mother was able to raise enough money to bring both of her children to the United States. "We ultimately came back. I didn't really know why I was coming or who I was, you know? I was lost. I would talk to my mom [on the phone] but not that much. I was confused [about] who are the figures in my life."

Yovany Diaz Tolentino returned to the United States when he was eight years old. "I'm crossing the Rio Grande and I'm like, where am I going, why am I going? And the first thing I see is all the lights, which I don't see in Mexico." After five years apart, Diaz Tolentino and his older brother reunited with their mother in Georgia, where she had relocated from California in search of more affordable living. Thinking back on his early years adjusting to the United States, he notes with regret, "I faced a lot of obstacles, in the sense that I didn't know English. Later on, it was more of an identity issue, because I didn't want to be Mexican. I didn't want to be brown. With that, I lost a little bit of Spanish, because I was ashamed to speak it."

———

NARRATIVES OF EXISTENCE, like Yovany Diaz Tolentino's story, assert the lives, experiences, and presence of undocumented people in the United States. In essence, these narratives affirm the *existence* of undocumented people. Claiming one's history and identity as unauthorized—sometimes referred to as "coming out of the shadows"—counters the narrative of illegality by highlighting the diversity, strength, and complexity of those who are "living unauthorized."[2] If illegality is a space of nonexistence, as Susan Bibler Coutin (2003) has suggested, or an underground and shadowy presence, as immigrant rights actors articulate, then coming out of the shadows is a direct confrontation with the invisibility of illegality.

Unauthorized immigrants, themselves, are not invisible. People often ascribe unauthorized status to Latinx residents and others based on perceptions of belongingness, and this is especially true in new destinations (Bohon and Macpherson Parrott 2011; Jones and Brown 2016). Moreover, the specter of the unauthorized dominates the contemporary national imagination, which often defines these immigrants as villainous others who menace citizens and other authorized residents. At the same time, the unauthorized—their voices, their experiences, and even their bodies—are rendered invisible on their own terms as narratives of illegality actively define the nature, being, and "problem" of unauthorized immigrants. Like the subaltern, unauthorized immigrants are defined primarily in terms of their relationship to power (Mignolo 2000; Spivak 1988). In "coming out" as undocumented, unauthorized immigrants articulate their actual bodies as they inhabit the world, making the invisible very much visible and present in everyday life. Unauthorized immigrants reject invisibility by occupying space in public life—not only physically through marches and demonstrations but also ideologically through narratives of existence.

Narratives of existence articulate the stories of those who are directly affected by the politics of illegality through the voices and standpoints of the directly affected. The right to tell one's own story—to articulate a claim to knowledge about oneself and one's experience—is itself a source of power. Too frequently, stories of and about unauthorized immigrants are told from the voices and standpoints of those who are not directly affected—including here in this book. In this way, even stories that embrace unauthorized immigrants may nonetheless reproduce their invisibility. Advocates who claim to speak for or on behalf of undocumented people, to be a "voice for the voiceless," often construct paternalistic narratives that portray unauthorized immigrants as defenseless, passive bystanders to their own devastation. Although immigrants and immigrant communities are vulnerable—after all, the sociopolitical condition of illegality is premised on reproduction of marginality—directly affected people are also vital in resisting their vulnerability. Omitting this story renders invisible the leadership and engagement of unauthorized immigrants and other directly affected people in immigrant rights movements.

In fact, undocumented people are central protagonists in their own liberation, a point that becomes apparent when they speak on their own behalf. Diaz Tolentino told me, "People advocate for immigrant rights, but they do it in a way where they're keeping us behind as well. Here's someone talking for me, instead of me talking, and so I'm not being a hero to [myself]." To emphasize his point, he continued, "Undocumented people are *really strong*, and I think the movement will grow if [we] come out of the shadows and say, 'I don't have any papers, but it's okay, this is *my country*.'"

In claiming their status, unauthorized immigrants bring their existence out of the shadows of illegality, establishing presence and asserting belongingness. Many speak of coming out as a liberatory experience, an act of defiance against the stigma associated with this identity. This process and its outcomes are not dissimilar to the experience of "coming out of the closet" for people who identify as gender and sexual minorities, where personal stories become part of political action to effect social change. In fact, the *undocuqueer* identity blends these marginalized identities to challenge norms of citizenship, migration, and sexuality (Seif 2014). Luís Escoto, who is both undocumented and gay, draws parallels in how he was imprisoned by the stigma of these identities and how he made himself visible and powerful by claiming his identities. He explained, "I'm a prisoner on two sides. I've had to come out twice." In coming out, Escoto embodied his existence as a gay, undocumented immigrant. He continued:

> The first time I came out [was] when I came out as gay. I was four-teen. Pretty dramatic moment in my life, but I don't want to look back because I know from that moment I decided to move forward, and grow, and be who I am, and embrace that. I have gained so much. I have gained more love from my family, more respect from my community. And coming out as undocumented, I've gained more power, I've gained more voice. And that's good. I've just gained so much more coming out from the shadows than I would have staying back in those creepy dark spaces.

Stepping out of the "creepy dark spaces" to claim one's status can be a freeing experience, a confrontation with the painful truth of a society that threatens unauthorized immigrants with the consequences of the enforcement lottery. Meetings and organizing workshops are often spaces where those who are directly affected by the politics of illegality share accounts of loss and hardship, hope and triumph—not just in campaign successes but in their immigration stories as well, sometimes in preparation for more public disclosure. Public storytelling sessions take the form of coming out ceremonies, where participants openly claim their status in front of a crowd of supporters. Participants share their names and stories with the audience, adding, "I am undocumented and unafraid" and, increasingly, "unashamed" and "unapologetic." These declarations, often punctuated by applause and cheers from the audience, normalize the bodies and stories of undocumented people.

Many people who are affected by the politics of illegality feel that their silence is more taxing than their voice. This is true of Alysa Medina, a U.S.-born citizen of the United States, and her husband, Luís Medina, who is undocumented. The Medinas and their children belong to a *comité*, Crossville Para una Acción Solidaria (Crossville for a Solidarity Action), in their Tennessee town. Despite the risks associated with public admission of Luís's status, the Medinas have grown accustomed to revealing their family's situation, a sentiment that has emerged over time through a process of small but steady steps. One evening, as we talked in their living room, Alysa Medina explained, "We're tired of hiding." She laughed then, a sharp exhalation that conveyed weariness rather than joy. Bouncing their infant daughter on her knee and then smiling at their son, who was playing on the floor nearby, she continued, "We're just tired of not being able to be who we really are, and this is part of who we are. We're a mixed [status] family with an undocumented parent, and we're fighting hard to change that. We've both decided that instead of hiding anymore, we really just . . . we want to . . . be more open about it."

––––––––––

YOVANY DIAZ TOLENTINO has not always been open about his status, and this, too, is part of his coming out story. More than a year after we first met, he recalled sharing with me an earlier version of his story that consisted simply of a declaration of his status. At the time, he had only just become involved with the Georgia Undocumented Youth Alliance, a group organized and led by undocumented youth. We were participating in a workshop on migrant rights at the Highlander Center, a social movement organizing school in East Tennessee, when Diaz Tolentino shared his status with me. "I told you [that I was undocumented]," he remembered later. "But I didn't fully tell you my whole story, where I would be open and vulnerable." He continued, "I was sorry for not telling you the story. Along the way, I learned that that's the way it will help you. That's one of the things I've learned, is your story, your life, it's something that you shouldn't take for granted."

In fact, narratives of existence serve strategic functions. Claiming one's identity is essential to making oneself the subject rather than the object of one's own biography and liberation. In coming out as unauthorized, immigrants may demand a role in reframing and resolving the "problem" of unauthorized migration. Tania Unzueta Carrasco, an undocumented organizer who was also present at the Highlander retreat, explained, "We realize that we need a seat at the table, if you will, in terms of discussing the solutions around immigration. And one of the ways in which . . . we are able to almost justify our seat at the table is by letting people know that we are directly affected and that we should be there."

What does it mean for undocumented people to have a "seat at the table" in discussions about immigration and immigration reform? To Pancho Argüelles, a popular educator, it is a question of power. "But then there are different *kinds* of power," he cautioned. "It's not just about creating the same kind of power that has been destroying our communities [or] becom[ing] better at using that [power]. It's a different kind of power that has moral authority, historical moral authority, that is connected to your identity." For Argüelles, this is about identity—in his words, knowing "who you are, where you come from, what are your needs, what are your resources, what is your vision, what do you want, what do you believe, what's your story." In understanding their identities as collective, undocumented activists build autonomy, which leads to power.

According to Tania Unzueta Carrasco, the collective process of coming out as undocumented has led grassroots immigrant rights groups to critically analyze leadership structures in conversations of immigration and criminalization. Unzueta Carrasco explained, "As we started to talk about being undocumented . . . we realized . . . that there is very little voice of undocumented people within the dialogue of what needs to happen around immigration reform." This point comes up again and again among immigrant rights actors in the Southeast, particularly in conversations about national immigrant rights organizations that have little skin in the game—in terms of leaders who do not personally face the costs and risks of illegality— and that nevertheless set the agenda around immigration reform through compromises that are increasingly restrictive and less inclusive. Emphasizing the importance of representation, Unzueta Carrasco continued, "Obviously, at a federal level, at a national level, none of our legislators are undocumented. There [are] very few undocumented people who are leading organizations, even. So even in our own movement it often becomes hard to have undocumented people at the forefront. I think it's important to listen to those people who are being directly affected by legislation and by the policies that we are trying to change. This doesn't mean that it should be the only voice, but if there are no undocumented voices I think that that's a problem."

Unzueta Carrasco's call for a seat at the table asserts the subjectivity of a population that is often spoken for and spoken about by those who are not directly affected by the policies and practices of illegality. In fact, when the United States Commission on Civil Rights (USCCR) organized a field hearing in Birmingham, Alabama, to gather information on the civil rights implications of state crimmigration laws, no unauthorized immigrants were originally invited to testify on the impact of such policies in their own lives. The agenda of speakers for the field hearing included policy makers and legislators (including Kris Kobach, the legal architect of Arizona S.B. 1070 and other self-deportation policies), law enforcement officials, educators, and social services providers. The hearing also included testimony from civil rights organizations such as the Southern Poverty Law Center, the Mexican American Legal Defense Fund, and the South Carolina Appleseed Legal Justice Center as well as from immigration restrictionist groups like Numbers USA, the Center for Immigration Studies, and the Federation for American Immigration Reform. However, no undocumented immigrants were included on the agenda.

When I asked Commissioner Martin R. Castro, chair of the USCCR and a Democratic appointee, about the composition of the panels, he sighed and explained, "Both sides recommended panelists that they wanted to see. The conservatives, of course, recommended conservative panelists, and those on the Democratic side suggested and recommended more progressive panelists in an effort to try to find a balance. My conservative colleagues invited folks with whom I strongly disagree." Chairman Castro's original proposal for the hearing included space for the testimony of an unauthorized immigrant, but the commission was unable to identify anyone who was willing to testify publicly, on the record.

In the moments preceding the hearing's commencement, it became apparent that something had changed. Several undocumented people arrived to witness the meeting, and many wore white T-shirts emblazoned with the words "*Sin papeles, sin miedo*" (No papers, no fear) and an image of the migratory monarch butterfly. During the testimony of Kris Kobach, undocumented activists rose from their seats and lifted banners with the word *undocumented* printed in bold, capital letters. The group was part of the Undocubus, a bus of undocumented people traveling deliberately and visibly through communities where policy makers had implemented harsh immigration policies—places like Arizona, Alabama, Georgia, and Tennessee—en route to the 2012 Democratic National Convention in Charlotte, North Carolina. Modeled consciously, in part, after the Freedom Rides of the civil rights movement, the idea for the Undocubus was conceived during the Highlander workshop where Yovany Diaz Tolentino publicly came out as undocumented. As the USCCR field hearing drew to a close and all the invited panelists had spoken, Commissioner Castro insisted on additional time for two undocumented activists to present their testimony. In coming out during the hearing, undocumented people asserted their right to articulate their experiences of illegality and obligated those present at the hearing to recognize their existence.

Coming out of the shadows of illegality is crucial to narratives of existence, but these narratives encompass much more than acknowledgement of undocumented status. Just as the BRIDGE curriculum's immigration history time line recontextualizes and rehistoricizes international migration within policies and practices that structure immigration, narratives of existence situate people's individual immigration statuses within their broader migration stories. Diaz Tolentino's "whole story," in which—in his words—he could be "open and vulnerable," locates his undocumented status in a narrative of hardship that is connected to the global economy, family separation, confusion, and shame. And yet his narrative of existence is just as much about triumphant reunification with his mother and defiance of the shadowy spaces of illegality.

Immigration status is often regarded as a private issue rather than a sociopolitical condition, and a person's unauthorized status (or the perception thereof) is construed as a personal failing. But as Pancho Argüelles told me, "People are under attack, not just because of our individuality, but because

Coming out in Birmingham. (Author's collection)

of the communities we are and [who] we represent. A lot of those policies, a lot of those ideological forces, and all this hatred . . . it is really a fear and an anger directed to a community, not just individuals." Narratives of existence challenge the individualistic frame by converting the unauthorized from a nameless, faceless, monolithic other into a collection of people with specific, and often shared, biographies. In this way, narratives of existence function as a consciousness-raising tactic, enabling individual immigrants to bring their personal stories into dialogue with collective histories of immigration and the enforcement of illegality (Richardson 1990).

The act of making visible the invisible also strategically reframes conversations around immigration status and illegality for those who are not directly affected. Yovany Diaz Tolentino's story is powerful in part because themes of hardship, separation from loved ones, and perseverance are relatable to—or at least evoke sympathy among—not just other undocumented people and their families but also those who are not directly affected by the politics of illegality. When I asked Tania Unzueta Carrasco to reflect on coming out as an organizing strategy, she paused, quiet in thought, and then replied, "It's a lot easier to connect what was happening at a federal level with what's happening in our everyday communities when people know that it affects me and my friends. When people know that, you know, that when we're talking about immigrants and 'criminals' and all those people who 'should' be deported, that it's not these numbers, that it's people, that it's people like me, people like my mom, my sister. . . . We think that changed how debate happens, that we've become a face, instead of a number."

Coming out ceremonies, as public narratives of existence, embody those who inhabit the status of unauthorized, making them present and relevant to those who are not directly affected by the politics of illegality. This, in turn, is crucial to reframing popular narratives of unauthorized immigrants and unauthorized immigration; the unauthorized other is humanized into an individual with triumphs and strengths rather than an abstract representation of the more than eleven million unauthorized immigrants in the United States.

Some anecdotal evidence supports the strategic value of this tactic. Former Utah Republican representative Stephen Sandstrom, who once championed his state's copycat version of Arizona S.B. 1070, later hoped that such laws would be overturned and called for passage of the DREAM Act. According to Sandstrom, his conversion happened after a young undocumented woman approached him during a town hall and confided that she had little future in the United States without a social security number, despite the fact that she had excelled in school. Sandstrom explained, "Nothing else I'd heard . . . shook me to the core more than that statement. . . . I thought this girl who put her hand over her heart and said the Pledge of Allegiance was in every way an American, and she really is an American" (Montero 2013).[3]

It is significant that Sandstrom's opinions about (some) unauthorized immigrants apparently shifted in the wake of his interaction with this undocumented woman, and that people who support strict enforcement measures in the abstract may disagree with enforcement against people they know. What remains unspoken, however, is that the individual histories and biographies of those who publicly come out as undocumented structure not only the face of the unauthorized but also the resistance; some biographies are framed as more deserving than others, even by movement actors—a point I return to later in this chapter.

Coming out publicly as undocumented can serve a related function: it provides immigrant rights actors the ability to organize collectively against enforcement proceedings that target specific people. As immigrant rights movements raise public awareness about enforcement and challenge illegality through narratives that render visible those who inhabit the status of unauthorized, they also create space to intervene in enforcement outcomes. Unzueta Carrasco explained, "Just on a strategy level, it is a lot safer to organize as an undocumented person when people know that you are undocumented." Many undocumented organizers in the Southeast agree with this principle. Yovany Diaz Tolentino, for example, told me that this was one of several reasons that he decided to reveal his status. "If you come out as undocumented," he explained, "you're actually a little safer because the public

knows, and so you have a better way of staying here, where you belong."
Tania Unzueta Carrasco elaborated on this strategy: "What we have seen is
that people who are 'out' and who have the public support of their community, and sometimes public support from their legislators, are going to get
noticed if they get placed in deportation proceedings, if they have an ICE
hold, and their detention could lead to action. And we know that people who
are supported by the public, when people pay attention to their deportations,
they're less likely to be deported. Coming out really plays into survival of
being undocumented in the United States."

Of course, coming out does not guarantee one's safety from the enforcement lottery. But some unauthorized immigrants may benefit from being
connected to an organized community that can be mobilized to action, because this action may influence administrative decisions on an immigrant's
removal. Azadeh Shahshahani of Project South noted that this was especially true under the latter years of the Obama administration, when ICE
implemented measures for prosecutorial discretion. She explained, "It was
our experience that if a case came to our attention, the grassroots groups'
attention, if there was a campaign mounted to get that person released, they
didn't have a criminal record, and they were considered so-called 'low priority,' then there was a good chance that the person would be released." Even
under Obama, however, the strategy's efficacy was limited. Shahshahani
noted, "There are thousands of other cases where the family may not be in
touch with any organizations, they may not have the resources, and so that
person could languish in the local jail, and then eventually they are picked
up and deported. The onus is on the community to be super vigilant."

Shahshahani's qualification of the power of community organizing un-
derscores that resistance to one person's deportation does not create structural change in the enforcement lottery. Each case—each person apprehended through policies and practices that structure illegality—must be defended
from removal on an individual basis. Not only does this mean that unauthorized immigrants and their advocates carry the burden of remaining
"super vigilant," it also means that the individual histories and biographies
of unauthorized immigrants, often expressed through a rhetoric of deservingness that prefers "noncriminals" and other low-priority cases, will influence the outcomes of cases. There are limits to this movement strategy, especially for immigrants marked as enforcement priorities under the Obama
administration or in the absence of reasonable guidelines for prosecutorial
restraint under the Trump administration.

Most undocumented immigrants are probably unwilling to speak publicly about their status or the status of family members. This includes many
in the Southeast who are active in immigrant rights work. One such person—
who agreed to share their[4] story under condition that their identity be kept
confidential—expressed their fear as follows:

It really affects me not being able to know if my [partner] will make it home tonight, or if [my partner] is going to be able to see [our] kids tomorrow. We were separated for almost two years, and we still can't fix [my partner's] immigration status. So I know what it's like to be separated from a family member. I know what you suffer. I know that the system is broken, me being a citizen, our children being citizens, and [my partner] still can't get papers. I know what it's like to live in the shadows, having to hide, having to be careful.

Speaking through tears, the person continued:

It scares me a lot because [my partner] has to drive an hour [to work] and an hour back. It was always, "When you're leaving your work-place, call me. When you get home, call me. If you're halfway, call me. When you get there, call me." I won't see [my partner] until 5:30, because I'm working, but [my partner] sends me a text: "OK, I've left work." [My partner] sends me another text: "I'm here." [My partner] sends me another text: "I'm at home," because [my partner] has to pass by the school to pick up the kids. So, firsthand, I know what it's like. I know what it's like to be separated from your family.

This couple is deeply involved in immigrant rights work in the Southeast. Like Luís and Alysa Medina in Tennessee, they hold leadership positions in their local *comité* and work with other *comités* throughout the region to raise awareness about immigrants' civil and legal rights and advocate for policy reforms. Their situation is an open secret to friends. For the most part, however, they do not share personal reasons for their involvement in the work, even with movement allies, or publicly acknowledge their family's mixed immigration status. Living in a rural town in the Southeast, they have good reason to be circumspect. Even though many of their neighbors, coworkers, and children's teachers may turn out to be welcoming, coming out as undocumented in a small town does not afford much anonymity should the opposite be true. The undocumented partner has also defied an order of removal to remain with their family, a violation that—combined with a previous deportation and ongoing unauthorized presence—makes this person a prime target for enforcement, including a possible permanent bar. For this couple, and for many immigrant families in the Southeast, disclosing existence could be more burdensome than maintaining silence.

Narratives of Deservingness

Narratives of existence create space for, and often precede, narratives of deservingness. These narratives challenge illegality by arguing that some unauthorized people are, in fact, deserving of legality. The idea of deservingness has been used to legitimize or delegitimize a variety of rights and privileges. With regard to illegality, narratives of deservingness contrast with dominant accounts of immigrants as undeserving, which are often expressed through inflammatory rhetoric, myths, and popular misperceptions. Narrative accounts of immigrants as undeserving are abundant; in these stories, immigrants are often imagined through the lens of violence and destruction. Radio "shock jock" Michael Savage once claimed, for example, that unauthorized immigrants are "killing our police for sport, raping, murdering like a scythe across America," and Donald Trump campaigned for president on a platform that framed Mexican migrants as rapists, murderers, and drug dealers.

Narratives that portray immigrant women specifically as undeserving often focus on sexuality, particularly the idea of "unrestrained childbearing" (Luibhéid 2008) and the "threat" this poses to the nation's economic welfare (Hondagneu-Sotelo 1995; Huang 2008). For example, Tennessee representative Curry Todd compared unauthorized immigrant women to rats who "multiply" uncontrollably, suggesting that undocumented women have children to exploit social welfare programs. These stories of deservingness cannot be separated from the implied threat to the nation's demographic composition and narratives of who counts as an "American," as in Iowa representative Steve King's tweet in 2017, "We can't restore our civilization with somebody else's babies." In accounts such as these, unauthorized immigrants subvert the United States by breaking laws, exploiting resources, and sabotaging the nation's integrity; consequently, unauthorized immigrants are undeserving of the United States—and, by extension, of legality.

In contrast, narratives of deservingness challenge the idea that unauthorized immigrants are "bad" (i.e., lawbreakers, criminals, abusers of public assistance) by showing instead that they are "good" (i.e., hard workers, taxpayers, innocents) and therefore merit special consideration in terms of access to the United States and legality. Here, I discuss three variations on narratives of deservingness: immigrants as martyrs, workers, and criminals; immigrants as DREAMers; and immigrants paying restitution. These narratives strive to combat negative rhetoric of unauthorized immigrants and their impacts to the economy, perceived criminality, and use of services. In articulating the deserving, however, these stories often rely on underlying foundations of illegality.

Martyrs, Workers, and Criminals

Narratives of deservingness often manifest through claims of substantial suffering in the service of family commitments. Many unauthorized immigrants have stories of hardship through pain and suffering, even martyrdom, a fact that reflects their status and the consequences of illegality in their daily lives. At a hearing on the impact of crimmigration policies on undocumented communities, an undocumented woman testified:

I came to the United States when I was sixteen years old. I came for extreme poverty. My dad died from cancer when I was eight years old. My mother had to work a lot. And when I was sixteen years old, my mother got sick because she worked so much. And at that point, I decided I couldn't take it anymore, and I had to do whatever it takes to support my family, because it was *my* turn. They offer me to come to the United States, and I cross the desert and I risk my life. It was a tremendous fear. It was . . . we run out of water, we run out of food, and I thought I was going to die. I never wanted to come here illegally [*sic*], I promise you. None of the people that was there wanted to come here illegally [*sic*], none of us looked for it. It was a group of twenty people, and I was the only woman, sixteen years old. I was terrified. But my thoughts were on my mom and my sister in Mexico, and I was willing to give my life for them. I came to the United States. I trust in [God], he gave me the strength to come here. . . . I graduated from high school, because that's why I came here, that's why immigrants came here, to work hard. . . . I'm sure that the 99 percent of undocumented [people] are like me, 'cause I don't know anybody that is not here for a good reason and are not suffering, because we're not with our loved ones. I graduated from high school and I—I'm in college. I'm trying to get my degree. And it's obstacle over obstacle over obstacle. And now this law [Alabama H.B. 56] that's trying to punish . . . people like me. . . . I can't understand why you want to punish people like me, put them in jail, put me in jail, or . . . take me away from working. 'Cause I never got tuition . . . for free. I work every [day], three jobs sometimes. I have to support myself and my family in Mexico.

Migration stories such as these are commonplace for unauthorized immigrants, particularly those from Mexico and Central America, who are more likely to enter the United States without inspection rather than overstay their visas (Massey and Riosmena 2010). In these stories, unauthorized immigrants are people who have left their homes, countries—even family— to provide for themselves and their families. These narratives appeal to directly affected people and advocates. For some immigrants, the desire to *superarse*—to overcome, or better oneself, often through self-sacrifice to provide younger generations with better opportunities—justifies their experiences of hardship. These stories also fit into U.S.-centric cultural narratives of rugged individualism and the American dream—complementary and deeply held beliefs that everyone can succeed as long as they work hard enough.

The framing of unauthorized immigrants as hard workers is pervasive in narratives of deservingness, and it is used alike by immigrants and their advocates. Accounts often emphasize the fact that unauthorized immigrants have never taken or received anything "for free" despite their need; instead, unauthorized immigrants are framed as exceptionally dedicated workers who provide for themselves and their families by any sacrifice necessary (Coutin and Chock 1996). In so doing, deservingness narratives push against accusations that immigrants abuse welfare programs, such as the Supplementary Nutrition Assistance Program or Emergency Medicaid—accusations primarily leveled at immigrant women (Huang 2008).[5] Simultaneously, these stories suggest that those who need public assistance are somehow less deserving. The racialization of welfare recipients and hard workers is implicit in commonly held stereotypes of "lazy" African Americans and "efficient" Latinx workers (Neal and Bohon 2003).

Accounts of deservingness also manifest through rhetoric that immigrants—especially the unauthorized—are eager to "do the jobs no one else will" to provide for themselves and their families. This frame implies that unauthorized immigrants are willing to labor in dirty, dangerous, and demeaning jobs that are arduous and tenuous; under conditions that may be risky, uncomfortable, and exploitative; and often in exchange for low pay and few benefits. Accordingly, this reasoning assumes that U.S.-born workers are unwilling to work under such conditions, a belief that naturalizes exploitation of unauthorized labor. Just so, one prominent scholar joked during his plenary address at a 2011 national conference on immigrant integration about whether there was "any way you can get landscaping done without undocumented workers." Looking around the packed conference hall, I noticed that everyone was laughing. But I could not help but catch my breath at the subtext of the message.

Unauthorized immigrants embrace this story just as much as well-intentioned advocates do. After the passage of Georgia's state crimmigration law, when farmers reported that they were unable to hire U.S.-born workers to fill positions vacated by immigrants, some policy makers tried to require incarcerated people—disproportionately people of color—to work the fields as a condition of parole. One undocumented activist in Georgia told me, "They try to get jail people to pick the crops, but they don't pick as fast as Mexicans." I must have looked shocked by his assertion, because he assured me, "It's true. One Mexican will pick ten trucks of fruit, like tomatoes or oranges; the jail people would pick one truck. So it's one versus ten trucks." When I asked him to reflect on this difference, he responded, "They [incarcerated people] don't have the drive to live, to contribute, to get money."

I pushed back lightly, wondering aloud if policies and practices of crim-inalization—of both immigrants and U.S.-born people of color—were about creating vulnerability, making it easier to exploit and abuse workers. He shrugged and said, "That doesn't make any sense. It just doesn't help nobody, it's a no-win situation." Then he continued, "I don't think America has a problem with undocumented people. The white people's houses that I cleaned, they wanted us there. We cleaned their house for cheap." Stories like these tell us that undocumented people are deserving of legality because they are motivated to work, and they are willing to work for low wages—unlike *certain other people.*

Claims that allude to unauthorized immigrants as hard workers articu-late a narrative of deservingness that juxtaposes those who deserve leniency from enforcement and illegality against the nondeserving. This is clear in the exhortation by unauthorized immigrants, "We are workers, not criminals"— a catchphrase that appears through speeches and protest signs at immigrant rights rallies. Workers are constructed as desirable (and deserving), while "criminals" are both undesirable and undeserving. To confront the specter of criminality, unauthorized immigrants argue that they migrate to the United States to work, not to break laws; they are workers—not criminals.

Just as claims of welfare dependency and indolence are racialized, the subject of crime and the figure of the criminal are racialized such that people of color—particularly African Americans and Latinx people—are dispro-portionately likely to be criminalized (Russell-Brown 1998). Targeted polic-ing of low-income communities of color shapes disparate detection of criminalized activities in these communities. Disproportionate arrests and sentencing of people of color, combined with media coverage that portrays black and brown people as criminals, fuel public perceptions of criminality (Ghandnoosh 2014). Latinx and black immigrants are criminalized and il-legalized based on perceptions of language, skin color, and appearance (Menjívar and Abrego 2012; Romero 2006) as well as their portrayals in popular culture (Chavez 2001, 2008). Thus, the assertion that "we are work-ers, not criminals" confronts criminalization and illegalization by articulat-ing an alternative narrative of an identity seen as more deserving: workers—and *hard* workers at that.

This narrative takes for granted the framing of criminality and implica-tions for deservingness (Escobar 2009). That is, to dispute who counts as a criminal, we must first accept the condition and meaning of criminality. To distance unauthorized immigrants from criminalization, immigrants and ad-vocates create wedges of deservingness separating unauthorized immigrants who are "here to work" from those who are, ostensibly, legitimately labeled as "criminals," including U.S.-born people of color and unauthorized immi-grants who engage in criminalized activities unrelated to immigration status.

"We are workers, not criminals." (Author's collection)

Concerns such as these weigh heavily on many who advocate for the rights of unauthorized immigrants, including Mónica Hernández of SEIRN. Hernández's appraisal of the framing of criminality reveals experience organizing around immigrant rights through a racial justice lens that emphasizes the structural and systemic roots of racism. Hernández critiques narratives that juxtapose the racialized language of criminality against hard work. She explained, "[We need to] understand what it means to say 'We do the jobs that nobody wants to do; we're not the criminals.' Always from a very compassionate point, right? Because from my perspective, community members were defending themselves from these attacks that were being made against them. And they didn't know the context. They didn't know that this rhetoric has been historically used against African Americans. But *we* should know." She continued, "It's different—I'm not saying that it's good—but it's different when a person grabs a marker and just puts that because that's their thought in the moment, than a group—an organized group—that's printing out all these little placards that say any of these messages. It's very dangerous."

Hernández highlights a distinction in contextual awareness with how the imposed label of criminality has historically been used as a controlling narrative against people of color, particularly black people. Grassroots organizations that are composed of unauthorized immigrants and other directly affected people may not understand the implicit racialization in framing immigrants as "workers, not criminals," but longer-term activists and organizers—and certainly formal organizing institutions with paid staff and some history in a U.S. context—must be acquainted with this history. Otherwise, immigrant rights actors reproduce a racialized framework of dominant beliefs about criminality and deservingness.

Accounts that rely on the language of criminality help perpetuate policies and practices of enforcement. Instead of challenging the idea of criminality and the reality of criminalization, these narratives limit the framework of deservingness to the assumption that *criminal* equates to bad and undeserving, while *noncriminal* equates to good and deserving. However, the ubiquity of illegality, through the enforcement lottery, may create a disconnect between the rhetoric of criminality and people's lived experiences. One undocumented person related just such an experience:

> My uncle went to pick me up. I see a cop, because we're aware of these things. [The cop] goes that way. [My uncle] calmed down. We're going into the neighborhood, but [the cop] was behind us, I completely missed him. He stops [my uncle] in front of the neighborhood. We were almost home. So, for not having a license, he was detained and he was criminalized. Is he a criminal because he doesn't have a driver's license? No. [But] he's labeled a criminal. Now he's not what America wants, and so he's out of the picture. You get stopped, you get labeled as a criminal, and you get deported, and something that small just stopped you.

In this account, the storyteller's uncle was deported over his lack of a driver's license, something that should not have labeled him a criminal.

If those who are directly affected by the politics of illegality as well as their advocates assume that *criminal* is a term applied only to people convicted of violent crimes, they may pause at learning that people like Alejandro Guizar and Juana Villegas were arrested and processed for removal based on minor violations. In Hernández's view, this disparity encourages reflection on components of deservingness. She noted, "There's been a lot more consciousness and awareness of the issue of criminalization as part of the discourse and approach to immigration policy. It's easier when you're in defensive mode against these policies that do this widespread criminalization that people can really relate to—I mean, there's this danger still, right, about how do we make sure we don't buy into this rhetoric. Obama even said, 'We're going after the criminals.' There's still that danger. But at the same time, people are seeing that the reality is really different, and that these enforcement policies are really targeting everybody."[6]

The risk in negotiating deservingness based on degrees of criminality— such as minor misdemeanors versus felonies—is that this nevertheless upholds foundations of illegality through a racialized system of enforcement and incarceration. By reinforcing the space between deserving and nondeserving through the specter of the criminal, immigrant rights actors and advocates strengthen the rhetoric of the homeland security state, unintentionally accepting the right of the nation to deport those who are defined as criminals. Once we agree to this framing of the problem, we limit ourselves to a debate over which behaviors constitute crime and which crimes justifiably result in deportation.

The Deservingness of DREAMers

Not all unauthorized immigrants are equally criminalized or labeled as criminals. Unauthorized youth, for example, are often portrayed and perceived as innocent casualties in their parent's violation of immigration law. The U.S. public overwhelmingly supports a pathway to citizenship for undocumented youth (Tyson 2018)—though these boundaries of belongingness often exclude youth who arrive as older adolescents, especially young Latino men who are portrayed as gang members based on attire and activities (Atiles and Bohon 2002) as well as immigrant youth who are in the workforce rather than in school (Patler and Gonzales 2015). Certainly, some policy makers strive to criminalize unaccompanied minors—youth who arrive at the U.S. border without a parent or legal guardian—such as Iowa representative Steve King, who contended that undocumented youth have "calves the size of cantaloupes because they're hauling 75 pounds of marijuana across the desert" (Reeve 2013).

Obama's Deferred Action for Childhood Arrivals (DACA), which provided some undocumented youth with temporary deferral of deportation and work visas, suggests that some young people are perceived as qualitatively different from their adult counterparts, at least by some (Nicholls 2013). Leisy Abrego's (2011) research indicates that different contexts of reception for unauthorized immigrants who migrated to the United States as children and those who migrated as adults impact the extent to which immigrants are willing to speak openly about their status. Unauthorized immigrant youth have used this perception of belongingness to their strategic advantage in organizing against restrictionist policies and practices, recognizing, perhaps, that they are less likely to be removed than unauthorized adults. In fact, unauthorized immigrant youth are a consistent and vocal presence in immigrant rights work in the Southeast and around the nation, particularly around access to higher education (Corrunker 2012; Seif 2011).

Narratives of deservingness are abundant in discussions of unauthorized immigrant youth, who are often referred to as DREAMers. In adopting the name of the DREAM Act, DREAMers assert a claim to deservingness based on the right to education, which is unobtainable for many unauthorized im-

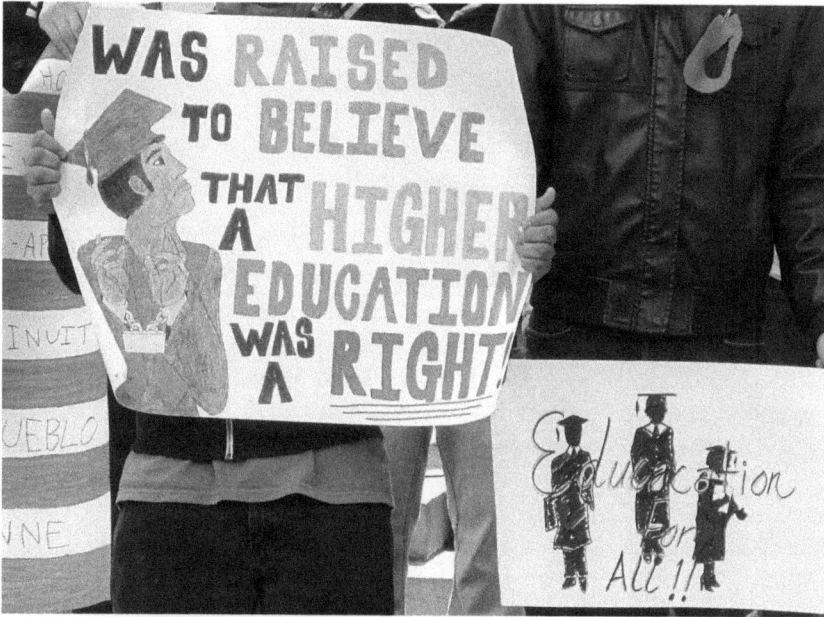

Protesting the Georgia ban on undocumented students in Athens, GA.
(Author's collection)

migrants. In most states, unauthorized immigrant students must pay out-of-state or international tuition rates to attend public colleges and universities, even if they complete primary and secondary education in the United States and even if their parents pay federal, state, and local taxes. Unauthorized students cannot receive federal scholarships or federally funded student financial aid. In some cases, state laws or university policies may prohibit unauthorized students from attending public institutions of higher education. In Georgia, for example, the board of regents voted overwhelmingly in 2010 to ban unauthorized immigrant youth from attending any of the top five public colleges and universities in the state. In 2012, the Georgia legislature attempted, but failed, to extend the ban to the entire public higher education system.

Such policies make it virtually impossible for many unauthorized students to attend college and impact educational aspirations of youth (Bohon, Macpherson, and Atiles 2005; Seif 2011). Yovany Diaz Tolentino, who migrated to Georgia when he was eight, remembered,

In high school I went into 'zombie mode' where I didn't think I was going to go to college. And so I just, kind of, just went, just go, just pass. And ultimately I graduated, but without any hope of, 'Okay, I'm going to college!' And so I worked at McDonald's my junior year. I became [a] manager. And my mom works there too, and she was a crew member, so we worked together, we got to travel [to work] together. But ultimately I didn't see . . . the prosperity, success, or what I imagined, or what I wanted, as a career. It really sucked, getting minimum wage, and me being there six days a week. And you don't see it really going anywhere, and the time you have free time you want to rest. I felt trapped.

Diaz Tolentino's aspirations changed when he heard about the Georgia Undocumented Youth Alliance, which advocated against the Georgia ban on undocumented students, and he quickly became involved in immigrant rights organizing. When I first met Diaz Tolentino, he was in the middle of his first semester at Freedom University, a nonaccredited Georgia-based institution organized by volunteer faculty that offers college-level coursework to unauthorized students. At that time, Diaz Tolentino had never attended a march or rally. Barely a year later, he attended the migrant rights retreat at Highlander. Shortly thereafter, he rode the Undocubus to the Democratic National Convention in Charlotte, North Carolina, and participated in civil disobedience to protest Obama's escalation of immigration enforcement and lack of progress on immigration reform.

Being young does not automatically exempt unauthorized immigrants from the enforcement lottery, as illustrated by Alejandro Guizar's experiences. However, Yovany Diaz Tolentino's experience in North Carolina during his arrest for civil disobedience illustrates a dividing line of belongingness often drawn between unauthorized youth and adults. In anticipation of protests, the Charlotte police had set up outdoor encampments to detain arrestees. It was cold and rainy that day, and Diaz Tolentino remembers taking off his water-logged socks, trying to warm up while he waited to be processed. "Twenty minutes in, ICE comes. And I was sleeping." He continued, "[The ICE agent] was talking to my friends who were arrested, and he was bullying them. And then he asked me to help him. He said that I would be free. He was like, 'Okay, you look American. I'm sure you don't belong with them. Help me help you, and we'll get you out. These people have no right to be here.' And I was like, 'No, I'm actually with them.'"

Like many undocumented youth who grow up in the United States, Diaz Tolentino looks "American." As he sat across from me at a coffee shop one day, casually draped over a chair and wearing the same long-sleeved white shirt he wore on the day he was arrested, I could not help but notice that Diaz Tolentino easily blended in as a typical U.S. teenager, and with good reason: he had spent his entire adolescence in the United States. Perhaps more importantly, though, Yovany Diaz Tolentino also stands out as deserving of his belongingness: wide-eyed, fresh-faced, and politely mannered, Diaz Tolentino appears as though he deserves to belong to the United States, and he is often treated accordingly.

Even after revealing his immigration status to ICE on the day of his arrest, the ICE agent articulated a difference between Diaz Tolentino and the older unauthorized participants of the action. Diaz Tolentino recalled, "Ultimately [the ICE agent] is like, 'Your friends here don't have a lot going for them. They're gonna be . . . you know, they have family back home, they're going to go back home. You—you should be here, you look like you're not a troubled kid.'" In many ways, then, the DREAMer identity buffers some unauthorized youth from the enforcement lottery. As a result of their perceived deservingness—expressed through their belongingness—some youth are able to avoid the criminal label that is applied to older immigrants with the same status.

The idea of belongingness suggests another component of deservingness: the right to remain in the United States based on one's length of residency within the country regardless of status during that time. This argument is reflected in Joseph Carens's (2010) work, which articulates that unauthorized immigrants have a moral claim to belongingness based on amount of time lived in the United States. After a certain number of years—Carens suggests that five years should be sufficient—people have rooted themselves in their neighborhoods and communities. People build their homes where they are: they go to work, make friends, join churches and social clubs. Children are born and raised. Lives are lived. Thus, unauthorized immigrants who are deported are not only forced to leave the United States but the very homes they have created over time. For many, this alone provides motivation for unauthorized immigrants and their advocates to resist restrictionist policies and practices.

For Carens, it is this process of living one's life in a community that conveys moral claims to belongingness, a type of deservingness related to one's entrenchment in the United States rather than to one's formal status. In this sense, length of residency is a convenient but arbitrary substitute for "integration"—a concept that is much more difficult to measure and apply across populations. Despite the fact that length of stay is not the best stand-in for the development and elaboration of relationships (Bosniak 2013), Carens's argument is that, over time, a person begins to belong to her or his community; in turn, the community comes to belong to the people who inhabit it. As Mae Ngai (in Carens 2010: 55) elaborates, "The social ties that migrants establish over time . . . make them de facto members of society, even if they lack formal legal status." It is to this version of deservingness that many DREAMers and their advocates appeal.

Unauthorized youth often measure their belongingness in terms of the amount of time lived in their countries of origin versus in the United States.

I have met many young people who migrated to the United States as adolescents and who subsequently feel less entitled to—less deserving of—a claim on belongingness compared to those who arrived as infants or children. Those who migrated at older ages have memories of lives lived in their countries of origin. They grew up learning how to read and write in Spanish in their early schooling, and perhaps they speak a heavily accented, and somewhat limited, English. These undocumented youth—who may be no less DREAMers in technicality than those who came to the United States as young children—exist in a liminal status, divided between their well-remembered past in their countries of origin and their relatively recent present and future in the United States.

In comparison, those who came to the United States as infants or children have memories of childhoods lived in the United States, and these memories are used to justify their deservingness through their belongingness. Like many advocates, I, too, have been complicit in supporting this narrative, especially when coaching young people to speak in public, memories I look back on now with shame. I have encouraged undocumented youth, like Alejandro Guizar, to share their memories of growing up in the Southeast, to talk about friendships developed in elementary school, to joke about speaking Spanish with a Southern accent. Such stories are intended to make undocumented youth seem fully "American," so deeply integrated into the United States that it should be impossible to deny their deserving claim to belongingness regardless of where they were born. However, in defining deservingness through this form of belongingness, undocumented youth and their advocates underscore the non-belongingness of unauthorized immigrants with different histories—adolescents who come to the United States primarily to work, people who migrate at older ages, those with briefer residencies in the United States, and those who are—in this shorthand, at least—less integrated into the "American" community.

Just as accounts of belongingness may exclude some unauthorized immigrants from perceptions of deservingness, accounts that focus on unauthorized immigrant youth through the lens of the DREAM Act easily become wedges. Unauthorized youth and their advocates may invoke accounts of deservingness that separate exemplary (Nicholls 2013), high-performing, high-achieving youth—who are often referred to as "the best and the brightest" or, more cynically, the "darlings" of the movement—from those who appear to be less dedicated to their studies, who are therefore constructed as less deserving. One young undocumented activist in Tennessee articulated a clear difference between deserving youth and the nondeserving:

> The United States [should] finally give out the DREAM Act. Pass the
> DREAM Act. Finally get an opportunity, you know, for students *who*

are not doing anything wrong. Or at least to give it to the *good* students, maybe not to the students who really don't want to give a good shot for it, okay, but *for the ones that do want to improve themselves, they deserve it, because they're working harder* than probably any regular student out there. Because you have the students that are involved in sports, the student that's involved with gangs. You have your students that are just completely stuck to the books, they never want to fail. Those are the students that I believe do *deserve* it, because *they're working harder* than other ones. But really, just pass the DREAM Act. That's what everybody is shooting for. (emphasis added)

Here, the deservingness of DREAMers is conflated with another narrative of deservingness—unauthorized immigrants as hard workers. In this story, it is not enough to be young to be deserving; unauthorized immigrant youth must also work hard in school, achieve good grades, and aspire to greater success through higher education in order to qualify. Just as Representative Sandstrom was convinced of the necessity of the DREAM Act by the appeal of an exemplary undocumented student who could not go to college, movement actors, too, imply degrees of deservingness.

DREAMers assert a claim to deservingness based on their particular experience of illegality—the experience of those who came to the United States "through no fault of their own" but who nonetheless suffer the consequences of their status. In this sense, unauthorized youth are constructed as more deserving of legality than their parents or other adult unauthorized immigrants, who are said to have deliberately violated immigration laws (Bosniak 2013). Of course, many undocumented youth reject this frame (Nicholls 2013), often referring to their parents as the original dreamers— those who first dreamed of a better life for themselves and their children and made it happen by migrating to the United States. One young activist in Georgia told me, "The DREAM [Act] itself, it's BS. It's directly for alien [*sic*] minors. It excludes other undocumented people who are maybe not the glorious one, what America would want."

Still, some activists differentiate between types of immigration reform, expressed in degrees of legality that should be conferred on youth versus adults. One young undocumented person told me,

The way I see it is that *people who have been here ten or twenty years, who are good people, do their jobs, and don't have any problems,* they should be able to live here. And maybe America doesn't think they should be citizens, but they should be included because *they already live here and this is their country too.* And so with that, maybe they can have some kind of a permit to be here, not maybe citizens, but a permit. Like my mom—she's been here twenty years, and I don't think she would want to go back [to school] to [get an] education, but she certainly wouldn't go looking for a CEO job. She's not going to take that away from you. What she will do is she will keep doing what she likes to do, which is clean houses, and be *a good, moral person*. So, I think, some kind of visa just to stay here would be great for that category. And for *innocent people who came here at a young age*, certainly, citizenship is just the way to go, because *they're committed to this country, it's their own.* (emphasis added)

In many ways, this account inadvertently endorses taken-for-granted assumptions about unauthorized immigrants that support policies and practices of illegality. That is, even as the account suggests alternative ways of dealing with the "problem" of unauthorized immigrants (permits rather than removal), it sustains illegality through a dichotomy between those deserving of legal residency and those deserving of enforcement. Not only does this account suggest a distinction between unauthorized immigrant youth ("innocents") and unauthorized adults, it also emphasizes other aspects of deservingness: unauthorized immigrants are deserving of legality as long as they are hard workers who will not take prestigious, high-paying jobs from authorized (perhaps even citizen) residents and are "good, moral" people who cause no problems—in other words, as long as they are not "criminals."

Paying Restitution

Claims of deservingness can also be viewed as accounts of restitution. That is, stories that focus on unauthorized immigrants as martyrs, hardworking employees, and dedicated students illustrate how such individuals "give back" to the United States in payment for their violation of immigration laws, often in ways that subtly imply their deservingness over others who provide fewer benefits to the nation. One undocumented woman in Alabama captured several different accounts of deservingness through the lens of restitution when she declared, "We are here, and *we are hardworking people*, and we [are] just . . . begging for the opportunity to be legal. *We [are] willing to do whatever it takes* to be legal." Her voice trembling and anguished, she pleaded,

Let's work together. Let's find a way to be legal. Because *we're willing to pay*, if that's what we have to pay, fines or whatever. Because when you have a ticket, you pay your fine, right? *It's not like you're a criminal*, because you break the law when you speed. It's the same. We came here and *our crime is to risk our lives to provide for our families.*

Let's—we just need to work together. We need an opportunity for the people that are here now, *we don't commit a crime, we are good people, we work, we are studying.* We just need an opportunity. And we are willing, and we are desperate to be legal. And we can work for the economy of this country because we [are] already here and we love this country. (emphasis added)

According to these stories, unauthorized immigrants deserve legality because they are willing to offer recompense for violating immigration laws, which, in these accounts, is expressed as an act of survival. Accounts of restitution operate within the frame of illegality even as they seek reforms to policies that illegalize some unauthorized immigrants. That they are reformist does not imply that they are not beneficial: small, incremental measures, including the DREAM Act, DACA, expanded access to visas, and similar measures, should not be dismissed lightly, because pathways to authorization or citizenship or deferral of deportation doubtless have far-reaching implications for many who are currently unauthorized. Yet reformist arguments are also premised on the concession that not all will benefit through such measures. Much like principles of comprehensive immigration reform, reformist arguments compromise in anticipation of policies that may benefit some, but not all. Advancing arguments for deserving immigrants, who agree to pay restitution through fines or other compensation, requires not only that we acknowledge the legitimacy of these policies but also that we accept that others are undeserving. Fundamentally, these accounts limit how illegality can be resisted.

Some immigrant rights actors recognize that narratives of deservingness can be problematic for social justice movements, because such narratives support oppressive power structures and undermine solidarity. Mónica Hernández of SEIRN noted,

Where I really see the danger is that right now everybody's focused on trying to combat repressive laws—and yes, there are calls for—there will always be calls for comprehensive immigration reform. But people's energy and focus is in trying to combat repressive laws. But if the momentum builds again for the type of proposal where you have some type of comprehensive immigration reform, legalization, whatever you want to call it, I think that's where the real danger is, because that's where there's this . . . attempt to create wedges, and where bargains are made to include some people and exclude other people. That's the big problem, because that's where people try to distance themselves from the "bad," the "undeserving," and, well, end up playing into those wedges.

Narratives of deservingness do far more than encourage wedges between different constituencies of unauthorized immigrants. In attempting to resist the policies and practices that structure everyday illegality, unauthorized immigrants and their advocates simultaneously and unintentionally re-create illegality through these same narratives. In defining those who deserve access to legality by articulating those who are undeserving of access, immigrant rights actors accept the framing of unauthorized immigrants and unauthorized immigration as a/the problem.

Narratives of deservingness are constructed around frames that implicitly acknowledge the legitimacy of illegality. They stem from the premise that exceptions must be made for those who "deserve" access to lawful residency, thereby implying the existence of shadowy others who do not deserve access—those who take more than they give, who do not contribute productively to their communities, who do not sufficiently belong, and who are "real" criminals—in short, those who are, to repurpose Bosniak's (2013: 438) term, "unproblematically deportable." In contrast, many immigrant rights actors define the deserving as those with various equities—those who contribute more than they receive, who have never been in trouble with the law, who have lived in the United States for an extended period, and who were brought to the United States "through no fault of their own." In arguing for such exceptions, these narratives tacitly accept the authority of immigration policies and practices that structure illegality.

Narratives of (Il)legitimacy

Unauthorized immigrants also redefine the legitimacy of policies and practices that structure illegality. In contrast to narratives of existence and deservingness, narratives of (il)legitimacy focus outwardly, specifically addressing the production of illegality by challenging the authority of policy makers and crimmigration policies and practices. Immigrant rights actors often express narratives of (il)legitimacy through two distinct yet interrelated techniques. Some narratives confront individual public officials for racist speech or actions to delegitimize their authority to create and implement structures of illegality. Other accounts appropriate the rhetoric of illegality in application to the structures themselves, juxtaposing illegalization of unauthorized immigrants against the (illegitimate) legality of the enforcement lottery.

"Do I Look Illegal?" The Racial Politics of Illegality

Unauthorized immigrants delegitimize those who make and implement structures of illegality by confronting racially charged speech or actions that appear to motivate crimmigration policies and practices. Mechanisms of

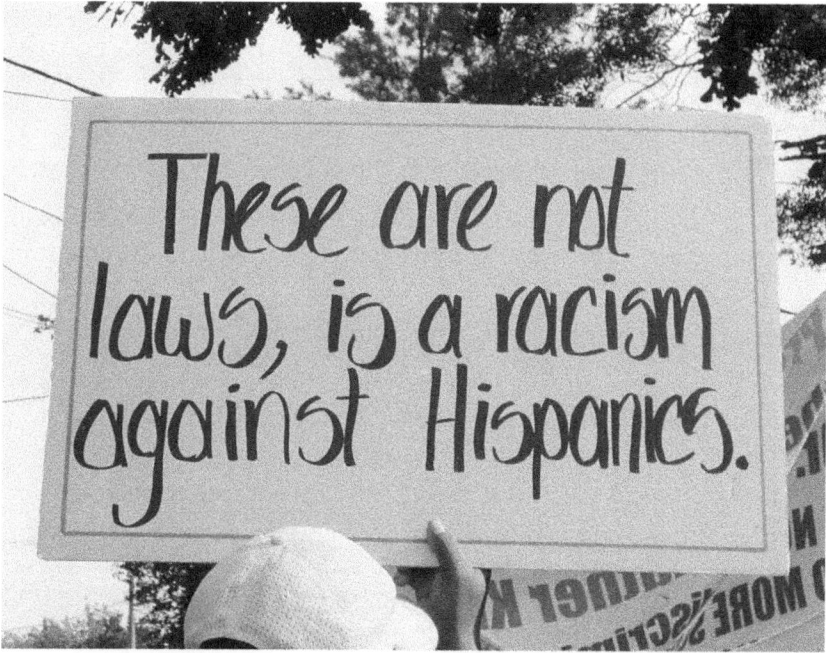

"Racism against Hispanics." (Author's collection)

immigration enforcement—including police-ICE collaboration and state crimmigration laws—are often experienced by Latinx people as discriminatory (Lopez, Morin, and Taylor 2010; Southern Poverty Law Center 2009), an unsurprising sentiment given that such policies have a disproportionate impact on Latinx people. Catchphrases such as "Brown is not a crime," "Driving while Latino," and "Do I look illegal?" highlight the anger and frustration of Latinx people over their experiences of racial profiling. These slogans, which allude to charges of racial profiling, are a method of delegitimizing policy makers and law enforcement officials.

This framing can be used to shame specific policy makers and those who enforce policies, but it can also be problematic. Those who write or implement policies that structure illegality dismiss accusations of racism by arguing that policies such as H.B. 56 and practices like police-ICE collaboration are "not in any way racially motivated" and that they are merely "asking the federal government [to] enforce the laws" (Robert Bentley, former Alabama governor, quoted in Pow 2011) or that they "don't arrest people based on the color of their skin" (Joe Arpaio, former sheriff of Maricopa County, Arizona, quoted in Billeaud 2012). Legally, the colorblind argument is a sturdy defense against allegations of racism. Challenges of racial bias require clear demonstration of intentional racial discrimination—definitive proof that those who

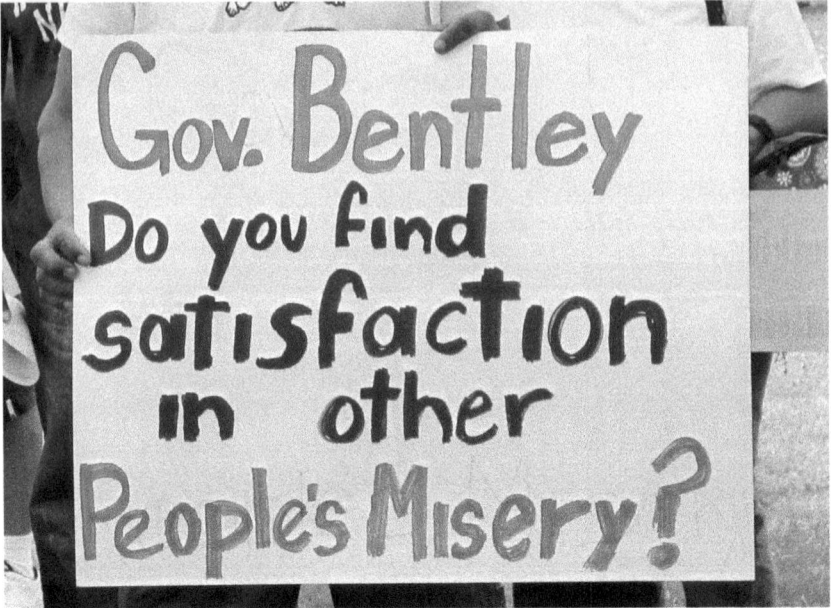

"Other people's misery." (Author's collection)

engage in actions that result in racially disproportionate outcomes explicitly intend to discriminate on the basis of race (Alexander 2012). Evidence of de facto discrimination in implementation and enforcement, through a clear pattern of racialized outcomes, for example, is not enough to prove racist intent.

Even if claims of race neutrality are true, intent is clearly distinct from outcome. Policies that are not specifically intended to be racially discriminatory may still have disproportionate and racialized impacts (Bohon, Conley, and Brown 2014; Bonilla Silva 2010; Jones and Brown 2016). Narratives that focus on the words and actions of individuals—even individual policy makers—risk treatment of racism as a discrete phenomenon. In this story, individual policy makers write legislation from their own racial biases, and individual police officers engage in racial profiling because of specific discriminatory intent. This version of the narrative of (il)legitimacy implies, subtly, that policies with racially discriminatory impact are acceptable as long as they stem from nonracially motivated speech and intent. They also overshadow analysis and articulation of structural and institutional patterns in the production of illegality. Accounts of structural and institutional racism emerge more pointedly when immigrant rights actors invoke messages about "Juan Crow" and the historical foundations that give rise to contemporary expressions of racism in the Southeast.

"La Migra, la Policía, la Misma Porquería": Retelling the Story of Police-ICE Collaboration

Immigrant rights actors also construct narratives of (il)legitimacy by appropriating the rhetoric of illegality, juxtaposing the misconduct of law enforcement officials against the illegalization of unauthorized immigrants. Building on narratives of deservingness, immigrant rights actors argue that policies and practices that structure illegality are illegitimate because they cause harm to unauthorized immigrants who seek only to contribute their energy and talents to the nation.

This account became apparent at an organizing retreat. During a break in the day's activities, participants dispersed throughout the room, chatting quietly in groups or strolling the building's narrow hallway. Several people stepped outside to smoke, though the chilly fall air kept most of the participants bundled in sweaters inside the building, filling Styrofoam cups with an endless supply of bitter coffee and watery hot chocolate. The group's collective exhaustion was palpable as we contemplated the magnitude of ideas that we had spent the week discussing. But there was also a quiet energy to the room, and our spirits were buoyed by the presence of so many people gathered together to resist illegality.

As we lingered over coffee, someone loaded a video of Manu Chao's *"Clandestino"* onto a computer that was hooked up to a projector and then cranked the volume on the speakers. The video projected large on the opposite wall, attracting the attention of those of us who had wandered across the room in search of a midday snack. Manu Chao may be relatively obscure in mainstream U.S. culture, but he is popular in the Spanish-speaking world. The original version of *"Clandestino"* is also well known to many who listen to Spanish-language music, and so we gathered in anticipation of a classic. This version, however, was different. The video, remade and produced in collaboration with the National Day Laborer Organizing Network, opened with film from a tent city in Maricopa County, Arizona—Sheriff Joe Arpaio's unique model for housing detained immigrants under his authority. As the camera lens peeped through the tent city's barbed-wire fences, we watched detained immigrants milling about beneath the tents and sitting on bunk beds. The men were clothed in bright pink undershirts, the signature color of the Maricopa County Sheriff's Office, which intended the clothing as a form of humiliation.

Like several progressive musicians and artists of color, Manu Chao's opposition to Arizona's crimmigration law was vocal. He was an early supporter of campaigns against S.B. 1070, and his support was reflected in this revision of *"Clandestino."* The music and lyrics, like the video, were slightly altered in this rendition. Instead of the original gritty sound, this version was lacking ornamentation and strummed in just a few chords. Accompanied by two acoustic guitars, Manu Chao's nimble voice echoed across the room. Here, I reproduce the song with my translations:

Solo voy con mi pena	I go alone with my sorrows
Sola va mi condena	Alone goes my sentence
Correr es mi destino	My destiny is to run
Para burlar la ley	To evade the law
Perdido en el corazón	Lost in the heart
De la grande Babylon	Of the great Babylon
Me dicen el clandestino	They call me clandestine
Yo soy el quiebra ley	I am the lawbreaker
Para una ciudad del Norte	To a city in the North
Yo me fui a trabajar	I went to work
Mi vida la dejé	I left my life
Entre Ceuta y Gibraltar	Between Ceuta and Gibraltar
Soy una raya en el mar	I am a (sting)ray in the sea
Fantasma en la ciudad	A ghost in the city
Mi vida va prohibida	My life is prohibited
Dice la autoridad	The authorities say
Mano Negra clandestina	*Mano Negra,*[8] clandestine
Mexicano clandestino	Mexican, clandestine
Guatemalteco clandestino	Guatemalan, clandestine
Maricopa ilegal	Maricopa, illegal

The group burst into laughter as the song ended, surprised and delighted by the revised ending. "*Otra vez,*" someone called—"[Play it] again!" A crowd had gathered, and the video was played once more for those who had missed it the first time.

The story of "*Clandestino*" was relatable to many at the workshop who had similar experiences through their own migration histories. Nodding along to the strumming guitar, we heard of an individual traveling to a "city in the North" to look for work, and it was quickly understood that this account—a narrative of existence—was from the perspective of an undocumented person. The immigrant left their entire life behind, carrying only grief on this journey. Manu Chao told us that the immigrant's sentence was to be alone, that their destiny was to live on the run. We heard that unauthorized immigrants were "clandestine"—furtive, hidden, underground. We also heard that authorities call such immigrants "lawbreakers," that the very lives of these individuals were *prohibida*—prohibited.

And yet, in Manu Chao's rendition, neatly summed up in the closing line, it is not the unauthorized immigrants who are "illegal" but rather Maricopa County, Arizona (and, by extension, the Maricopa County Sheriff's Office). In fact, both the office and its former sheriff, Arpaio, were sued over allegations of racially discriminatory treatment against Latinx residents. The Department of Justice under the Obama administration found that the Maricopa County Sheriff's Office engaged in a systemic pattern of unconstitutional policing against Latinx residents, including racial profiling (U.S. Department of Justice 2011). Then a federal judge ruled that Maricopa County, under Arpaio's leadership, racially profiled Latinx residents. In 2017, Arpaio was convicted of criminal contempt, a conviction that was pardoned later that same year by Donald Trump. Manu Chao used the term *ilegal* to imply that Maricopa County's racialized and degrading treatment of Latinx residents and unauthorized immigrants was criminal—or at least that it should be. In yet another version, Manu Chao concluded by singing, "Joe Arpaio *ilegal*"; now it is Joe Arpaio, the sheriff of Maricopa County, who is the criminal.

By and large, immigrant rights actors do not take lightly use of the term *illegal*. The slogan—"No human being is illegal"—is widely expressed in such circles, and it can be seen on placards and T-shirts at any pro-immigrant demonstration. "Drop the I-Word," a nationwide campaign, labeled the word a "racially charged slur" and championed its removal from public discourse. One of the campaign's organizers, Mónica Novoa (2012), explained that the term "illegal immigrant" is "1) legally inaccurate and misleading; 2) politically loaded and popularized by anti-immigrant strategists; and 3) experienced as racially biased and dehumanizing by the people it is used to describe." Following the lead of the National Association of Hispanic Journalists, which in 2006 publicly condemned use of the term and encouraged use of "undocumented immigrant," the "Drop the I-Word" campaign challenged people, organizations, and media outlets to discontinue *illegal* as a descriptor for immigrants. Instead, the campaign favored more humanizing language, such as *undocumented*, or more precise terminology, such as *unauthorized*.

Unauthorized entrants have long been referred to through demeaning euphemisms—including, for example, "tonks,"[9] "border jumpers," "wets," and "wetbacks"—but none of these carries the same cultural cachet and veneer of objectivity as "illegal immigrant." Other versions of this phrase, such as "illegal aliens" and "illegals," have been labeled dehumanizing and, for the most part, have lost acceptance in mainstream discourse.[10] Through widespread and uncritical use in media and public discourse, however, the term "illegal immigrant" seems neutral and accurate to many. I am often lambasted by those who favor the term over my preference for "unauthorized immigrant." After a presentation to a church, one congregant e-mailed me to scold, "By avoiding the use of 'illegal,' you put blinders on the fact that these people have broken the laws of this country by the manner in which they got here." This argument, as well as the semantic choice of "illegal," ignores nearly half of unauthorized immigrants who overstay their visas rather than crossing the border without inspection (Pew Hispanic Center 2006).

"Illegal" objectifies and decontextualizes immigration laws and policies, removing the status from its sociopolitical origins. As such, "illegal immigrant" is broadly considered to be neutral by the mainstream media, with few exceptions, and the term is used by pundits, politicians, and some scholars. When Jose Antonio Vargas (2012)—perhaps the highest-profile undocumented person in the United States—publicly urged media to discontinue using this "inflammatory, imprecise and, most of all, inaccurate" term, the *New York Times* public editor concluded that there was "no advantage . . . in a move away from . . . use of the phrase 'illegal immigrant.' It is clear and accurate; it gets its job done in two words that are easily understood" (Sullivan 2012). In 2013, the Associated Press announced that it "no longer sanctions the term 'illegal immigrant' or the use of 'illegal' to describe a person" (Colford 2013). A few other mainstream news organizations have disavowed the term, including the *Miami-Herald*, the *San Antonio Express-News*, and the *Huffington Post*.

Among unauthorized immigrants—particularly those active in organizing around immigrant rights—the term is largely considered unacceptable. For immigrant rights organizers, "illegal" has been used to frame unauthorized immigration from the perspective of the opposition, those who intend to dehumanize unauthorized immigrants. Manu Chao's play on words in *"Clandestino"* demonstrates how unauthorized immigrants and their advocates attempt to reframe the conversation around illegality rather than individual unauthorized immigrants. By juxtaposing the word *ilegal* against the Maricopa County Sheriff's Office and Sheriff Arpaio, the song articulates a narrative of illegitimacy regarding the role of state and local law enforcement agencies in matters of immigration enforcement.

This particular account manifests in various ways, though a clear favorite of immigrant rights actors in the Southeast is the *polimigra* wedding skit. This popular education sociodrama recounts the "marriage" of police and *la migra*—Spanish slang for immigration enforcement agents—and the consequences of such collaboration on Latinx immigrant communities. The following passage from my field notes describes a version of the skit:

> A crowd of more than a hundred guests sprawled lazily on the grass. Abuzz with excitement, we eagerly anticipated the culmination to the day's festivities. President Obama, our surprise host for the evening, emerged in a shabby gray suit coat and tattered brown pants to announce the beginning of the ceremony and a union so significant that it would have tremendous repercussions for years to come.
>
> The guests looked on in delight and bemused horror as the bride and groom stepped forward to pledge their vows to one another. On

one side stood the bride, resplendent in a navy midway cap and avia-
tor glasses. Across the aisle stood the groom, understated in a dark,
unmarked baseball cap, wearing equally reflective glasses. Both wore
simple necklaces made of string with cardboard placards, upon which
their names were respectively inscribed: Police and Immigration.

The minister's monologue on the sanctity of this union, punctuated by the occasional snickering and hissing of the audience, left
behind a grave impression. As the bride and groom exchanged their
solemn vows—to work together from this day forward to deport
workers, young people, and parents; to waste taxpayer dollars purs-
ing programs with a proven record of failure; and to undermine
years spent developing trusting relationships with the community—
the newlyweds flipped their necklaces to reveal their new shared
name: *PoliMigra*. (Conley 2012a)

I have seen this skit performed numerous times across the Southeast,
always with local flair, but the version described above was my first experience. During the summer of 2012, more than a hundred organizers—including representatives of *comités* from across the Southeast—gathered for a
workshop on migrant rights at the Highlander Center in East Tennessee.
Our work focused specifically on implementation of art activism and nonviolent civil disobedience. One division of the larger group planned, wrote,
and acted out the skit, complete with newly constructed giant papier-mâché
puppet heads of a police officer and an immigration agent.

These skits have been performed in countless communities across the
Southeast. They are not scripted by professional writers or performed by paid
actors. SEIRN has developed a "PoliMigra Wedding Toolkit" with a sample
script and cast of characters for groups interested in performing their own
polimigra wedding ceremony. However, the many performances that I have
seen vary widely in length, treatment, and complexity, demonstrating that
the telling of this story is eminently local, even as it is recounted in communities across the Southeast.

Those who participate in writing and acting such skits construct performances through the lenses of their own experiences and those of their family, friends, and neighbors who have been entangled in the enforcement
lottery. In one version of the skit, a woman is stopped at a police checkpoint
for driving without a license; in another, a youth (identified as a DREAMer
by his black mortarboard) is stopped for littering when he accidentally drops
a candy wrapper in a public park. As the skits suggest, these incidents might
have resulted in a simple fine before implementation of police-ICE collaboration and state crimmigration laws. After the wedding of *polimigra*, however,
unauthorized immigrants with even minor infractions face detention and
removal, meaning that all unauthorized immigrants are eminently deport-

Polimigra puppet head. (Author's collection)

able under the enforcement lottery. Some versions of the skit are even more disturbing: in one story, a migrant worker is arrested by *polimigra* at the behest of his employer after he protests unsafe working conditions; in another, a woman is arrested after she complains of sexual harassment.

In framing unauthorized immigrants as "illegal" immigrants, the "common sense" narrative justifies police-ICE interoperability and other practices that criminalize unauthorized immigrants. Building from the assumption that those who violate immigration laws will inevitably violate criminal laws, it is considered common sense to expect that local law enforcement should be enlisted to make it easier to detect, apprehend, and remove unauthorized immigrants before they cause harm. Conveniently, this framing fits neatly into a dominant narrative of villains, victims, and heroes. Implicit is the characterization of unauthorized immigrants as villains, the United States and its citizens and authorized residents as victims, and law enforcement (and others who implement policies of illegality) as heroes. An insidious form of cultural hegemony, common sense also conveys authority and a sense of moral imperative, such that policies and practices of illegality, and the narratives on which these are based, are broadly shielded from critical examination (Gramsci 1971). As a result, this narrative obscures the devastating consequences of *polimigra's* impact on the lives of unauthorized immigrants and their families.

As with *"Clandestino,"* however, the *polimigra* wedding skit appropriates the rhetoric of illegality to confront the legitimacy of policies and practices that criminalize unauthorized immigrants. Skits such as these subvert the commonsense rendition of police-ICE collaboration, and hence illegality, through an alternative narrative that points an accusatory finger at *polimigra*. Over and again, these skits draw on narratives of existence and deservingness to tell the stories of hardworking unauthorized immigrants whose attempts to thrive are threatened and thwarted by villainous others— the xenophobic legislator, the zealous white nationalist, the unscrupulous employer, and the fanatical *polimigra*. In these stories, Latinx immigrants are the victims, and *polimigra* enables their vulnerability. Grassroots resistance manifests through the reclaiming (and retelling) of the story in ways that resist the portrayal of unauthorized immigrants as villains and immigration agents as heroes.

Not only do these narratives challenge the roles of victim and villain; they also recast the hero. These sociodramas almost always incorporate a final act in which immigrants organize themselves in collective resistance to unjust policies and practices, delegitimizing structures of illegality even as they legitimize the heroic work of unauthorized immigrants in combating these structures. In one scene, immigrants interrupt the *polimigra* wedding to object to the marriage and demand an immediate moratorium on all deportations; in another, immigrants organize a monitoring system to alert communities to police checkpoints; in yet another, they organize a community hearing to testify against *polimigra* abuses. Through these dramas, performed by and for unauthorized immigrants and other directly affected community members, the audience learns that the organized community is the only community secure from the encroachment of *polimigra*. Just as these popular education performances exist to explain enforcement practices, so, too, do they demonstrate methods of resistance. Recognizing that they bear the burden of *polimigra's* induced vulnerabilities, immigrants also demand that they occupy the front lines of collective resistance. To borrow the words of Yovany Diaz Tolentino, undocumented immigrants become heroes to themselves.

These plays—and other counternarratives that question the legitimacy of policies and practices that structure illegality—are a form of resistance not just through the messages they convey but also from the audacity of their very existence. In defying the commonsense narrative of illegality and its legitimacy, counternarratives resist taken-for-granted assumptions about the nature of unauthorized immigrants. The *polimigra* skit challenges dominant articulations of unauthorized immigrants as villains and *polimigra* as heroes. Still, narratives of (il)legitimacy often function to assert accusations of harm against *deserving* immigrants. In these accounts, crimmigration policies and practices are illegitimate not because they create illegality but because they create vulnerability for those undeserving of the enforcement lottery: DREAMers, victims of abuse, hardworking people, and those with minor misdemeanors. Like narratives of existence and deservingness, narratives of (il)legitimacy rely on a subtext of worthiness, thereby reinscribing the illegality of some unauthorized immigrants.

Notes

1. A mixed-status family has members with different immigration statuses—one may be unauthorized, while others are U.S. citizens or authorized immigrants. Nine million people live in mixed-status families in the United States (Taylor et al. 2011).

2. The phrase "living unauthorized" is a variation on the title of Marquardt et al.'s (2013) *Living Illegal*.

3. Sandstrom's comments came as the Republican Party struggled to recruit Latinx voters following the 2012 presidential election.

4. I use gender-nonspecific pronouns to maintain the speaker's confidentiality to the greatest extent possible.

5. Noncitizens are prohibited or restricted from receiving many government assistance programs.

6. Hernández refers to Obama's 2012 presidential debate comments, where Obama argued: "If we're going to go after folks who are here illegally [*sic*], we should do it smartly and go after folks who are criminals, gang bangers, people who are hurting the community, not after students, not after folks who are here just because they're trying to figure out how to feed their families. . . . For young people who come here, brought here often times by their parents, had gone to school here, pledged allegiance to the flag, think of this as their country, understand themselves as Americans in every way except having papers . . . we should . . . give them a pathway to citizenship" (Commission on Presidential Debates 2012). This became a centerpiece of Obama's narrative on enforcement discretion. In 2014, when Obama announced Deferred Action for Parents of Americans and Lawful Permanent Residents, he stated, "We're going to keep focusing enforcement resources on actual threats to our security. Felons, not families. Criminals, not children. Gang members, not a mom who's working hard to provide for her kids" (Office of the Press Secretary 2014).

7. This chant, popular at protests in the Southeast, translates as "immigration, police, the same crap (or filth)."

8. *La Mano Negra* was an anarchist group in late nineteenth-century Spain and the name of Manu Chao's former band.

9. The meaning of the term *tonk* is disputed. Supposedly an acronym for "traveler origin not known," some Border Patrol agents claim it is the sound made when they hit an unauthorized entrant over the head with a metal flashlight (Urrea 2004). Alternatively, the term refers to Chinese immigrants who traveled by way of the Vietnamese Gulf of Tonkin when Chinese immigration was barred by the Chinese Exclusion Act.

10. The phrase "illegal alien" appears in some federal laws, such as the 1996 Illegal Immigration Reform and Immigrant Responsibility Act. Other laws, like the Immigration and Nationality Act, refer to unauthorized immigrants as "aliens" who are "deportable," "removable," "inadmissible" or "unauthorized."

8

Undoing Illegality

The Stories We Tell

This book explores policies and practices of illegality that structure the lives of unauthorized immigrants in the U.S. Southeast and how immigrant rights actors resist illegalization. Illegality is a legal phenomenon embedded in the creation and implementation of policies and practices that illegalize. It also emerges through ideological boundaries of belongingness, which separate those who belong from those who do not. In this way, storytelling is central to both the construction of and resistance to illegality. Hegemonic narratives of illegality and counternarratives of immigrant rights actors compete to frame the "problem" of unauthorized immigration and unauthorized immigrants, offer stories of threat and harm, and suggest solutions to these problems. These accounts also tell stories about the efficacy of proposed solutions in addressing problems as defined.

From the perspectives of those who champion policies and practices of illegality, unauthorized immigrants subvert the integrity of the United States by breaking laws, exploiting resources, and undermining the security of the nation. This rhetoric of harm suggests that unauthorized immigrants inevitably cause injury to the nation and to the people who are lawfully, "rightfully" present. In this framework, the United States, its people, and its way of life are the victims of villainous unauthorized immigrants. In support of this rhetoric are restrictionist policies and practices that illegalize unauthorized immigrants. Mechanisms to enforce illegality, such as police-ICE collaboration programs and bureaucratic enforcement policies, intend to constrain the lives of unauthorized immigrants so they cannot "harm" the nation. In practical terms, the mechanisms of illegality exclude unauthorized immigrants from full participation in public life, a form of "legal violence" (Menjívar and Abrego 2012) that perpetuates vulnerability for undocumented people. Unauthorized immigrants cannot work legally; in many states, they cannot drive. They cannot access public services and inhabit public spaces without risk or expect equal protection from the law and law enforcement officials. Stories of threat and harm offered by restrictionists naturalize and legitimize the effects of enforcement, carefully preserving boundaries of belongingness and excluding undocumented people as undeserving of dignity.

Restrictionists argue that widespread enforcement enables active and timely removal of unauthorized immigrants. It is certainly true that the homeland security state's enforcement regime has expanded the nation's capacity to detect, apprehend, detain, and deport more noncitizens. The enforcement lottery threatens unauthorized immigrants in their daily lives, and its impacts are especially relevant in places that actively engage in police-ICE collaboration and bureaucratic enforcement. In the Southeast, policy makers have enacted laws that criminalize unauthorized immigrants, encourage and/or mandate cooperation between state and local governments and federal immigration authorities, and prohibit sanctuary jurisdictions. Immigrants who live in jurisdictions that actively cooperate with ICE more readily engage the enforcement lottery and its consequences than those who live in places that actively limit police-ICE collaboration or in states that have enacted protective policies. This is compounded by racialized discourses that mark people of Latin American ancestry and origin as different and "illegal."

Restrictionist policy makers assume that the threat of enforcement will cause unauthorized immigrants to concede defeat and voluntarily return to their countries of origin. In reality, restrictionist laws have failed to encourage widespread "self-deportation" of unauthorized immigrants. Police-ICE collaboration and bureaucratic enforcement have not forced unauthorized immigrants to abandon the U.S. Southeast. Similarly, the United States has not experienced massive out-migration of unauthorized residents, nor has widespread enforcement consistently deterred unauthorized entry.

Policy makers have raised the stakes of unauthorized residency, but in ways that do not actually decrease the size of the unauthorized population. Policies and practices of illegality have not substantively addressed any of the root causes of unauthorized migration or unauthorized status, including real material conditions that push migrants to leave their countries of origin and pull them to the United States. Instead, the effect of widespread enforcement is to make unauthorized immigrants, and even the marginally authorized, more vulnerable. In "protecting" the nation from the "harm" of unauthorized immigrants and unauthorized immigration, those who make and implement the policies and practices of illegality actually generate harm for undocumented people and their communities.

It is fitting that immigrant rights actors resist illegality by questioning the nature of the "problem" that has been defined. In asserting that unauthorized immigrants are not problematic as they have been constructed, movement actors create space to reframe the problem, drawing on narratives of existence, deservingness, and (il)legitimacy to combat the illegalization of undocumented people. In these stories, unauthorized immigrants are not criminals but rather hard workers and exemplary students. They are not job takers; rather, they do the dirty, dangerous, and demeaning jobs that others will not do. Moreover, they do these jobs faster and cheaper than citizens. Unauthorized immigrants do not exploit social welfare programs; to the contrary, they martyr themselves for their families and the U.S. economy. In recasting unauthorized immigrants through the lens of deservingness, these stories create space for alternative narratives of threat. Crimmigration policies and practices render unauthorized immigrants vulnerable, forcing them into exploitative circumstances and preventing them from reporting victimization. Undocumented people do not harm the United States—they are harmed *by* the United States. Policy makers, ICE agents, police officers, and government bureaucrats who criminalize innocent DREAMers and their hardworking parents are the true villains. Deserving immigrants, in turn, are both the victims of illegality and the heroes of their own existence.

These narratives are powerful. However, stories such as these legitimize ideological foundations of illegality, the borders of belongingness that separate *"us* from *them"* (Anzaldúa 1987). Just as the rhetoric of illegality holds individual migrants accountable for their status, narratives of deservingness—which appear as subtext in narratives of existence and (il)legitimacy—suggest that some unauthorized immigrants must be held to greater account than others. Inasmuch as these narratives create wedges of belongingness, they legitimize enforcement of non-belongingness, thereby reinscribing the identity of "illegal." Narratives that articulate claims to legality through these wedges tacitly accept hegemonic framing of the problem of unauthorized immigration and unauthorized immigrants.

In recounting Jesús's story in the preface of this book, I noted that his immigration status should not have rendered him vulnerable to law enforcement, because, after all, he had "done nothing wrong." This sentiment resonates with those who are concerned about the rights of undocumented immigrants. People who are directly affected by the politics of illegality may see themselves and those they love in Jesús's story. Those who are not directly affected may express outrage when incidents like this happen to people in their community, such as those who attend their church or those whose children attend their own child's school. People who do not normally engage in immigrant rights activism are horrified when they hear about innocent families torn apart by the callous indifference of a mass deportation force or the casual cruelty of a zero-tolerance border enforcement strategy.

Movement actors emphasize the fact that unauthorized presence is a civil violation to assert that unauthorized residents are not criminals. We fight for undocumented youth because they did not break the law. We assert that their undocumented mothers and fathers are workers. Moreover, we argue that undocumented workers benefit the U.S. economy by doing the jobs that citizens will not do, often for low wages. We affirm that undocumented people like these are deserving, and we assert that deservingness underlies their right to remain in the United States.

It is not surprising that we tell stories in this way. Stories of good, hard-working, self-sacrificing immigrants contradict prevailing narratives of harm on which mechanisms of illegality are constructed. Certainly, these counternarratives challenge "commonsense," taken-for-granted assumptions about unauthorized immigration and unauthorized immigrants. A kernel of transgressiveness—a not insignificant challenge to the negative portrayals of unauthorized immigrants—emerges when I say that Jesús, an undocumented immigrant, has "done nothing wrong." In framing Jesús's immigration status as nonproblematic, I denaturalize the harm in his violation of immigration law and instead suggest that the consequence of illegality—in this case, his inability to report his victimization to the police—is the real problem.

I tell Jesús's story because it encapsulates many of the themes in this book. Jesús migrated to the United States in search of steady employment, elusive in his country of origin, to provide for his family. He moved to the Southeast specifically because friends told him that the region was safer for undocumented people and that he would be able to find a good job. Instead, he experienced increasing criminalization, first in North Carolina and then in Georgia. Like others, Jesús resisted. He attended a massive demonstration to protest a law that sought to make life so difficult that undocumented immigrants would give up and leave. In the midst of resistance, Jesús was made vulnerable by crimmigration policies and practices that reinforce exclusionary boundaries around his belongingness.

This incident is not the most appalling example of injustice that has come to my attention in the course of my involvement with immigrant rights work—far from it. As enforcement expands and intensifies across the country, both along the border and in the nation's interior, Jesús's experience is almost inconsequential, except in the impact it had on his ability to provide for himself and his family and to feel secure under the enforcement lottery. Rather, Jesús's story stands out because of its banality: it is the condition under which undocumented people live in the United States today, particularly in the Southeast, where the threat of enforcement is ubiquitous.

I also tell Jesús's story because this incident was the moment that I first confronted my own unexamined beliefs about deservingness and deportation. At the time, I thought of deportation as a serious consequence for serious crimes—not for everyone but perhaps permissible in certain circumstances. In this way, immigrant rights actors challenge the narrative framing of illegality, but we do so in ways that reaffirm its basic tenets, including the underlying legitimacy of the enforcement regime. That is: What if Jesús *had* done something wrong? At what point should undocumented immigrants rightly fear enforcement? I wonder whether and how we might think differently about Jesús if the details of his story distinguished him as less deserving. Similarly, what if some DREAMers do commit crimes? What if their undocumented parents only work as hard as U.S. citizens? What if they need charity or public assistance to survive? What then?

Even as stories of deservingness challenge illegality, they simultaneously restrict solutions to a debate over who may be *legitimately* illegalized. What threshold of criminality must immigrants cross to become "unproblematically deportable" (Bosniak 2013)? How hard must immigrants work and how well integrated must they be before their removal becomes problematic? What must undocumented people sacrifice to sufficiently compensate the United States and its authorized residents for the "harm" of unauthorized residency?

At the heart of the debate lies a straightforward question: Is deportation ever acceptable? If so, under what circumstances, and why? If immigrant rights actors continue to utilize narratives that are premised on, or that allude to, wedges of deservingness, then we must provide unequivocal answers to these questions. If, however, we do not wish to operate within a rhetoric of illegality that defines the deservingness of some unauthorized immigrants at the expense of those who are unproblematically deportable, then we must redefine the nature of the "problem" that we seek to resolve. Deportation is not, inherently, a reasonable or necessary solution to a problem that emerges through the creation and enforcement of arbitrary boundaries of belongingness.

Undoing Illegality

Structures and consequences of illegality defy the intentions of those who create, implement, and resist mechanisms of illegality. Thus, policy makers implement policies that do not actually result in "self-deportation," and movement actors employ narratives that often reinscribe the structures they intend to resist. We might assume that failed outcomes such as these result from complex interactions of social actors with different motivations and degrees of power. Some argue, for example, that policy disagreements between opposing factions lead to compromise, where neither side gets every-thing it wants and everyone gets something they oppose. Some anticipate that disputes over crimmigration laws may result in court challenges to con-strain the efficacy of policies and practices of illegality. Indeed, Alabama's crimmigration law was enjoined by judicial ruling, inspiring many to trust the courts to protect vulnerable people, including undocumented immi-grants.

Of course, policy changes could provide immediate, tangible benefits to many who are directly affected by illegality. Legislative reforms that expand and simplify access to residency and/or citizenship would provide pathways for more people to enter the country with authorization and live and work in peace. State laws that enable undocumented people to obtain driver's li-censes or policing standards that encourage alternatives to arrest for those caught driving without a license would limit the criminalization of undocu-mented people as they go about their daily lives. Sanctuary policies that dis-entangle local law enforcement from federal immigration authorities or that prohibit or resist bureaucratic enforcement policies would similarly impede the progression of the enforcement lottery for individual undocumented people.

Administrative reforms that promote targeted approaches to immigra-tion enforcement, such as implementation of enforcement priorities and fa-vorable exercise of prosecutorial discretion for people beyond those priorities, would reduce the number of undocumented immigrants pushed into the deportation machine. Decriminalization of unauthorized migra-tion, especially through the repeal or reform of laws such as the Illegal Im-migration Reform and Immigrant Responsibility Act and policies such as Operation Streamline, would deprioritize enforcement against vast numbers of unauthorized immigrants whose "crimes" are based entirely on immigra-tion violations. Likewise, universal access to legal representation for people in detention and deportation proceedings would help shield noncitizens from removal, particularly those who have compelling or "deserving" cases, such as asylum seekers. All of these reforms would limit the numbers of un-authorized immigrants who experience the full effects of illegalization.

Structurally speaking, however, illegality cannot be undone through modifications and restrictions to existing enforcement policies. This is be-cause illegality is not just a product of policies and practices that illegalize but a hegemonic paradigm that draws boundaries of belongingness around who belongs within the nation-state, who does not, and under what condi-tions. Discourses and policies of illegality can expand or contract bound-aries of belongingness; they can legalize or illegalize bodies; they can extend or restrict the enforcement lottery; and they can prioritize or deprioritize the removal of certain classes of migrants. Reforms to policies and practices of illegality decrease the likelihood that certain undocumented people will suffer many of the repercussions of illegalization—and, of course, this is not insignificant—but reforms do not address the ideological foundations of illegality, let alone the structural origins. For just this reason, illegality also cannot be undone through narratives that expand boundaries of belongingness to "deserving" immigrants by excluding others.

A movement to abolish ICE (and, in some circles, to abolish and prosecute ICE), has gained momentum among immigrant rights actors. Motivated in part by the Trump administration's indiscriminate escalation of enforcement, the movement seeks to abolish the agency responsible for immigration enforcement alongside eradication of the function of enforcement (McElwee 2018; Mijente 2018). How much ground this movement can gain in expanding boundaries of belongingness is yet to be known.

Still, illegality is built on a structural foundation of vulnerability. The United States has played a key role in undermining the political, social, and economic stability of other countries, particularly in Latin America. U.S. policies are implicated, directly and indirectly, in the forced or coerced migration of millions of people. Legacies of imperialism and military intervention, including U.S. financial and military backing of foreign anticommunist dictatorships and brutal civil wars, especially in Latin America, have provoked people to flee their countries of origin as a condition of survival. Neoliberal policies have devastated the local economies of peripheral nations (Frank 1969; Portes and Walton 1981); anti-labor policies have amplified the precarity of both U.S.- and foreign-born workers (Calavita 1992; Sassen 1990). Contemporary U.S. immigration policies, which provide few pathways for residency and citizenship, render millions of bodies unauthorized, and these bodies are further illegalized by policies and practices that enforce these boundaries.

In this framing of the problem, unauthorized immigrants are not vulnerable because they are unauthorized; they are unauthorized because they are vulnerable, and immigration status exacerbates their vulnerability. Once vulnerable people are present in the United States and out of status, the nation benefits from their legal and social construction as nonpersons (K. Johnson 1997). I do not mean to imply that individual citizens of the United States benefit—although many certainly do. As employers and consumers, citizens benefit when the real costs of labor are externalized to unauthorized workers or to workers whose status is under threat, even though they are not presently unauthorized. White (and perhaps white-adjacent) citizens benefit from the "psychological wages" of whiteness (DuBois 1935) built into racial hierarchies of belongingness.

More importantly, the United States benefits structurally from the production of illegality. Illegality is a primary means of ensuring the exploitability of all people, not just those who are unauthorized (Freeman 1986; Golash-Boza 2015a). As policy makers implement policies that do not result in "self-deportation," and immigrant rights actors resist these policies in ways that affirm wedges of deservingness, the structural effect is the maintenance of vulnerability. The sociopolitical conditions of illegality obscure histories and policies that impel international migration as well as the fact that the United States is dependent on "illegal" bodies. Policies and practices of illegality, and narratives of resistance embedded within the framing of illegality, do not change foundations of society; accordingly, they do not render society any less dependent on vulnerability and exploitation. In fact, the borderlands of illegality are precisely the defining boundaries of the United States.

————

THOSE WHO ARE INVOLVED in immigrant rights activism know that there is no such thing as a monolithic "immigrant rights movement." Instead, we approach our task through a variety of ethical, moral, empirical, and political lenses. If I were to identify one unifying strength of the movement, however, I offer that it is the commitment to community—and to people. After all, this is what immigrant rights activists are here for, broadly speaking: the desire to build community, to care for one another, to transition—in the words of Martin Luther King Jr.—from a "thing-oriented" society to a "person-oriented" society. People who care about immigrant rights implicitly believe that birth certificates and visas—perhaps even national borders—are just things and that these things are not more important than the people they represent.

The greatest weakness among immigrant rights activists is that we have not made explicit our assumptions about what it means to value people over things. Practically speaking, what does this mean for how we approach and articulate the "problem" of unauthorized immigration and unauthorized immigrants? What does it mean for the solutions we propose? As a movement, and sometimes even within the context of local organizing, we often sidestep discussions of root causes of international migration, the scope of rights deemed inalienable, and the role of deportation, let alone racism and colorism, the functions of law enforcement and incarceration, the trauma of forcible displacement, and the legitimacy of borders.

This is not a rebuke. After all, those who are committed to the rights of immigrants have been occupied for so long by so many fires. Directly affected people are fighting for their own dignity and survival. Together, immigrants and allies are monitoring and resisting criminalization and police-ICE collaboration, documenting and litigating abuses committed against unauthorized workers and immigrant detainees, defending people from deportation, expanding access to and awareness of civil and humanitarian rights, and much more. These fires did not begin with the Trump administration. Still, Trump's escalation of dehumanizing policies and practices has supplied fresh oxygen to those who support crimmigration and those who resist.

Even as the flames burn hotter, we must make time to consider what it means to value people over things. This is especially true for those who identify as allies and advocates and for those who have recently become active in the work. For all of us, though, the conversations we are *not* having shape our understanding of the problem and our approach to solutions. Indeed, to be a community of people united by anything but the vaguest notion of immigrant rights, to know how and when to act as a movement, it is necessary to seek consensus on who and what we are fighting for.

When we say that we are for immigrant rights, I am certain that we are for DREAMers and undocumented mothers and fathers, for family and friends who are undocumented, for those who embrace the American flag and suffer to achieve the American dream. For many, it is obvious that Jesús, who had "done nothing wrong," should be able to report his victimization without fear of deportation. I am less confident that we agree on what role deportation should play in the lives of other noncitizens, especially the "nondeserving"—or whether it should play any role at all. When we say we are *for* immigrant rights, we must be explicit about which immigrants we mean and what rights we are talking about.

In my travels across the Southeast, I find that movement actors—those who are directly affected and allies—are concerned less about the possibility that immigration reform will never happen than they are about the likelihood that reforms will make life worse for the vast majority of undocumented people. In the last two decades, each significant proposal for comprehensive immigration reform has offered amnesty to an increasingly smaller percentage of the resident unauthorized population—extended over long provisional periods during which more people may be disqualified by minor violations. This trend expands enforcement against those who fail to qualify and against the future flow of unauthorized entrants, and it increases militarization of the border. If we do not take seriously our diverse, conflicting, and even contradictory understandings of the depths and nuances of immigrant rights, I fear that the movement may collapse under the weight of our own collective relief at achieving a bare minimum of concessions from restrictionist forces, especially during times of unrestrained enforcement.

The answers to any problem are concealed within the boundaries of the problem as it is defined. It is foolish to expect that reforms premised on unauthorized immigration and unauthorized immigrants as a/the problem will substantively impact the conditions and consequences of illegality. Regardless of whether such reforms intend to resolve this "problem" through "self-deportation" (the preference of many restrictionists) or legalization (the preference of many immigrant rights actors), these solutions will never address the underlying conditions that structure illegality. Illegality, and the boundaries of belongingness, will continue to exist alongside the need for vulnerable bodies and the borders that create and constrain them. As long as our articulation of the problem obscures the fact that society requires "illegal" or otherwise exploitable bodies, the borderlands of illegality will continue to define the United States and its Southeast region.

Acknowledgments

FIRST AND FOREMOST, I am grateful to the movement activists and advocates across the Southeast who trusted me with their voices and stories, who allowed me to interview them and accompany them in their work, and who challenged my thinking every step of the way. I owe an unpayable debt for their words, their wisdom, and their time. I am humbled and inspired by their efforts to support and defend immigrants.

I am also thankful to the immigrant rights community in Knoxville, and especially to AKIN, for giving me hope in times of despair. I am encouraged by the work of Centro Hispano de East Tennessee, Comité Popular de Knoxville, Somos LASO, Kindred Futures, the Welcoming Immigrants Faith Network, Witnessing Wednesdays, and many others. It is hard to be pessimistic about the future of the Southeast when so many people are doing good work in my community and throughout the region.

Writing is a lonely process; luckily, editing is not. This book has benefited enormously from the generous insights of many people. I am grateful to the movement actors who made time, during periods of unrelenting assault on the rights of immigrants, to review parts of this work and offer critiques, including Alejandro Guizar Lozano, Yovany Diaz Tolentino, Mónica Hernández, Luis Escoto, Alysa Medina, Pancho Argüelles, César Bautista Sánchez, Tania Unzueta Carrasco, Azadeh Shahshahani, Isabel Rubio, Francisco Pacheco, Miguel Carpizo, and Adelina Nicholls. Many others were not able to read and respond to this work; I have tried to share their experiences as best as I can.

I am also grateful to friends, colleagues, and anonymous reviewers who read various chapters and earlier versions of this book, including Fran Ansley, De Ann Pendry, Stephanie Bohon, Steve Rabson, Jon Shefner, Louise Seamster, and Lois Presser. Valeria Gomez checked my legal descriptions for inaccuracies; all remaining mistakes are my own. I thank my editor, Ryan Mulligan, for seeing potential in this manuscript and for seeing me through to the end.

Last, but never least, I am thankful to Peter Fernandez for his patience and encouragement throughout this process. Thank you, Eamon and Rebecca Dawn, for being my whole world.

References

Abercrombie, Nicholas, Stephen Hill, and Bryan Turner. 1980. *The Dominant Ideology Thesis*. London: George Allen and Unwin.

Abrego, Leisy J. 2011. "Legal Consciousness of Undocumented Latinos: Fear and Stigma as Barriers to Claims-Making for First- and 1.5-Generation Immigrants." *Law and Society Review* 45 (2): 337–370.

Addy, Samuel. 2012. *A Cost-Benefit Analysis of the New Alabama Immigration Law*. Tuscaloosa: University of Alabama Center for Business and Economic Research. https://cber.cba.ua.edu/New%20AL%20Immigration%20Law%20-%20Costs%20and%20Benefits.pdf.

Alabama Department of Labor. 2013. *Alabama Labor Market News: January 2013 Newsletter*. Montgomery: Alabama Department of Labor.

Alabama House of Representatives. 2011. Beason-Hammon Alabama Taxpayer and Citizen Protection Act.

Alexander, Michelle. 2012. *The New Jim Crow: Mass Incarceration in the Age of Colorblindness*. New York: New Press.

Alonso, Alexsa, Kristin Macleod-Ball, Greg Chen, and Su Kim. 2011. *Immigration Enforcement Off Target: Minor Offenses with Major Consequences*. Washington, DC: American Immigration Lawyers Association. https://www.aila.org/File/Related/11081609.pdf.

American Civil Liberties Union. 2009. *Prolonged Immigration Detention of Individuals Who Are Challenging Removal*. New York: American Civil Liberties Union. https://www.aclu.org/other/issue-brief-prolonged-immigration-detention-individuals-who-are-challenging-removal.

Ansley, Fran. 2010. "Constructing Citizenship without a License." *Studies in Social Justice* 4 (2): 165–178.

Anzaldúa, Gloria. 1987. *Borderlands/La Frontera*. San Francisco: Aunt Lute Books.

Aranda, Elizabeth, and Elizabeth Vaquera. 2015. "Racism, the Immigration Enforcement Regime, and the Implications for Racial Inequality in the Lives of Undocumented Young Adults." *Sociology of Race and Ethnicity* 1 (1): 88–104.

Arizona Republic. 2010. "The Truth about SB 1070." July 28.

Armenta, Amada. 2015. "Between Public Service and Social Control: Policing Dilemmas in the Era of Immigration Enforcement." *Social Problems* 63 (1): 111–126.

———. 2017. *Protect, Serve, and Deport.* Berkeley: University of California Press.

Arthur, Rob. 2017. "Latinos in Three Cities Are Reporting Fewer Crimes since Trump Took Office." *Five Thirty Eight*, May 18. https://fivethirtyeight.com/features/latinos -report-fewer-crimes-in-three-cities-amid-fears-of-deportation/.

Atiles, Jorge, and Stephanie Bohon. 2002. *The Needs of Georgia's New Latinos: A Policy Agenda for the Decade Ahead.* Atlanta, GA: Carl Vinson Institute of Government.

———. 2003. "Camas Calientes: Housing Adjustments and Barriers to Social and Economic Adaptation among Georgia's Rural Latinos." *Southern Rural Sociology* 19 (1): 97–122.

Bada, Xochitl, Jonathan Fox, and Andre Selee. 2006. *Invisible No More: Mexican Migrant Civic Participation in the United States.* Washington, DC: Wilson Center. https:// www.wilsoncenter.org/sites/default/files/Invisible%20No%20More_0.pdf.

Baker, Bryan. 2017. *Immigration Enforcement Actions: 2016.* Washington, DC: Department of Homeland Security Office of Immigration Statistics. https://www.dhs.gov /sites/default/files/publications/Enforcement_Actions_2016.pdf.

Barkan, Elliot. 2003. "Return of the Nativists? California Public Opinion and Immigration in the 1980s and 1990s." *Social Science History* 27 (2): 229–283.

Bass, Jack, and Walter De Vries. 1995. *The Transformation of Southern Politics.* Athens: University of Georgia Press.

Beason, Scott. 2012. "Beason Statement on the Impact of HB 56 on Alabama Unemployment Rate." Press release. January 26.

Beckett, Katherine. 2016. "The Uses and Abuses of Police Discretion: Toward Harm Reduction Policing." *Harvard Law and Policy Review* 10:77–100.

Bedolla, Lisa Garcia. 2003. "The Identity Paradox: Latino Language, Politics and Selective Dissociation." *Latino Studies* 1 (2): 264–283.

Best, Joel. 1987. "Rhetoric in Claims-making: Constructing the Missing Children Problem." *Social Problems* 34 (2): 101–121.

Billeaud, Jacques. 2012. "Arizona Sheriff Taking the Stand over Racial Profiling Allegations." *Huffington Post*, July 24.

Black, Earl, and Merle Black. 2003. *The Rise of Southern Republicans.* Cambridge, MA: Harvard University Press.

Blitzer, Johnathan. 2017. "The Woman Arrested by ICE in a Courthouse Speaks Out." *The New Yorker.* February 23.

Bohon, Stephanie. 2006. "Georgia's Response to New Immigration." Pp. 67–100 in *Immigration's New Frontiers*, edited by G. Anrig and T. A. Wang. New York: Century Foundation.

Bohon, Stephanie, and Meghan Conley. 2015. *Immigration and Population.* Cambridge: Polity.

Bohon, Stephanie, Meghan Conley, and Michelle Brown. 2014. "Unequal Protection under the Law: Encoding Racial Disparities for Hispanics in the Case of *Smith v. Georgia*." *American Behavioral Scientist* 58 (14): 1910–1926.

Bohon, Stephanie, Heather Macpherson, and Jorge Atiles. 2005. "Educational Barriers for New Latinos in Georgia." *Journal of Latinos and Education* 4 (1): 43–58.

Bohon, Stephanie, and Heather MacPherson Parrot. 2011. "The Myth of Millions: Socially Constructing 'Illegal Immigration.'" Pp. 99–113 in *Being Brown in Dixie*, edited by C. D. Lippard and C. A. Gallagher. Boulder, CO: First Forum.

Bonilla Silva, Eduardo. 2010. *Racism without Racists: Colorblind Racism and Racial Inequality in Contemporary America*. Boulder, CO: Rowman and Littlefield.

Borden, Tessie. 2000. "INS: Border Policy Failed." *Arizona Republic*, August 10.

Bosniak, Linda. 2013. "Arguing for Amnesty." *Law, Culture and the Humanities* 9 (3): 432–442.

Breakthrough. 2009. *Shackled and Detained: A Pregnant Woman's Story*. New York: Breakthrough.

Brodzinsky, Sibylla, and Ed Pilkington. 2015. "US Government Deporting Central American Migrants to the Deaths." *The Guardian*, October 12.

Bustamante, Juan Jose, and Eric Gamino. 2018. "'La Polimigra': A Social Construct behind the 'Deportation Regime' in the Greater Northwest Arkansas Region." *Humanity and Society* 42 (3): 344–366.

Calavita, Kitty. 1992. *Inside the State: The Bracero Program, Immigration, and the INS*. New York: Routledge.

———. 1998. "Immigration, Law, and Marginalization in a Global Economy." *Law and Society Review* 32 (3): 529–566.

Camia, Catalina. 2011. "GOP Lawmaker Blasted for 'Shooting' Immigrants Rant." *USA Today*, July 13.

Campbell, Kristina M. 2011. "The Road to S.B. 1070: How Arizona Became Ground Zero for the Immigrants' Rights Movement and the Continuing Struggle for Latino Civil Rights in America." *Harvard Latino Law Review* 14 (1): 1–21.

Capps, Randy, Marc R. Rosenblum, Cristina Rodriguez, and Muzzafar Chishti. 2011. *Delegation and Divergence: A Study of 287(g) State and Local Immigration Enforcement*. Washington, DC: Migration Policy Institute. https://www.migrationpolicy.org/research/delegation-and-divergence-287g-state-and-local-immigration-enforcement.

Carens, Joseph H. 2010. *Immigrants and the Right to Stay*. Cambridge, MA: MIT Press.

Castillo, Andrea. 2017. "Immigrant Arrested by ICE after Dropping Daughter Off at School, Sending Shockwaves through Neighborhood." *Los Angeles Times*, March 3.

CBS News. 2009. "Rove Protégé behind Racy Tennessee Ad." February 11.

Chandler, Kim. 2011. "Alabama House Passes Arizona-Style Immigration Law." *Birmingham News*, April 5.

Chavez, Leo. 2001. *Covering Immigration: Popular Images and the Politics of the Nation*. Berkeley: University of California Press.

———. 2007. "The Condition of Illegality." *International Migration* 45 (3): 192–196.

———. 2008. *The Latino Threat: Constructing Immigrants, Citizens, and the Nation*. Stanford, CA: Stanford University Press.

Chishti, Muzaffar, Sarah Pierce, and Jessica Bolter. 2017. *The Obama Record on Deportations: Deporter in Chief or Not?* Washington, DC: Migration Policy Institute. https://www.migrationpolicy.org/article/obama-record-deportations-deporter-chief-or-not.

Coleman, Matthew. 2007. "Immigration Geopolitics beyond the Mexico-US Border." *Antipode* 39:54–76.

———. 2008. "Between Public Policy and Foreign Policy: US Immigration Law Reform and the Undocumented Migrant." *Urban Geography* 29 (1): 4–28.

———. 2012. "The 'Local' Migration State: The Site-Specific Devolution of Immigration Enforcement in the US South." *Law and Policy* 34 (2): 159–190.

Coleman, Matthew, and Austin Kocher. 2011. "Detention, Deportation, Devolution and Immigrant Incapacitation in the US, Post 9/11." *Geographic Journal* 177 (3): 228–237.

Colford, Paul. 2013. "Illegal Immigrant No More." *Definitive Source*, April 2.

Commission on Presidential Debates. 2012. Debate transcript, President Barack Obama and Former Gov. Mitt Romney. Hofstra University, Hempstead, New York. October 16. https://www.debates.org/voter-education/debate-transcripts/october-16-2012-the -second-obama-romney-presidential-debate/.

Congressional Budget Office. 2007. *The Impact of Unauthorized Immigrants on the Budgets of State and Local Governments*. Washington, DC: Congressional Budget Office. https:// www.cbo.gov/sites/default/files/110th-congress-2007-2008/reports/12-6-immigration .pdf.

Conley, Meghan. 2012a. "'I Now Pronounce You PoliMigra': Narrative Resistance to Police-ICE Interoperability." *Societies without Borders* 8 (3): 373–383.

———. 2012b. "Nativism Is Big Business." *Z Magazine* 25 (3): 33–35.

———. 2015. "In Times of Uncertainty: The Great Recession, Immigration Enforcement, and Latino Immigrants in Alabama." Pp. 147–162 in *Immigrant Vulnerability and Resilience*, edited by M. Aysa-Lastra and L. Cachón Rodriguez. Cham, Switzerland: Springer.

———. 2019. "Police-ICE Collaboration in the Knox County Jail." Department of Sociology, University of Tennessee, Knoxville, TN. Unpublished manuscript.

Conley, Meghan, and Stephanie A. Bohon. 2010. "The Spectrum's Other End: Solidarity and Distrust in a New Latino Destination." *Journal of Latino-Latin American Studies* 3 (4): 13–30.

Constable, Pamela. 2012. "Alabama Law Drives Out Illegal Immigrants but Also Has Unexpected Consequences." *Washington Post*, June 17.

Cornelius, Wayne. 2001. "Death at the Border: Efficacy and Unintended Consequences of US Immigration Control Policy." *Population and Development Review* 27 (4): 661–685.

Corrunker, Lauren. 2012. "Coming Out of the Shadows: DREAM Act Activism in the Context of Global Anti-Deportation Activism." *Indiana Journal of Global Legal Studies* 19 (1): 143–168.

Coutin, Susan Bibler. 1993. *The Culture of Protest: Religious Activism and the US Sanctuary Movement*. Boulder, CO: Westview.

———. 2000a. "Denationalization, Inclusion, and Exclusion: Negotiating the Boundaries of Belonging." *Indiana Journal of Global Legal Studies* 7:585–591.

———. 2000b. *Legalizing Moves*. Ann Arbor: University of Michigan Press.

———. 2003. "Illegality, Borderlands, and the Space of Nonexistence." Pp. 171–202 in *Globalization under Construction*, edited by R. W. Perry and B. Maurer. Minneapolis: University of Minnesota Press.

Coutin, Susan Bibler, and Phyllis Pease Chock. 1996. "'Your Friend, the Illegal': Definition and Paradox in Newspaper Accounts of US Immigration Reform." *Identities* 2 (1–2): 123–148.

Crane, Ken R., and Ann V. Millard. 2004. "'To Be with My People': Latino Churches in the Rural Midwest." Pp. 172–195 in *Apple Pie and Enchiladas: Latino Newcomers in the Rural Midwest*, edited by A. V. Millard and J. Chapa. Austin: University of Texas Press.

Datel, Robin, and Dennis Dingemans. 2008. "Immigrant Space and Place in Suburban Sacramento." Pp. 171–199 in *Twenty-First Century Gateways*, edited by A. Singer, S. W. Hardwick, and C. B. Brettel. Washington, DC: Brookings.

Deeb-Sossa, Natalia, and Jennifer Bickham Mendez. 2008. "Enforcing Borders in the Nuevo South: Gender and Migration in Williamsburg, Virginia, and the Research Triangle, North Carolina." *Gender and Society* 22 (5): 613–638.

De Genova, Nicholas. 2002. "Migrant 'Illegality' and Deportability in Everyday Life." *American Review of Anthropology* 31:419–447.

———. 2004. "The Legal Production of Mexican/Migrant 'Illegality.'" *Latino Studies* 2:160–185.

———. 2007. "The Production of Culprits: From Deportability to Detainability in the Aftermath of 'Homeland Security.'" *Citizenship Studies* 11 (5): 421–448.

De Jong, Gordon F., and Quynh-Giang Tran. 2001. "Warm Welcome, Cool Welcome: Mapping Receptivity toward Immigrants in the US." *Population Today* 29 (8): 4–5.

Delgado, Richard. 1989. "Storytelling for Oppositionists and Others." *Michigan Law Review* 87 (8): 2411–2441.

Donato, Katharine, and Amada Armenta. 2011. "What We Know about Unauthorized Migration." *Annual Review of Sociology* 37:529–543.

Donato, Katharine, Melissa Stainbeck, and Carl L. Bankston. 2005. "The Economic Incorporation of Mexican Immigrants in Southern Louisiana." Pp. 76–100 in *New Destinations: Mexican Immigration in the United States*, edited by V. Zúñiga and R. Hernández-León. New York: Russell Sage Foundation.

Dove, April Lee. 2010. "Framing Illegal Immigration at the U.S.-Mexican Border: Anti-Illegal Immigration Groups and the Importance of Place in Framing." *Research in Social Movements, Conflict and Change* 30:199–237.

Downes, Lawrence. 2006. "In Immigrant Georgia, New Echoes of an Old History." *New York Times*, March 6.

———. 2013. "Comparing Immigrants to Cordwood." *New York Times*, August 22.

Dreby, Joanna. 2012. "The Burden of Deportation on Children in Mexican Immigrant Families." *Journal of Marriage and Family* 74:829–845.

———. 2015. *Everyday Illegal: When Policies Undermine Immigrant Families*. Berkeley: University of California Press.

DuBois, W.E.B. 1935. *Black Reconstruction in America*. New York: Harcourt, Brace.

Dunbar-Ortiz, Roxanne. 2015. *An Indigenous People's History of the United States*. Boston: Beacon Press.

Duncan Roy et al v. County of Los Angeles. 2018. United States District Court Central District of California. Feb 7, 2018. https://www.aclusocal.org/sites/default/files/aclu_socal_roy_20180208_order_re_msjs.pdf.

Dunn, Timothy, Ana Maria Aragones, and George Shivers. 2005. "Recent Mexican Migration in the Rural Delmarva Peninsula: Human Rights versus Citizenship Rights in a Local Context." Pp. 155–183 in *New Destinations: Mexican Immigration in the United States*, edited by V. Zúñiga and R. Hernandez Leon. New York: Russell Sage Foundation.

Durand, Jorge, Douglas Massey, and Chiara Capoferro. 2005. "The New Geography of Mexican Immigration." Pp. 1–20 in *New Destinations: Mexican Immigration in the United States*, edited by V. Zúñiga and R. Hernández-León. New York: Russell Sage Foundation.

Durand, Jorge, Douglas Massey, and Fernando Charvet. 2000. "The Changing Geography of Mexican Immigration to the United States: 1910–1996." *Social Science Quarterly* 81 (1): 1–15.

Eagleton, Terry. 1991. *Ideology*. London: Verso.

Ennis, Sharon R., Merarys Ríos Vargas, and Nora Albert. 2011. "The Hispanic Population: 2010." 2010 Census Briefs. Washington, DC: United States Census Bureau. https://www.census.gov/prod/cen2010/briefs/c2010br-04.pdf.

Escobar, Martha. 2009. *Reinforcing Gendered Racial Boundaries: Unintended Consequences of the Mainstream Immigrant Rights Discourse.* Los Angeles: UCLA Center for the Study of Women. https://cloudfront.escholarship.org/dist/prd/content/qt75x6w42n/qt75x6w42n.pdf?t=lnpv9m.

Espenshade, Thomas. 1995. "Unauthorized Immigration to the United States." *Annual Review of Sociology* 21:195–216.

Espenshade, Thomas, and Charles Calhoun. 1993. "An Analysis of Public Opinion toward Undocumented Immigration." *Population Research and Policy Review* 12:189–224.

Executive Office of the President. 2006. *The Federal Response to Hurricane Katrina.* Washington, DC: Government Printing Office.

Executive Order 13768. 2017. *Enhancing Public Safety in the Interior of the United States.* Washington, DC: Government Printing Office.

Fan, Mary. 2012. "Rebellious State Crimmigration Enforcement and the Foreign Affairs Power." *Washington University Law Review* 89:1269–1308.

Fennelly, Katherine. 2006. "State and Local Policy Responses to Immigration in Minnesota." Pp. 101–142 in *Immigration's New Frontiers,* edited by G. Anrig and T. A. Wang. New York: Century Foundation.

Fernández Campbell, Alexia. 2018. "Trump Doesn't Need to Put Families in Detention Centers to Enforce His Immigration Policy." *Vox,* June 22.

Fertig, Todd. 2011. "Lawmaker's Immigrant Remark Draws Gasps." *Wichita Eagle,* March 14.

Fink, Leon. 2003. *The Maya of Morganton: Work and Community in the Nuevo New South.* Chapel Hill: University of North Carolina Press.

Finnie, Nicole, Roman Guzik, and Jennifer Pinales. 2013. *Freed but Not Free: A Report Examining the Current Use of Alternatives to Immigration Detention.* Newark, NJ: Rutgers School of Law. https://www.afsc.org/document/freed-not-free-report-examining-current-use-alternatives-to-immigration-detention.

Fleischauer, Eric. 2011. "Decatur Utilities: No Water or Power for Illegal Immigrants." *Decatur Daily,* November 6.

Flores, Lisa. 2003. "Constructing Rhetorical Borders: Peons, Illegal Aliens, and Competing Narratives of Immigration." *Critical Studies in Media Communication* 20 (4): 362–387.

Foley, Elise. 2017. "ICE Director to All Undocumented Immigrants: 'You Need to Be Worried.'" *Huffington Post,* June 13.

Forbes, Jack D. 1973. *Aztecas del Norte.* Greenwich, CT: Fawcett.

Frank, Andre Gunder. 1969. *Capitalism and Underdevelopment in Latin America.* New York: Monthly Review Press.

Freeden, Michael. 2003. *Ideology: A Very Short Introduction.* Oxford: Oxford University Press.

Freeman, Gary P. 1986. "Migration and the Political Economy of the Welfare State." *Annals of the American Academy of Political and Social Science* 485:51–63.

Freire, Paulo. 2013. *Education for Critical Consciousness.* London: Bloomsbury Academic.

Fujiwara, Lynn H. 2005. "Immigrant Rights Are Human Rights: The Reframing of Immigrant Entitlement and Welfare." *Social Problems* 52 (1): 79–101.

Furuseth, Owen, and Heather Smith. 2006. "From Winn-Dixie to Tiendas: The Remaking of the New South." Pp. 1–17 in *Latinos in the New South*, edited by H. A. Smith and O. J. Furuseth. Burlington, VT: Ashgate.

Garcia, Maria Cristina. 1996. *Havana, USA: Cuban Exiles and Cuban Americans in South Florida*. Berkeley: University of California Press.

García Hernández, César Cuauhtémoc. 2014. "Immigration Detention as Punishment." *UCLA Law Review* 61:1346–1414.

———. 2015. "Naturalizing Immigration Imprisonment." *California Law Review* 103 (6): 1449–1514.

Gentsch, Kerston, and Douglas Massey. 2011. "Labor Market Outcomes for Legal Mexican Immigrants under the New Regime of Immigration Enforcement." *Social Science Quarterly* 92 (3): 875–893.

Georgia House of Representatives. 2011. Illegal Immigration Reform and Enforcement Act of 2011.

Ghandnoosh, Nazgol. 2014. *Race and Punishment: Racial Perceptions of Crime and Support for Punitive Policies*. Washington, DC: Sentencing Project. https://sentencing project.org/wp-content/uploads/2015/11/Race-and-Punishment.pdf.

———. 2015. *Black Lives Matter: Eliminating Racial Inequity in the Criminal Justice System*. Washington, DC: Sentencing Project. https://sentencingproject.org/wp-content/uploads/2015/11/Black-Lives-Matter.pdf.

Golash-Boza, Tanya. 2012. *Immigration Nation: Raids, Detentions and Deportations in Post-911 America*. Boulder, CO: Paradigm.

———. 2015a. *Deported: Immigrant Policing, Disposable Labor and Global Capitalism*. New York: New York University Press.

———. 2015b. "From Legal to 'Illegal': The Deportation of Legal Permanent Residents from the United States. Pp. 203–222 in *Constructing Immigrant "Illegality,"* edited by C. Menjívar and D. Kanstroom. Cambridge: Cambridge University Press.

Gomez, Alan. 2011. "Alabama Immigration Law Marked by Hispanic School Absences." *USA Today*, October 4.

Goss, Jon, and Bruce Lindquist. 1995. "Conceptualizing International Labor Migration: A Structuration Perspective." *International Migration Review* 29 (2): 317–351.

Goss, Stephen, Alice Wade, J. Patrick Skirvin, Michael Morris, K. Mark Bye, and Danielle Huston. 2013. *Effects of Unauthorized Immigration on the Actuarial Status of Social Security Trust Funds*. Baltimore: Social Security Administration Office of the Chief Actuary. https://www.ssa.gov/oact/NOTES/pdf_notes/note151.pdf.

Gouveia, Lourdes. 2006. "Nebraska's Responses to Immigration." Pp. 143–198 in *Immigration's New Frontiers*, edited by G. Anrig and T. A. Wang. New York: Century Foundation.

Gouveia, Lourdes, Miguel Carranza, and Jasney Cogua. 2005. "The Great Plains Migration: Mexicans and Latinos in Nebraska. Pp. 23–49 in *New Destinations: Mexican Immigration in the United States*, edited by V. Zúñiga and R. Hernandez Leon. New York: Russell Sage Foundation.

Gouveia, Lourdes, and Rogelio Saenz. 2000. "Global Forces and Latino Population Growth in the Midwest." *Great Plains Research* 10:305–328.

Graff, Garrett. 2014. "The Green Monster: How the Border Patrol Became America's Most Out-of-Control Law Enforcement Agency." *Politico*, November/December.

Gramsci, Antonio. 1971. *Selections from the Prison Notebooks of Antonio Gramsci*. New York: International Publishers.

Greenwald, Robert. 2017. "A Look inside Our Abusive Immigrant Prisons." *The Nation*, October 18.

Grey, Mark. 1999. "Immigrants, Migration, and Worker Turnover at the Hog Pride Pork Packing Plant." *Human Organization* 58 (1): 16–27.

Grey, Mark, and Anne Woodrick. 2002. "Unofficial Sister Cities: Meatpacking Migration between Villachuato, Mexico, and Marshalltown, Iowa." *Human Organization* 61 (4): 364–376.

Griffith, David. 2005. "Rural Industry and Mexican Immigration and Settlement in North Carolina. Pp. 50–75 in *New Destinations: Mexican Immigration in the United States*, edited by V. Zúñiga and R. Hernandez Leon. New York: Russell Sage Foundation.

Guthey, Greg. 2001. "Mexican Places in Southern Spaces: Globalization, Work and Daily Life in and around the North Georgia Poultry Industry." Pp. 57–67 in *Latino Workers in the Contemporary South*, edited by A. D. Murphy, C. Blanchard, and J. A. Hill. Athens: University of Georgia Press.

Hagan, Jaqueline. 1998. "Social Networks, Gender, and Immigrant Incorporation." *American Sociological Review* 63 (1): 55–67.

Hay, Douglas. 1975. "Property, Authority and the Criminal Law." Pp. 17–63 in *Albion's Fatal Tree*, edited by E. P. Thompson, D. Hay, P. Linebaugh, J. Rule, and C. Winslow. New York: Pantheon.

Heath, Brad. 2013. "Immigration Tactics Aimed at Boosting Deportations." *USA Today*, February 17.

Hellman, Judith Adler. 2008. *The World of Mexican Migrants: The Rock and the Hard Place*. New York: New Press.

Heredia, Luisa. 2011. "From Prayer to Protest: The Immigrant Rights Movement and the Catholic Church." Pp. 101–122 in *Rallying for Immigrant Rights*, edited by K. Voss and I. Bloemraad. Berkeley: University of California Press.

Hernández, Arelis, Wesley Lowery, and Abigail Hauslohner. 2017. "Federal Immigration Raids Net Many without Criminal Records, Sowing Fear." *Washington Post*, February 16.

Hernández-León, Rubén, and Víctor Zúñiga. 2000. "Making Carpet by the Mile: The Emergence of a Mexican Immigrant Community in an Industrial Region of the US Historic South." *Social Science Quarterly* 81 (1): 49–66.

———. 2003. "Mexican Immigrant Communities in the South and Social Capital." *Southern Rural Sociology* 19 (1): 20–45.

Heyman, Josiah M. 2014. "'Illegality' and the U.S.-Mexico Border." Pp. 111–135 in *Constructing Immigrant "Illegality,"* edited by C. Menjívar and D. Kanstroom. New York: Cambridge University Press.

Hincapié, Marielena. 2009. *"Aqui Estamos y No Nos Vamos"*: Unintended Consequences of Current Immigration Law," Pp. 89–128 in *Global Connections and Local Receptions*, edited by F. Ansley and J. Shefner. Knoxville: University of Tennessee Press.

Hing, Bill Ong. 2004. *Defining America through Immigration Policy*. Philadelphia: Temple University Press.

Hoefer, Michael, Nancy Rytina, and Bryan Baker. 2012. *Estimates of the Unauthorized Immigrant Population Residing in the United States*. Washington, DC: Department of Homeland Security. https://www.dhs.gov/sites/default/files/publications/Unau thorized%20Immigrant%20Population%20Estimates%20in%20the%20US%20January %202012_0.pdf.

Homeland Security Advisory Council. 2015. *Interim Report of the CBP Integrity Advisory Panel.* Washington, DC: US Department of Homeland Security. https://www.dhs .gov/sites/default/files/publications/DHS-HSAC-CBP-IAP-Interim-Report.pdf.

Hondagneu-Sotelo, Pierrette. 1995. "Women and Children First: New Directions in Anti-Immigrant Politics." *Socialist Review* 25 (1): 169–190.

———. 2001. *Doméstica: Immigrant Workers Cleaning and Caring in the Shadows of Affluence.* Berkeley: University of California Press.

Horton, John. 1995. *The Politics of Diversity: Immigration, Resistance, and Change in Monterey Park, California.* Philadelphia: Temple University Press.

Huang, Priscilla. 2008. "Anchor Babies, Over-Breeders, and the Population Bomb: The Reemergence of Nativism and Population Control in Anti-Immigration Policies." *Harvard Law and Policy Review* 2:385–406.

International Association of Chiefs of Police. 2007. *Police Chiefs Guide to Immigration Issues.* Alexandria, VA: International Association of Chiefs of Police.

Jackson, Regine. 2011. "The Shifting Nature of Racism." Pp. 25–51 in *Being Brown in Dixie*, edited by C. D. Lippard and C. A. Gallagher. Boulder, CO: First Forum.

Jacobson, Robin Dale. 2008. *The New Nativism: Proposition 187 and the Debate over Immigration.* Minneapolis: University of Minneapolis Press.

Johnson, James, Karen Johnson-Webb, and Walter Farrell. 1999. "A Profile of Hispanic Newcomers in North Carolina." *Popular Government* 65 (1): 2–12.

Johnson, Kevin. 1997. "'Aliens' and US Immigration Laws." *Inter-American Law Review* 28 (2): 263–292.

Johnson, Kevin, Raquel Aldana, Bill Ong Hing, Leticia Saucedo, and Enid Trucios-Haynes. 2015. *Understanding Immigration Law.* LexisNexis.

Johnson, Kevin, and Bill Ong Hing. 2007. "The Immigrant Rights Marches of 2006 and the Prospects for a New Civil Rights Movement." *Harvard Civil Rights–Civil Liberties Law Review* 42:99–138.

Johnson-Webb, Karen. 2002. "Employer Recruitment and Hispanic Labor Migration." *Professional Geographer* 54 (3): 406–421.

Jones, Jennifer, and Hana Brown. 2017. "American Federalism and Racial Formation in Contemporary Immigration Policy." *Ethnic and Racial Studies*, 1–21.

Kalhan, Anil. 2010. "Rethinking Immigration Detention." *Columbia Law Review* 110: 42–58.

Kandel, William, and Emilio Parrado. 2004. "Industrial Transformation and Hispanic Migration to the American South." Pp. 266–276 in *Hispanic Spaces, Latino Places*, edited by D. D. Arreola. Austin: University of Texas Press.

———. 2005. "Restructuring of the US Meat Processing Industry and New Hispanic Migrant Destinations." *Population and Development Review* 31 (3): 447–471.

Kanstroom, Daniel. 2007. *Deportation Nation.* Cambridge, MA: Harvard University Press.

Kee, Lindsay. 2012. *Consequences and Costs: Lessons Learned from Davidson County, Tennessee's Jail Model 287(g) Program.* Nashville: ACLU of Tennessee. https://www .aclu-tn.org/wp-content/uploads/2015/01/287gF.pdf.

Kennedy, Veronica. 2011. "Library Card Requires Proof of Citizenship at North Shelby." *Birmingham News*, October 24.

Kerwin, Donald. 2014. "'Illegal' People and the Rule of Law." Pp. 327–352 in *Constructing Immigrant "Illegality,"* edited by C. Menjívar and D. Kanstroom. Cambridge: Cambridge University Press.

Kerwin, Donald, and Serena Yi-Ying Lin. 2009. *Immigration Detention: Can ICE Meet Its Legal Imperatives and Case Management Responsibilities?* Washington, DC: Migration Policy Institute. https://www.migrationpolicy.org/research/immigrant-detention-can-ice-meet-its-legal-imperatives-and-case-management-responsibilities.

Khashu, Anita. 2009. *The Role of Local Police: Striking a Balance between Immigration Enforcement and Civil Liberties.* Washington, DC: Police Foundation. https://www.policefoundation.org/publication/the-role-of-local-police-striking-a-balance-between-immigration-enforcement-and-civil-liberties/.

Kilty, Keith, and Maria Vidal de Haymes. 2000. "Racism, Nativism, and Exclusion." *Journal of Poverty* 4 (1–2): 1–25.

King, D. A. 2009. "Should Local Public Safety Units Enforce Immigration Laws?" *Atlanta Journal-Constitution*, October 19.

Kochar, Rakesh, Roberto Suro, and Sonya Tafoya. 2005. *The New Latino South: The Context and Consequences of Rapid Population Growth.* Washington, DC: Pew Hispanic Center. https://www.pewresearch.org/wp-content/uploads/sites/5/reports/50.pdf.

Koh, Jennifer Lee, Jayashri Srikantiah, and Karen Tumlin. 2011. *Deportation without Due Process.* Los Angeles: National Immigration Law Center. https://www.nilc.org/wp-content/uploads/2016/02/Deportation-Without-Due-Process-2011-09.pdf.

Koskela, Hille. 2011. "'Don't Mess with Texas!' Texas Virtual Border Watch Program and the (Botched) Politics of Responsibilization." *Theoretical Criminology* 15:269–282.

Koslowski, Rey. 2011. *The Evolution of Border Controls as a Mechanism to Prevent Illegal Immigration.* Washington, DC: Migration Policy Institute. https://www.migrationpolicy.org/research/evolution-US-border-controls-illegal-immigration.

Koulish, Robert. 2016. "Using Risk to Assess the Legal Violence of Mandatory Detention." *Laws* 5 (3): 30.

Lacy, Elaine. 2011. "Integrating into New Communities: The Latino Perspective." Pp 115–132 in *Being Brown in Dixie,* edited by C. D. Lippard and C. A. Gallagher. Boulder, CO: First Forum.

Lakoff, George, and Sam Ferguson. 2006. "The Framing of Immigration." Rockridge Institute.

Lakoff, George, and Mark Johnson. 1980. *Metaphors We Live By.* Chicago: University of Chicago Press.

Lamis, Alexander. 1999. *Southern Politics in the 1990s.* Baton Rouge: Louisiana State University Press.

Larrain, Jorge. 1983. *Marxism and Ideology.* Atlantic Highlands, NJ: Humanities Press.

Law Enforcement Immigration Task Force. 2018a. "50 Law Enforcement Leaders Send Letter to Senate on Proposals Related to 'Sanctuary Cities.'" February 15. https://leitf.org/2018/02/nearly-50-law-enforcement-leaders-send-letter-senate-proposals-related-sanctuary-cities/.

———. 2018b. "LEITF Co-Chairs Write to House Judiciary Committee, Subcommittee on Immigration and Border Security." February 13. https://leitf.org/2018/02/leitf-co-chairs-write-house-judiciary-committee/.

Leadership Conference on Civil Rights. 2006. "Civil Rights Coalition Joins Widespread Calls for Comprehensive, Fair Immigration Reform." Press release. March 15.

Lee, Jennifer, and Frank Bean. 2007. "Reinventing the Color Line." *Social Forces* 86 (2): 561–586.

Levin, Brian. 2016. *Special Status Report: Hate Crime in the United States.* San Bernardino, CA: Center for the Study of Hate and Extremism.

Lewis, Brooke. 2017. "HPD Chief Announces Decrease in Hispanics Reporting Rape and Violent Crimes Compared to Last Year." *Houston Chronicle*, April 6.

Lewis, Paul, and S. Karthick Ramakrishnan. 2007. "Police Practices in Immigrant Destination Cities?" *Urban Affairs Review* 42 (6): 874–900.

Light, Ivan, and Michael Francis Johnston. 2009. "The Metropolitan Dispersion of Mexican Immigrants in the United States, 1980 to 2000." *Journal of Ethnic and Migration Studies* 35 (1): 3–18.

Lippard, Cameron, and Charles Gallagher, eds. 2011. *Being Brown in Dixie: Race, Ethnicity, and Latino Immigration in the New South.* Boulder, CO: First Forum.

Lipset, Seymour Martin. 1996. *American Exceptionalism.* New York: W. W. Norton.

Lopez, Mark Hugo, Ana Gonzalez-Barrera, and Seth Motel. 2011. *As Deportations Rise to Record Levels, Most Latinos Oppose Obama's Policy.* Washington, DC: Pew Hispanic Center. https://www.pewhispanic.org/2011/12/28/as-deportations-rise-to-record-levels -most-latinos-oppose-obamas-policy/.

Lopez, Mark Hugo, Rich Morin, and Paul Taylor. 2010. *Illegal Immigration Backlash Worries, Divides Latinos.* Washington, DC: Pew Hispanic Center. https://www.pew research.org/wp-content/uploads/sites/5/reports/128.pdf.

Lugo-Lugo, Carmen, and Mary Bloodsworth-Lugo. 2010. "475° from September 11: Citizenship, Immigration, Same-Sex Marriage, and the Browning of Terror." *Cultural Studies* 24 (2): 234–255.

Luibhéid, Eithne. 2008. "Queer/Migration: An Unruly Body of Scholarship." *GLQ: A Journal of Lesbian and Gay Studies* 14 (2–3): 169–190.

Lukes, Steven 2005. *Power: A Radical View.* London: Palgrave Macmillan.

Lydgate, Joanna. 2010. *Assembly-Line Justice: A Review of Operation Streamline.* Berkeley, CA: Chief Justice Earl Warren Institute on Race, Ethnicity and Diversity. https:// www.law.berkeley.edu/files/Operation_Streamline_Policy_Brief.pdf.

Lyman, Brian. 2011. "MPS Parent Says Child Asked for Immigration Status." *Montgomery Advertiser*, October 4.

Macaraeg, Sarah. 2018. "Fatal Encounters: 97 Deaths Point to Pattern of Border Agent Violence across America." *The Guardian*, May 2.

Magnus, Chris. 2017. "Sessions's Anti-Immigrant Policies Will Make Cities More Dangerous." *New York Times*, December 6.

Mahony, Roger. 2006. "Called by God to Help." *New York Times*, March 22.

Mariscal, Jorge. 2005. "Homeland Security, Militarism, and the Future of Latinos and Latinas in the United States." *Radical History Review* 93:39–52.

Markowitz, Peter. 2011. "Deportation Is Different." *Journal of Constitutional Law* 13:1299 –1361.

Marquardt, Marie Freidman, Timothy Steigenga, Philip Williams, and Manuel Vasquez. 2011. *Living Illegal: The Human Face of Unauthorized Immigration.* New York: New Press.

Marrow, Helen. 2005. "New Destinations and Immigrant Incorporation." *Perspectives on Politics* 3 (4): 781–799.

———. 2009. "New Destinations and the American Colour Line." *Ethnic and Racial Studies* 32 (6): 1037–1057.

———. 2011a. "Intergroup Relations: Reconceptualizing Discrimination and Hierarchy." Pp 53–76 in *Being Brown in Dixie*, edited by C. D. Lippard and C. A. Gallagher. Boulder, CO: First Forum.

———. 2011b. *New Destination Dreaming: Immigration, Race, and Legal Status in the Rural American South.* Stanford, CA: Stanford University Press.

———. 2011c. "Race and the New Southern Migration, 1986 to the Present." Pp. 125–160 in *Beyond La Frontera*, edited by M. Overmyer-Velázquez. New York: Oxford University Press.

Martinez, Lisa. 2008. "Flowers from the Same Soil: Latino Solidarity in the Wake of the 2006 Immigrant Mobilizations." *American Behavioral Scientist* 52 (4): 557–579.

Massey, Douglas. 1987. "Understanding Mexican Migration to the United States." *American Journal of Sociology* 92 (6): 1372–1403.

———. 1999. "International Migration at the Dawn of the Twenty-First Century: The Role of the State." *Population and Development Review* 25 (2): 303–322.

———. 2005. *Backfire at the Border*. Washington, DC: Cato Institute.

Massey, Douglas, Jorge Durand, and Nolan Malone. 2002. *Beyond Smoke and Mirrors: Mexican Immigration in an Era of Economic Integration*. New York: Russell Sage Foundation.

Massey, Douglas, Jorge Durand, and Karen Pren. 2016. "Why Border Enforcement Backfired." *American Journal of Sociology* 121 (5): 1557–1600.

Massey, Douglas, and Fernando Riosmena. 2010. "Undocumented Migration from Latin America in an Era of Rising US Enforcement." *Annals of the American Academy of Political and Social Science* 630 (1): 294–321.

Mayer, Jeremy. 2002. *Running on Race: Racial Politics in Presidential Campaigns 1960–2000*. New York: Random House.

McAdam, Doug. 1982. *Political Process and the Development of Black Insurgency, 1930–1970*. Chicago: University of Chicago Press.

McClain, Paula. 2006. "North Carolina's Response to Latino Immigrants and Immigration." Pp 7–32 in *Immigration's New Frontiers*, edited by G. Anrig and T. A. Wang. New York: Century Foundation.

McConnell, Eileen Diaz. 2011. "Racialized Histories and Contemporary Population Dynamics in the New South." Pp. 77–98 in *Being Brown in Dixie*, edited by C. D. Lippard and C. A. Gallagher. Boulder, CO: First Forum.

McDaniel, Josh, and Vanessa Casanova. 2003. "Pines in Lines: Tree Planting, H2B Guest Workers, and Rural Poverty in Alabama." *Southern Rural Sociology* 19 (1): 73–96.

McElwee, Sean. 2018. "It's Time to Abolish ICE." *The Nation*, March 9.

McKanders, Karla. 2007. "Welcome to Hazelton! 'Illegal' Immigrants Beware." *Loyola University Chicago Law Journal* 39 (1): 1–49.

McKissick, John, and Sharon Kane. 2011. *An Evaluation of Direct and Indirect Economic Losses Incurred by Georgia Fruit and Vegetable Producers in Spring 2011*. Athens: University of Georgia Center for Agribusiness and Economic Development. https://athenaeum.libs.uga.edu/bitstream/handle/10724/34040/GeorgiaFruitandVegetableSurveyAnalysis-3.pdf?sequence=1&isAllowed=y.

Menjívar, Cecilia. 2006. "Liminal Legality: Salvadoran and Guatemalan Immigrants' Lives in the United States." *American Journal of Sociology* 111 (4): 999–1037.

———. 2011. "The Power of the Law: Central Americans' Legality and Everyday Life in Phoenix, Arizona." *Latino Studies* 9 (4): 377–395.

Menjívar, Cecilia, and Leisy J. Abrego. 2012. "Legal Violence: Immigration Law and the Lives of Central American Immigrants." *American Journal of Sociology* 117 (5): 1380–1421.

Menjívar, Cecilia, and María Enchautegui. 2015. "Confluence of the Economic Recession and Immigration Laws in the Lives of Latino Immigrant Workers in the United States." Pp. 105–126 in *Immigrant Vulnerability and Resistance*, edited by M. Aysa-Lastra and L. Cachón. Cham, Switzerland: Springer.

Mignolo, Walter. 2000. *Local Histories/Global Designs*. Princeton, NJ: Princeton University Press.

Mijente. 2018. *Free Our Future: An Immigration Policy Platform for Beyond the Trump Era*. Mijente. https://mijente.net/wp-content/uploads/2018/06/Mijente-Immigration-Policy-Platform_0628.pdf.

Millard, Ann, and Jorge Chapa. 2004. *Apple Pie and Enchiladas: Latino Newcomers in the Rural Midwest*. Austin: University of Texas Press.

Mindiola, Tatcho, Yolanda Flores Niemann, and Nestor Rodriguez. 2002. *Black-Brown Relations and Stereotypes*. Austin: University of Texas Press.

Mittelstadt, Michelle, Burke Speaker, Doris Meissner, and Muzzaffar Chishti. 2011. *Through the Prism of National Security: Major Immigration Policy and Program Changes in the Decade since 9/11*. Washington, DC: Migration Policy Institute. https://www.migrationpolicy.org/research/post-9-11-immigration-policy-program-changes.

Mohl, Raymond. 2003. "Globalization, Latinization, and the Nuevo New South." *Journal of American Ethnic History* 22 (4): 31–66.

Molina, Natalia. 2014. *How Race Is Made in America: Immigration, Citizenship, and the Historical Power of Racial Scripts*. Berkeley: University of California Press.

Montero, David. 2013. "Sandstrom Says Immigration Law He Pushed Should Be Axed." *Salt Lake Tribune*, March 14.

Morgan-Trostle, Juliana, Kexin Zheng, and Carl Lipscombe. 2016. *Black Immigrants in the Mass Criminalization System*. New York: Black Alliance for Just Immigration.

Morton, John. 2011. "Exercising Prosecutorial Discretion Consistent with the Civil Immigration Enforcement Priorities of the Agency for the Apprehension, Detention, and Removal of Aliens." Memorandum. Washington, DC: Department of Homeland Security, Immigration and Customs Enforcement. https://www.ice.gov/doclib/secure-communities/pdf/prosecutorial-discretion-memo.pdf.

Motomura, Hiroshi. 2011. "The Discretion That Matters: Federal Immigration Enforcement, State and Local Arrests, and the Civil-Criminal Line." *UCLA Law Review* 58: 1819–1858.

Mountz, Alison. 2011. "Border Politics: Spatial Provision and Geographical Precision." *Political Geography* 30 (2): 65–66.

Naples, Nancy. 2007. "The Social Regulation of Community: An Intersectional Analysis of Migration and Incorporation in the Heartland." *Journal of Latino-Latin American Studies* 2 (3): 16–23.

National Commission on Terrorist Attacks upon the United States. 2004. *The 9/11 Commission Report*. Washington, DC: Government Printing Office. http://govinfo.library.unt.edu/911/report/911Report.pdf.

National Community Advisory Commission. 2011. *Restoring Community: A National Community Advisory Report on ICE's Failed "Secure Communities" Program*. Pasadena, CA: National Day Laborer Organizing Network.

Neal, Micki, and Stephanie Bohon. 2003. "The Dixie Diaspora: Attitudes towards Immigrants in Georgia." *Sociological Spectrum* 23 (2): 181–212.

Nevins, Joseph. 2002. *Operation Gatekeeper and Beyond*. New York: Routledge.

Newton, Lina. 2008. *Illegal, Alien, or Immigrant: The Politics of Immigration Reform*. New York: New York University Press.

Ngai, Mae. 2004. *Impossible Subjects: Illegal Aliens and the Making of Modern America*. Princeton, NJ: Princeton University Press.

Nguyen, Mai Thi, and Hannah Gill. 2010. *The Costs and Consequences of Local Immigration Enforcement in North Carolina Communities.* Chapel Hill: University of North Carolina Press.

Nicholls, Walter. 2013. *The DREAMers: How the Undocumented Youth Movement Transformed the Immigrant Rights Debate in the United States.* Palo Alto, CA: Stanford University Press.

No More Deaths. 2011. *A Culture of Cruelty: Abuse and Impunity in Short-Term and U.S. Border Patrol Custody.* Tucson, AZ: No More Deaths. http://forms.nomoredeaths.org/wp-content/uploads/2014/10/CultureOfCruelty-full.compressed.pdf.

Novoa, Mónica. 2012. "Open Letter from Drop the I-Word to *The New York Times.*" *Colorlines,* October 1.

Nowrasteh, Alex. 2018. *The State of Immigration Enforcement.* Washington, DC: Cato Institute. https://www.cato.org/blog/state-immigration-enforcement.

Obama, Barack. 2010. *Remarks by the President at Naturalization Ceremony for Active-Duty Service Members.* April 23. Washington, DC: White House, Office of the Press Secretary. https://obamawhitehouse.archives.gov/the-press-office/remarks-president-naturalization-ceremony-active-duty-service-members.

———. 2014. *Remarks by the President in Address to the Nation on Immigration.* November 20. Washington, DC: White House, Office of the Press Secretary. https://obamawhitehouse.archives.gov/the-press-office/2014/11/20/remarks-president-address-nation-immigration.

Oberhaus, Daniel. 2018. "ICE Modified Its 'Risk Assessment' Software So It Automatically Recommends Detention." *Motherboard,* June 26.

Office of Inspector General, Department of Homeland Security. 2017. *Concerns about ICE Detainee Treatment and Care at Detention Facilities.* OIG-18-32. Washington, DC: Department of Homeland Security. https://www.oig.dhs.gov/sites/default/files/assets/2017-12/OIG-18-32-Dec17.pdf.

Ogletree, Charles. 2000. "America's Schizophrenic Immigration Policy: Race, Class, and Reason." *Immigration and Nationality Law Review* 21:3–18.

Omi, Michael, and Howard Winant. 1994. *Racial Formation in the United States: From the 1960s to the 1990s.* New York: Routledge.

Ono, Kent, and John Sloop. 2002. *Shifting Borders: Rhetoric, Immigration and California's Proposition 187.* Philadelphia: Temple University Press.

Padin, Jose Antonio. 2005. "The Normative Mulattoes: The Press, Latinos, and the Racial Climate on the Moving Immigration Frontier." *Sociological Perspectives* 48 (1): 49–75.

Papadimitriou, Demetrios, and Philip Martin. 1991. *The Unsettled Relationship: Labor Migration and Economic Development.* Westport, CT: Greenwood Press.

Pardo, Mary. 1990. "Mexican American Women Grassroots Community Activists: 'Mothers of East Los Angeles.'" *Frontiers: A Journal of Women Studies* 11 (1): 1–7.

———. 1995. "Doing It for the Kids: Mexican American Community Activists, Border Feminists?" Pp. 356–371 in *Feminist Organizations: Harvest of the New Women's Movement,* edited by M. Marx Ferree and P. Yancey Martin. Philadelphia: Temple University Press.

Passel, Jeffrey, and D'Vera Cohn. 2009. *A Portrait of Unauthorized Immigrants in the United States.* Washington, DC: Pew Hispanic Center. https://www.pewresearch.org/wp-content/uploads/sites/5/reports/107.pdf.

———. 2011. *Unauthorized Immigrant Population: National and State Trends, 2010.* Washington, DC: Pew Hispanic Center. https://www.pewresearch.org/wp-content/uploads/sites/5/reports/133.pdf.

———. 2016. *Overall Number of U.S. Unauthorized Immigrants Holds Steady Since 2009.* Washington, DC: Pew Hispanic Center. https://www.pewhispanic.org/wp-content /uploads/sites/5/2016/09/PH_2016.09.20_Unauthorized_FINAL.pdf.

Passel, Jeffrey, D'Vera Cohn, and Ana Gonzalez-Barrera. 2012. *Net Migration from Mexico Falls to Zero—and Perhaps Less.* Washington, DC: Pew Hispanic Center. https://www .pewresearch.org/wp-content/uploads/sites/5/2012/04/PHC-Net-Migration-from -Mexico-Falls-to-Zero.pdf.

Pastor, Ed. 1996. "Immigration and Naturalization Service Comprehensive Southwest Border Enforcement Strategy." *Congressional Record* 142 (39). Washington, DC: Government Printing Office.

Patler, Caitlin, and Roberto Gonzales. 2015. "Framing Citizenship: Media Coverage of Anti-deportation Cases Led by Undocumented Immigrant Youth Organizations." *Journal of Ethnic and Migration Studies* 41 (9): 1453–1474.

Pessar, Patricia R. 1999. "Engendering Migration Studies: The Case of New Immigrants in the United States." *American Behavioral Scientist* 42 (4): 577–600.

Pew Hispanic Center. 2006. *Modes of Entry for the Unauthorized Migrant Population.* Fact sheet. Washington, DC: Pew Hispanic Center. https://www.pewresearch.org/wp -content/uploads/sites/5/2011/10/19.pdf.

Pew Research Center. 2010. *Broad Approval for New Arizona Immigration Law: Democrats Divided, But Support Key Provisions.* Washington, DC: Pew Research Center. https://www.pewresearch.org/wp-content/uploads/sites/4/legacy-pdf/613.pdf.

Phillips, Julie, and Douglas Massey. 1999. "The New Labor Market: Immigrants and Wages after IRCA." *Demography* 36 (2): 233–246.

Pickering, Sharon. 2006. "Border Narratives: From Talking Security to Performing Borderlands." Pp. 45–62 in *Borders, Mobility and Technologies of Control*, edited by S. Pickering and L. Weber. Dordrecht, The Netherlands: Springer.

Pierson, Emma, Camelia Simoiu, Jan Overgoor, Sam Corbett-Davies, Vignesh Ramachandran, Cheryl Phillips, and Sharad Goel. 2017. *A Large-Scale Analysis of Racial Disparities in Police Stops across the United States.* Working paper. Stanford Open Policing Project, Stanford University. https://5harad.com/papers/100M-stops.pdf.

Pilkington, Ed. 2011. "Alabama Immigration Threat: Prove Your Legal Status or Lose Water Supply." *The Guardian*, October 7.

Piven, Frances Fox, and Richard Cloward. 1977. *Poor Peoples' Movements.* New York: Vintage Books.

Poe, Ryan. 2017. "Feds Arrest Memphis Immigrants in Sunday 'Surge,' Outraging Activists." *Commercial Appeal*, July 23.

Pollner, Melvin, and Robert Emerson. 1983. "The Dynamics of Inclusion and Distance in Field Work Relations." Pp. 235–252 in *Contemporary Field Research: Perspectives and Formulations*, edited by R. M. Emerson. Boston: Little, Brown.

Portes, Alejandro. 1978. "Toward a Structural Analysis of Illegal (Undocumented) Immigration." *International Migration Review* 12 (4): 469–484.

———. 1998. "Social Capital: Its Origins and Applications in Modern Sociology." *Annual Review of Sociology* 24:1–24.

Portes, Alejandro, and Robert Bach. 1985. *Latin Journey: Cuban and Mexican Immigrants in the United States.* Berkeley: University of California Press.

Portes, Alejandro, and Rubén Rumbaut. 1996. *Immigrant America.* Berkeley: University of California Press.

Portes, Alejandro, and Alex Stepick. 1993. *City on the Edge: The Transformation of Miami.* Berkeley: University of California Press.

Portes, Alejandro, and John Walton. 1981. *Labor, Class, and the International System.* New York: Academic Press.

Pow, Chris. 2011. "Gov. Robert Bentley Responds to Immigration Law Criticism." *Alabama Media Group,* November 15.

Preston, Julia. 2011. "In Alabama, a Harsh Bill for Residents Here Illegally." *New York Times,* June 3.

Price, Marie, and Audrey Singer. 2008. "Immigrants, Suburbs, and the Politics of Reception in Metropolitan Washington." Pp. 137–168 in *Twenty-First Century Gateways,* edited by A. Singer, S. W. Hardwick, and C. B. Brettell. Washington, DC: Brookings.

Provine, Doris Marie, and Roxanne Lynn Doty. 2011. "The Criminalization of Immigrants as a Racial Project." *Journal of Contemporary Criminal Justice* 27 (3): 261–277.

Purvis, Trevor, and Alan Hunt. 1993. "Discourse, Ideology, Discourse, Ideology, Discourse, Ideology." *British Journal of Sociology* 44 (3): 473–499.

Queally, James. 2017. "Latinos Are Reporting Fewer Sexual Assaults amid a Climate of Fear in Immigrant Communities, LAPD Says." *Los Angeles Times,* March 21.

Ramakrishnan, S. Karthick, and Tom Wong. 2010. "Partisanship, Not Spanish: Explaining Municipal Ordinances Affecting Undocumented Immigrants." Pp. 73–96 in *Taking Local Control,* edited by M. W. Varsanyi. Stanford, CA: Stanford University Press.

Reeve, Elspeth. 2013. "Steve King Wants to Protect the Border from Cantaloupe-Sized Calves." *The Atlantic,* July 23.

Regan, Margaret. 2010. *The Death of Josseline.* Boston: Beacon Press.

Richardson, Laurel. 1990. "Narrative and Sociology." *Journal of Contemporary Ethnography* 19 (1): 116–135.

Riosmena, Fernando. 2004. "Return versus Settlement among Undocumented Mexican Migrants, 1980 to 1996." Pp. 265–281 in *Crossing the Border: Research from the Mexican Migration Project,* edited by J. Durand and D. Massey. New York: Russell Sage Foundation.

Robertson, Campbell. 2011. "After Ruling, Hispanics Flee an Alabama Town." *New York Times,* October 3.

Roche, Kathleen, Elizabeth Vaquera, Rebecca M. B. White, and Maria Ivonne Rivera. 2018. "Impacts of Immigration Actions and News and the Psychological Distress of U.S. Latino Parents Raising Adolescents." *Journal of Adolescent Health* 62 (5): 525–531.

Roemer, John, Woojin Lee, and Karina Van der Straeten. 2007. *Racism, Xenophobia, and Distribution.* Cambridge, MA: Harvard University Press.

Rolley, Sam. 2011. "Beason: Dems Don't Want to Solve Illegal Immigration Problem." *Cullman Times,* February 6.

Romero, Mary. 2006. "Racial Profiling and Immigration Law Enforcement." *Critical Sociology* 32 (2–3): 447–473.

Rosenberg, Mica, and Reade Levinson. 2018. "Trump's Catch-and-Detain Policy Snares Many Who Have Long Called U.S. Home." *Reuters,* June 20.

Rosenblum, Marc, and Kristen McCabe. 2014. *Deportation and Discretion: Reviewing the Record and Options for Change.* Washington, DC: Migration Policy Institute. https://www.migrationpolicy.org/research/deportation-and-discretion-reviewing -record-and-options-change.

Rosenblum, Marc, Doris Meissner, Claire Bergeron, and Faye Hipsman. 2014. *The Deportation Dilemma.* Washington, DC: Migration Policy Institute. https://www.mig rationpolicy.org/research/deportation-dilemma-reconciling-tough-humane-enforce ment.

Russell-Brown, Katheryn. 1998. *The Color of Crime: Racial Hoaxes, White Fear, Black Protectionism, Police Harassment, and Other Macroaggressions*. New York: New York University Press.

Sáenz, Rogelio, Cecilia Menjívar, and San Juanita Edilia García. 2013. "Arizona's SB 1070: Setting Conditions for Violations of Human Rights Here and Beyond." Pp. 165–180 in *Governing Immigration through Crime*, edited by J. A. Dowling and J. X. Inda. Stanford, CA: Stanford University Press.

Salter, Mark. 2012. "Theory of the /: The Suture and Critical Border Studies." *Geopolitics* 17:734–755.

Santa Ana, Otto. 2002. *Brown Tide Rising: Metaphors of Latinos in Contemporary American Public Discourse*. Austin: University of Texas Press.

Sapp, Leslie. 2011. *Apprehensions by the US Border Patrol, 2005–2010*. Washington, DC: Department of Homeland Security, Office of Immigration Statistics.

Sassen, Saskia. 1990. *The Mobility of Labor and Capital: A Study in International Investment and Labor Flow*. Cambridge: Cambridge University Press.

Schriro, Dora. 2009. *Immigration Detention Overview and Recommendations*. Washington, DC: Department of Homeland Security. https://www.ice.gov/doclib/about/offices/odpp/pdf/ice-detention-rpt.pdf.

———. 2010. "Improving Conditions of Confinement for Criminal Inmates and Immigrant Detainees." *American Criminal Law Review* 47 (4): 1441–1451.

Seif, Hinda. 2011. "Unapologetic and Unafraid: Immigrant Youth Come Out from the Shadows." *New Directions for Child and Adolescent Development* 2011 (134): 59–75.

———. 2014. "'Coming Out of the Shadows' and 'Undocuqueer': Latina/o Undocumented Immigrants Transforming Sexuality Discourse and Activism." *Journal of Language and Sexuality* 3 (1): 87–120.

Shahshahani, Azadeh. 2009. *Terror and Isolation in Cobb: How Unchecked Police Power under 287(g) Has Torn Families Apart and Threatened Public Safety*. Atlanta: ACLU of Georgia. https://www.aclu.org/other/terror-and-isolation-cobb-how-unchecked-police-power-under-287g-has-torn-families-apart-and.

———. 2010. *The Persistence of Racial Profiling in Gwinnett: Time for Accountability, Transparency, and an End to 287(g)*. Atlanta: ACLU of Georgia. https://www.acluga.org/sites/default/files/gwinnett_racial_profiling_report_1.pdf.

Shefner, Jon. 2008. *The Illusion of Civil Society: Democratization and Community Mobilization in Low-Income Mexico*. University Park: Pennsylvania State University Press.

Shutika, Debra Latanzi. 2008. "The Ambivalent Welcome: *Cinco de Mayo* and the Symbolic Expression of Local Identity and Ethnic Relations." Pp. 274–307 in *New Faces in New Places*, edited by D. S. Massey. New York: Russell Sage Foundation.

Singer, Audrey. 2004. *The Rise of New Immigrant Gateways*. Washington, DC: Brookings.

Singer, Audrey, Jill Wilson, and Brooke DeRenzis. 2009. *Immigrants, Politics, and Local Response in Suburban Washington*. Washington, DC: Brookings.

Siskin, Alison. 2012. *Immigration-Related Detention*. Washington, DC: Congressional Research Service.

Skop, Emily, and Tara Buentello. 2008. "Austin: Immigration and Transformation Deep in the Heart of Texas." Pp. 257–280 in *Twenty-First Century Gateways*, edited by A. Singer, S. W. Hardwick, and C. B. Brettell. Washington, DC: Brookings.

Smith, Rebecca, Ana Ana Avendaño, and Julie Martínez Ortega. 2009. *Iced Out: How Immigration Enforcement Has Interfered with Workers' Rights*. Washington, DC: AFL-CIO.

Snow, David. 1980. "The Disengagement Process: A Neglected Problem in Participant Observation Research." *Qualitative Sociology* 3 (2): 100–122.

Snow, David, and Robert Benford. 1988. "Ideology, Frame Resonance, and Participant Mobilization." *International Social Movement Research* 1:197–217.

Snow, David, E. Burke Rochford, Jr., Steven Worden, and Robert Benford. 1986. "Frame Alignment Processes, Micromobilization, and Movement Participation." *American Sociological Review* 51 (4): 464–481.

Southern Poverty Law Center. 2009. *Under Siege: Life for Low-Income Latinos in the South.* Montgomery, AL: Southern Poverty Law Center. https://www.splcenter.org/20090331 /under-siege-life-low-income-latinos-south.

———. 2012. *Alabama's Shame: HB 56 and the War on Immigrants.* Montgomery, AL: Southern Poverty Law Center. https://www.splcenter.org/20120131/alabamas-shame -hb-56-and-war-immigrants.

———. 2016a. "1,094 Bias-Related Incidents in the Month Following the Election." Montgomery, AL: Southern Poverty Law Center. https://www.splcenter.org/hatewatch /2016/12/16/update-1094-bias-related-incidents-month-following-election.

———, National Lawyers Guild, and Adelante Alabama Worker Center. 2016b. *Shadow Prisons: Immigrant Detention in the South.* Montgomery, AL: Southern Poverty Law Center. https://www.splcenter.org/20161121/shadow-prisons-immigrant-detention -south.

Speri, Alice. 2018. "Detained, then Violated." *The Intercept*, April 11.

Spivak, Gayatri. 1988. "Can the Subaltern Speak?" Pp. 271–317 in *Marxism and the Interpretation of Culture*, edited by C. Nelson and L. Grossberg. Chicago: University of Chicago Press.

Stave, Jennifer, Peter Markowitz, Karen Berberich, Tammy Cho, Danny Dubbaneh, Laura Simich, Nina Siulc, and Noelle Smart. 2017. "Evaluation of the New York Immigrant Family Unity Project: Assessing the Impact of Legal Representation on Family and Community Unity." Vera Institute of Justice. https://storage.googleapis.com/vera -web-assets/downloads/Publications/new-york-immigrant-family-unity-project -evaluation/legacy_downloads/new-york-immigrant-family-unity-project-evaluation .pdf.

Stillman, Sarah. 2018. "When Deportation is a Death Sentence." *The New Yorker*, January 8.

Striffler, Steve. 2005. *Chicken: The Dangerous Transformation of America's Favorite Food.* New Haven, CT: Yale University Press.

———. 2009. "Immigration Anxieties: Policing and Regulating Workers and Employers in the Poultry Industry. Pp. 129–154 in *Global Connections and Local Receptions*, edited by F. Ansley and J. Shefner. Knoxville: University of Tennessee Press.

Studstill, John, and Laura Nieto-Studstill. 2001. "Hospitality and Hostility: Latin Immigrants in Southern Georgia." Pp. 68–81 in *Latino Workers in the Contemporary South*, edited by A. D. Murphey, C. Blanchard, and J. A. Hall. Athens: University of Georgia Press.

Stuesse, Angela. 2016. *Scratching Out a Living: Latinos, Race, and Work in the Deep South.* Berkeley: University of California Press.

Stuesse, Angela, and Matthew Coleman. 2014. "Automobility, Immobility, Altermobility: Surviving and Resisting the Intensification of Immigrant Policing." *City and Society* 26 (1): 51–72.

Stumpf, Juliet. 2006. "The Crimmigration Crisis: Immigrants, Crime, and Sovereign Power." *American University Law Review* 56:367–318.

Sullivan, Margaret. 2012. "Readers Won't Benefit If *Times* Bans the Term 'Illegal Immigrant.'" *New York Times,* October 2.

Suro, Roberto, and Audrey Singer. 2002. *Latino Growth in Metropolitan America.* Washington, DC: Brookings.

Taylor, Paul, Mark Hugo Lopez, Jeffrey Passel, and Seth Motel. 2011. *Unauthorized Immigrants: Length of Residency, Patterns of Parenthood.* Washington, DC: Pew Hispanic Center. https://www.pewresearch.org/wp-content/uploads/sites/5/2011/12/Unauthorized-Characteristics.pdf.

Tennessee House of Representatives. 2010. House Joint Resolution 1253.

Theodore, Nik. 2013. *Insecure Communities: Latino Perceptions of Police Involvement in Immigration Enforcement.* Oakland, CA: Policy Link.

Thompson, Christie, and Anna Flagg. 2016. "Who Is ICE Deporting?" *Marshall Project,* September 26.

Thompson, John. 1984. *Studies in the Theory of Ideology.* Cambridge: Polity.

Thorne, Barrie. 1979. "Political Activist as Participant Observer." *Symbolic Interaction* 2 (1): 73–87.

Torres, Rebecca, E. Jeffrey Popke, and Holly Hapke. 2006. "The South's Silent Bargain: Rural Restructuring, Latino Labor and the Ambiguities of Migrant Experience. Pp. 37–67 in *Latinos in the New South,* edited by H. A. Smith and O. J. Furuseth. Burlington, VT: Ashgate.

Transactional Records Access Clearinghouse. 2012. *Sharp Decline in ICE Deportation Filings: Targeting of Serious Criminals Fails to Improve.* Syracuse, NY: Syracuse University. https://trac.syr.edu/immigration/reports/274/.

———. 2013. *Who Are the Targets of ICE Detainers?* Syracuse, NY: Syracuse University. https://trac.syr.edu/immigration/reports/310/.

———. 2018. *Deportations under ICE's Secure Communities Program.* Syracuse, NY: Syracuse University. https://trac.syr.edu/immigration/reports/509/.

———. 2019. *Immigration and Customs Enforcement Detainers.* Syracuse, NY: Syracuse University. https://trac.syr.edu/phptools/immigration/detain/.

Trowbridge, Alexander, and Mackenzie Weinger. 2011. "Alabama Immigration Law Is Working, Rep. Mo Brooks Says." *Politico,* October 6.

Tucker, Robert C., ed. *The Marx-Engels Reader.* 1978. New York: W.W. Norton & Company.

Tyson, Alec. 2018. *Public Backs Legal Status for Immigrants Brought to U.S. Illegally as Children, but Not a Bigger Border Wall.* Washington, DC: Pew Research Center. https://www.pewresearch.org/fact-tank/2018/01/19/public-backs-legal-status-for-immigrants-brought-to-u-s-illegally-as-children-but-not-a-bigger-border-wall/.

Urrea, Luis Alberto. 2004. *The Devil's Highway.* New York: Little, Brown and Company.

USA Today. 2011. "Alabama Passes Arizona-Style Immigration Bill." June 3.

U.S. Census Bureau. 2009. "Selected Characteristics of the Native and Foreign-Born Populations." 2005–2009 American Community Survey 5-Year Estimates. US Census Bureau's American Community Survey Office.

———. 2011. "Selected Characteristics of the Native and Foreign-Born Populations." 2007–2011 American Community Survey 5-Year Estimates. US Census Bureau's American Community Survey Office.

U.S. Customs and Border Protection. 2017a. *CBP Border Security Report, Fiscal Year 2017.* Washington, DC: Department of Homeland Security.

———. 2017b. *U.S. Border Patrol Fiscal Year Budget Statistics (FY 1990–FY 2017).* Washington, DC: Department of Homeland Security.

———. 2017c. *U.S. Border Patrol Fiscal Year Staffing Statistics (FY 1992–2017).* Washington, DC: Department of Homeland Security.

———. 2017d. *United States Border Patrol Nationwide Illegal Alien Apprehensions, Fiscal Years 1925–2017.* Washington, DC: Department of Homeland Security.

U.S. Department of Homeland Security. 2013. *Budget-in-Brief Fiscal Year 2013.* Washington, DC: Department of Homeland Security.

———. 2014a. *Policies for the Apprehension, Detention, and Removal of Undocumented Immigrants.* Washington, DC: Department of Homeland Security.

———. 2014b. *Secure Communities.* November 20. Washington, DC: Department of Homeland Security.

———. 2017. *Yearbook of Immigration Statistics: 2016.* Washington, DC: Department of Homeland Security, Office of Immigration Statistics.

U.S. Department of Justice. 2011. *Department of Justice Releases Investigative Findings on the Maricopa County Sheriff's Office.* Press release. December 15. Washington, DC: U.S. Department of Justice. https://www.justice.gov/opa/pr/department-justice -releases-investigative-findings-maricopa-county-sheriff-s-office.

———. 2012a. "Assistant Attorney General Thomas E. Perez Speaks at the American Civil Liberties Union's Plyler v. Doe 30th Anniversary Event." Transcript, June 11. https:// www.justice.gov/opa/speech/assistant-attorney-general-thomas-e-perez-speaks-amer ican-civil-liberties-union-s-plyler.

———. 2012b. "Justice Department Releases Investigative Findings on the Alamance County, N.C., Sheriff's Office." Press release. September 18. Washington, DC: U.S. Department of Justice. https://www.justice.gov/opa/pr/justice-department-releases -investigative-findings-alamance-county-nc-sheriff-s-office.

U.S. Government Accountability Office. 2009. *Immigration Enforcement: Better Controls Needed over Program Authorizing State and Local Enforcement of Federal Immigration Laws.* GAO-09-109. Washington, DC: U.S. GAO. https://www.gao.gov/assets /290/285583.pdf.

U.S. Immigration and Customs Enforcement. 2010a. *The ICE 287(g) Program: A Law Enforcement Partnership.* Washington, DC: U.S. Immigration and Customs Enforcement. https://www.hsdl.org/?view&did=29593.

———. 2010b. "Knox County First in Tennessee to Benefit from ICE Strategy." Press release. June 17. Washington, DC: U.S. Immigration and Customs Enforcement. https://www.ice.gov/news/releases/knox-county-first-tennessee-benefit-ice-strategy -enhance-identification-removal.

———. 2011. "Enforcement Actions at or Focused on Sensitive Locations." Memorandum. Washington, DC: U.S. Immigration and Customs Enforcement. https://www .ice.gov/doclib/ero-outreach/pdf/10029.2-policy.pdf.

———. 2014. "Secure Communities: Monthly Statistics through August 31, 2014. IDENT/IAFIS Interoperability." Washington, DC: U.S. Immigration and Customs Enforcement. https://www.ice.gov/doclib/foia/sc-stats/nationwide_interop_stats-fy 2014-to-date.pdf.

———. 2017a. "Fiscal Year 2017 ICE Enforcement and Removal Operations Report." Washington, DC: U.S. Immigration and Customs Enforcement. https://www.ice.gov/re moval-statistics/2017.

———. 2017b. "ICE Announces 18 New 287(g) Agreements in Texas." Press release. Washington, DC: U.S. Immigration and Customs Enforcement. https://www.ice.gov/news /releases/ice-announces-18-new-287g-agreements-texas.

———. 2018a. "Civil Immigration Enforcement Actions inside Courthouses." Directive 11072.1, January 10. Washington, DC: U.S. Immigration and Customs Enforcement. https://www.ice.gov/sites/default/files/documents/Document/2018/ciEnforcement ActionsCourthouses.pdf.

———. 2018b. "Secure Communities." Washington, DC: U.S. Immigration and Customs Enforcement. https://www.ice.gov/secure-communities.

Varano, Sean, Joseph Schafer, Jeffrey Michael Cancino, and Marc Swatt. 2009. "Constructing Crime: Neighborhood Characteristics and Police Recording Behavior." *Journal of Criminal Justice* 37 (6): 553–563.

Vargas, Jose Antonio. 2012. "Immigration Debate: The Problem with the Word *Illegal.*" *Time*, September 21.

Vitiello, Domenic, and Thomas Segrue. 2017. *Immigration and Metropolitan Revitalization in the United States.* Philadelphia: University of Pennsylvania Press.

Voss, Kim, and Irene Bloemraad, eds. 2011. *Rallying for Immigrant Rights.* Berkeley: University of California Press.

Walker, Thomas, and Ariel G. Armony. 2000. *Repression, Resistance, and Democratic Transition in Central America.* Wilmington, DE: Scholarly Resources.

Wallsten, Peter. 2006. "GOP Attack Ad Draws Heat for Racial Overtones." *Los Angeles Times*, October 24.

Wang, Ted, and Robert Winn. 2006. *Groundswell Meets Groundwork.* Sebastapol, CA: Four Freedoms Fund.

———. 2011. "Groundswell Meets Groundwork: Building on the Mobilizations to Empower Immigrant Communities." Pp. 44–62 in *Rallying for Immigrant Rights*, edited by K. Voss and I. Bloemraad. Berkeley: University of California Press.

Warren, Patricia, Donald Tomaskovic-Devey, William Smith, Matthew Zingraff, and Marcinda Mason. 2006. "Driving While Black: Bias Processes and Racial Disparity in Police Stops." *Criminology* 44 (3): 709–738.

Waslin, Michelle. 2010. "Immigration Enforcement by State and Local Police." Pp. 97–114 in *Taking Local Control*, edited by M. W. Varsanyi. Stanford, CA: Stanford University Press.

Weissman, Deborah, and Rebecca Headen. 2009. *The Policies and Politics of Local Immigration Enforcement Laws: 287(g) Program in North Carolina.* Raleigh, NC: American Civil Liberties Union. https://www.acluofnorthcarolina.org/sites/default/files/field_documents/ACLUNC_Report_PoliciesandPoliticsofLocalImmigrationLaws_Feb2009_1.pdf.

Wessler, Seth Freed. 2011. *Shattered Families: The Perilous Intersection of Immigration Enforcement and the Child Welfare System.* New York: Race Forward. https://www.raceforward.org/research/reports/shattered-families.

White, David. 2011. "Alabama Legislature Passes Arizona-Style Immigration Bill." *Birmingham News*, June 2.

Willen, Sarah. 2007. "Toward a Critical Phenomenology of 'Illegality.'" *International Migration* 45 (3): 8–38.

Wilson, Jill, and Audrey Singer. 2011. *Immigrants in 2010 Metropolitan America: A Decade of Change.* Washington, DC: Brookings.

Wilson, Pete. 1994. "Closing the Door." *Spectrum: The Journal of State Government* 67 (1): 14–15.

Wonders, Nancy. 2006. "Global Flows, Semi-permeable Borders and New Channels of Inequality." Pp. 63–86 in *Borders, Mobility and Technologies of Control*, edited by S. Pickering and L. Weber. Dordrecht, The Netherlands: Springer.

Wong, Janelle. 2007. "Two Steps Forward: The Slow and Steady March toward Immigrant Political Mobilization." *Du Bois Review* 4 (2): 457–467.

Wong, Tom. 2012. "287(g) and the Politics of Interior Immigration Control in the United States." *Journal of Ethnic and Migration Studies* 38 (5): 737–756.

Yukich, Grace. 2013. *One Family under God.* New York: Oxford University Press.

Zhou, Min. 1992. *New York's Chinatown: The Socioeconomic Potential of an Urban Enclave.* Philadelphia: Temple University Press.

Zlolniski, Christian. 2006. *Janitors, Street Vendors, and Activists.* Berkeley: University of California Press.

Zolberg, Aristide. 2006. *A Nation by Design.* Cambridge, MA: Harvard University Press.

Zúñiga, Víctor, and Rubén Hernández-León. 2005. *New Destinations: Mexican Immigration in the United States.* New York: Russell Sage Foundation.

Index

Meghan Conley is the Director of Community Partnerships in the Department of Sociology at the University of Tennessee. She is the co-author of *Immigration and Population*.

www.ingramcontent.com/pod-product-compliance
Lightning Source LLC
Chambersburg PA
CBHW051433270326
41935CB00018B/1809